Reformation, Dissent and Diversity

Reformation, Dissent and Diversity

The Story of Scotland's Churches,
1560–1960

ANDREW T. N. MUIRHEAD

Bloomsbury Academic
An imprint of Bloomsbury Publishing Plc

B L O O M S B U R Y
LONDON · NEW DELHI · NEW YORK · SYDNEY

Bloomsbury T&T Clark

An imprint of Bloomsbury Publishing Plc

50 Bedford Square
London
WC1B 3DP
UK

1385 Broadway
New York
NY 10018
USA

www.bloomsbury.com

BLOOMSBURY and the Diana logo are trademarks of Bloomsbury Publishing Plc

First published 2015

British Library Cataloguing-in-Publication Data
A catalogue record for this book is available from the British Library.

ISBN: HB: 978-0-5676-6145-6
PB: 978-1-4411-3903-0
ePDF: 978-1-4411-6842-9
ePub: 978-1-4411-1776-2

Library of Congress Cataloging-in-Publication Data
A catalogue record for this book is available from the Library of Congress

Typeset by Integra Software Services Pvt. Ltd.
Printed and bound in India

Dedicated with love to Sheena and
to the memory of Ian A. Muirhead, 1913–1983

Contents

List of Tables and Maps

Acknowledgements

A considerable number of people have aided me in the writing of this book, whether wittingly or unwittingly. It started many years ago when Anand Chitnis and David Bebbington aided my first faltering steps in historical research in Stirling University, and David's encouragement continues.

My first research was also greatly helped by the archivists of the then Central Regional Council, Connie Brodie and George Dixon, and the present archivists in Stirling, Pam McNicol and Jane Petrie, continue to support in an ever friendly and professional manner.

Countless libraries have played their part in providing information. Chief among them were the public and university libraries in Stirling. The National Library of Scotland's efforts in making digitized material available to users throughout the country make it indeed a national treasure and a wonderful resource. Scotland's libraries are a pearl beyond price.

A glance at the 'Further reading' section shows a huge reliance on the *Records of the Scottish Church History Society* for information on the highways and byways of the Scottish churches. Work is currently underway by the Society to make the entire back issues of the Records available online. This should open up a rich mine of information for anyone interested.

Many of the authors of the papers and books which I have used have also provided me with information personally, and I thank them for it. Any mistakes, howlers, misconceptions or opinionated nonsense are however entirely my own.

To those of my friends and family not interested in church history (and I regret that there are some), thank you for tolerating and encouraging my enthusiasm.

My greatest thanks go to two people: my wife Sheena, who has lived with this project for three years without throttling me or filing for divorce, and my father, Ian Muirhead, who passed on to me his love and enthusiasm for the heritage of the churches of Scotland. It was he who first kindled my interest when I studied history at school by answering questions and explaining with endless patience. He should have written this book and would have done it better.

Introduction

'Tradition', said a wise man addressing the General Assembly of the Church of Scotland in 2012, 'is passing on a flame, not worshipping the ashes.' The purpose of this book is not to worship the ashes of past controversies but to rake them over in the course of trying to explain what was important in the past lives of our ancestors, aiming to help the family historian or the local historian puzzled at all the varieties of Christianity that abounded in the times of our ancestors and still can be found today.

There are many books dealing with the varied and often troubled history of Scottish churches. Nineteenth-century bookshelves groaned under the weight of partisan volumes and pamphlets designed to prove that the authors' own church was the true embodiment of Christ's Kingdom on earth and that all other churches were at best weak shadows of the real thing and at worst the chosen vehicles for the devil to destroy souls. Some writers still pursue this particular vein as can easily be found by visiting web-sites.

More recently, and rather more healthily, historians are striving to fit the developments in the Scottish church into the wider context of Scottish history as a whole, but meanwhile much of the detail of that history is consigned to footnotes. This book aims to serve anyone puzzled about what it meant for their ancestor to be a member of the Relief Church or the Free Church, a Cameronian or a member of the Evangelical Union. It aims to serve anyone interested in putting their ancestors into historical context, in establishing why their local community had eight different varieties of church for a population of 3000 in 1860 or puzzled as to the significance of all the various brands of Christianity and looking for a brief explanation of how they arose. For a diagram of the situation in the Presbyterian churches, (see Figure 1, Splits and unions in Scottish Presbyterianism, see page 213)

In the modern world some of these churches may seem tyrannical, obsessed with tiny theological details, always ready to discipline the unruly in thought, word or deed, yet these were the churches that were the centre and anchor point of so many lives, churches which claimed a tremendous loyalty among their members.

No history is written in a vacuum; if the nineteenth-century glorifiers of the Covenanters were influenced by their own upbringing and society, so too are modern historians. The story of Scotland's churches is no exception. At its most obvious, people who were taught history in Roman Catholic schools will inevitably have a different attitude towards the Reformation from those taught their history in non-denominational schools. Even the use of the phrase 'Roman Catholic' immediately tends to imply that the author comes from a Protestant tradition which looks on the 'catholic church' as including all mainstream Christian traditions, Roman, Orthodox, Lutheran, Presbyterian, Anglican and many other traditions that exist throughout the world. Equally, a historian from an unchurched background will have a different perspective from one who has rejected the church and a different perspective again from someone still involved with their faith.

But even within the Protestant tradition, individual congregations and Christians are consciously or unconsciously moulded by the tradition of an individual denomination or congregation. Many a minister battling to unite two neighbouring congregations knows that to his or her cost. For the sake of record then, and to define the author's own prejudices and background, he (and of course gender can define outlooks on history as well) was brought up and continues in the Presbyterian mainstream, with a father who was a Church of Scotland minister, one grandfather ordained a minister of the Free Church and the other grandfather ordained a minister of the United Presbyterian Church, with both uniting successively into the United Free Church and finally into the Church of Scotland. Meanwhile, many of his other ancestors put their pennies into a variety of other Seceder and independent collection plates.

This book does not apologize for the history of the great diversity of churches to which our ancestors belonged but tries to explain how and why and where and when they flourished. Sometimes there are aspects of our history that we would want to disassociate ourselves from; the violence, the intolerance, the 'unco guid'-ness and self-righteousness which permeated most denominations at some time in their history. On the other hand, those same denominations produced people of courage and principle who were prepared to suffer and to sacrifice everything for what they believed in, and it is right to celebrate those heroes and to recognize them in all strands of our churches' history.

But if it is the heroes, the saints and the martyrs that are best remembered, the real subjects of this book are the people of Scotland who worshipped each in their own way. They passed their views and attitudes on to their descendants helping to make, for good or ill, the Scottish character and heritage what it is today.

The chapters described as 'Overviews' will look at the general history of the church in Scotland, from the sixteenth century to 1960, concentrating on the Church of Scotland as National Church. Why 1960? Aside from being the 400th anniversary of the Reformation in Scotland, 1960 also represented a high water mark in church membership. It was probably the year which had the greatest number of Scots ever being affiliated to a church. Although the numbers of members have declined since then, history is still being created. Sadly, denominational splits and schisms still occur, but this work will not cover the more recent schisms in the Free Church and the Free Presbyterian Church nor will it cover the current controversies in the Church of Scotland which threaten the unity of that strand of that church. So, 1960 is our concluding point.

Most of the remaining chapters take a denominational view of church history, showing the background and broad history of each of the major (and many of the minor) denominations in turn and showing how they fit into the broader picture of Scottish life. Chapter 2 covers the two main 'episcopal' traditions, Roman Catholic and Episcopalian. Chapters 4 and 8 deal with the Presbyterian churches which had their origins in the eighteenth and nineteenth century respectively. Chapter 6 considers the three denominations that are most like English dissenting churches. Chapter 9 looks at some of the smaller churches in the mainstream of Christian belief with Chapter 10 looking at some churches which are further from the main body of Scottish Christianity.

The two other chapters cover disparate themes. Chapter 5 looks at the way that churches had an impact on individual lives. Chapter 11 looks at the geography of Scottish Churches under four headings: the way that the Highlands and Islands have stories that run in parallel with the rest of Scotland at times; the way that certain areas were more sympathetic to differing points of view than others; the architectural styles of Scottish churches; and the way in which Scottish churches have carried a part of Scotland to other countries.

The tendency of Scottish churches to have an official legal name, a name used by its members, and a variety of other informal names used by other people is further complicated by the way that successive unions and schisms have multiplied a considerable number of very similar names. The index therefore serves as a means to cross reference all these names.

1

Reformation to Revolution; 1560–1688; An Overview

A nyone visiting the Perthshire village of Doune, with a population of about 1635, will find that it has three functioning churches, a large empty decaying church in the centre and four former churches converted to other uses. Further delving around the parish area will find the sites of six mediaeval chapels and of at least three more churches, even if little or nothing remains of them above the ground.

This pattern can be found all over Scotland, with many communities having 'rival' churches planted next door to each other in an attempt to claim moral, numerical, theological or indeed any kind of superiority that could be claimed. One particular crossroads in Edinburgh is known as 'Holy Corner' because each of the four corners had a different variety of Church set splendidly on it, with two other equally imposing churches within a hundred yards down the road. The situation can be summarized by looking at the 1851 Census of Scotland which shows twenty denominations (not counting fifty-eight 'isolated congregations'), all competing for the souls, or perhaps the money, of our ancestors. The purpose of this work is therefore to untangle the various threads of the churches' story in Scotland in an attempt to help readers understand the history of particular communities or the belief system of their ancestors (see Figure 2, the churches of Scotland according the Census of 1851, see page 214).

Prior to 1560, Scotland, like most of the rest of western Europe, was part of the western Catholic tradition, offering religious obedience to the pope. Admittedly, it did not always recognize the same pope as England, but the principle of papal rule was shared even if the identity of the 'true' pope was not always agreed. By 1560, England had thrown off papal control twice and was establishing its own variety of Christianity, now generally known as Anglicanism. Much of Germany, Switzerland, France and the rest of north western Europe was in the process of challenging papal authority. Some of the forces that had caused the English Reformation were at work in Scotland, not the prime cause of a king wanting to divorce his queen and marry his mistress but a recognition that the Church was not serving the spiritual needs of the people, a recognition that it controlled much of the wealth of the country for little benefit to the country and a recognition that much of this wealth could be transferred to the landowners greatly to their benefit.

Pre-Reformation Scotland did not figure highly on the Renaissance papacy's list of priorities nor did the loss of Scotland to the Protestant heresy create much more than polite regret, for Scotland was largely irrelevant or at best a bit-player in the power struggles of Europe. The other side to this was that the papacy wasn't actually very important in the religious life of the average Scot prior to 1560. Part of the reason lies in the three roles that the papacy tried to fulfil, not often successfully. In one role, it was a major military power in Italy itself, with borders to protect, alliances to preserve and wars to fight. Secondly, it was a political power throughout Europe and the rest of the western Christian world supporting or withholding support from Catholic countries according to the needs of the day. At its most paradoxical, in 1690 this was to lead to a situation where the Protestant King William's troops at the Battle of the Boyne, beloved of Northern Irish Orangemen, were fighting Catholic King James' troops thanks to being paid by Pope Innocent XI. The Pope gave King William his blessing and ordered a Te Deum to be sung in the Vatican when he heard the news of his victory. Thirdly, and in some ways a long way thirdly, the Pope was the spiritual leader of the Western world. But if the Pope was the spiritual leader of the Western world, including Scotland, why was Catholic Scotland disastrously attacking Catholic England in 1513 at the request of Catholic France while England attacked France at the request of Pope Julius II? Following that, how could the Scottish bishops be spiritually loyal to a Pope who was supporting their country's enemy?

The fact of the matter is that prior to the Reformation, the rule of the papacy was pretty light and remote, and it was more the needs of the reformed church both in Scotland and in England that made the pope of the day the bogeyman, one to be feared and exaggerated. Bishops needed to be confirmed by the pope on their appointment but in many cases they were actually appointed by the ruling monarch of the country in which they served. The pope's role in appointing Scottish bishops was considerably less in 1500 than it is in present-day Scotland.

The one area where the Pope might take a personal interest in matters in Scotland was where it concerned a Catholic monarch. James V and Mary were not spiritually subject to their local bishops, whom they might have appointed anyway, but directly to the pope. In this the case of Mary, her marriage to the Earl of Bothwell in 1567 had much the same effect on Pope Pius V as it had on her own Protestant lords, for he wrote to her telling her that he had broken off all communication with her until such time as he 'could see some better sign in her life and religion than he has in the past'.

This is not to say that pre-Reformation Scotland was ignored by the Vatican, only that it was not a country of great importance. Published volumes of 'supplications to Rome' give plenty of evidence of requests for benefices or to marry within forbidden degrees and give ample evidence of the way in which the Scottish nobility and court used the church to provide income for their children, legitimate and otherwise. Henry VIII may have suggested to his nephew James V that he should follow the English example and suppress the abbeys, but in fact there was no need to; James V was particularly successful in bestowing the revenue of Scottish abbeys on his friends and relatives.

On top of this laxity over appointments, the Papal courts also gave the church in Scotland the right to try its own cases rather than transmit them to Rome so there was little or no supervision from the mother church. One of the papacy's great efforts to face up to the rising tide of Protestantism in northern Europe was the Council of Trent (1545–1564), which tried to put right many of the problems of the mediaeval church and was the critical event in the Catholic- or Counter-Reformation. And Scotland's part in this? It was absolutely non-existent. No Scottish bishop attended any session throughout the nineteen years of existence of arguably the most important Catholic gathering prior to the twentieth century. Nor was this entirely because the Scottish bishops were so tied up in the Scottish Reformation crises that they could not leave the country; at least two were in France during the period.

So, the Scottish hierarchy showed little interest in trying to mount a concerted attempt to stem Protestantism. They did, it is true, hunt out individual Protestants, often ex-priests, a handful of whom died a martyr's death but the death toll was never comparable to the flood of English martyrs on either side of the Reformation divide.

Part of this comparative lack of strife was due to the nature of Queen Mary's father, King James V. Sixteenth-century Scotland was ruled by the House of Stewart. Although the country had been racked by local wars and rebellions against the ruling house and regularly had a monarch succeeding as a child or indeed an infant, the Stewarts had actually maintained an unbroken dynastic line for two hundred years. Few, if any, other European countries had monarchs whose legitimacy was as unchallengeable but equally few countries has as many monarchs succeeding as children. The oldest of the seven new monarchs between 1406 and 1600 succeeded at the ripe old age of fifteen.

Having succeeded his father, James V finally took control of his kingdom in 1528 at the age of sixteen and deserves much of the credit for bringing Scotland out of the Middle Ages and into the Renaissance. The first cousin of Henry VIII of England, he encouraged learning and the arts to flourish in his kingdom, giving rise to a golden age of literature, music and architecture which was sadly to survive all too short a time. He also, incidentally, reached an accommodation with the pope, managing to provide for at least four of his many illegitimate children by having them appointed as priors or abbots of Scottish religious houses. The encouragement he gave to literature gave rise to a freedom of speech at the court. David Lindsay, Lyon King of Arms and therefore a senior courtier, was able to write and to have performed (probably in 1540) a play, *Ane Satire of the Thrie Estatis*, which attacked and satirized corruption throughout the government of the kingdom and particularly within the Church. It was the recognition of the split between 'the Church' as an institution, seen as money-grabbing at every level of society, and the spiritual worth of the Church in the parish that gave rise to the support for a reformed Church unconnected to the institution which was seen by many as sucking the country dry.

The fact that such satire was tolerated at court gave a clear signal to those in power that the king was open to new ideas, despite the considerably less tolerant views of those who helped him rule the kingdom.

Meanwhile, the situation was further complicated by the politics of the day. The conversion of England to schismatic Catholicism under Henry VIII, followed by a more extreme form of Protestantism under Edward VI had its effect on Scotland. On the one hand, the sacrament of Communion celebrated in Holyrood Abbey in Edinburgh to seal the betrothal of Henry's son Edward to Scotland's Queen Mary apparently showed a 'never-to-be-challenged amity' between the two nations. On the other hand, a scant four years later, there was a huge amount of damage done to southern Scotland by the marauding armies of the Earl of Hertford who was of the slightly odd view that burning abbeys and towns like Haddington would persuade the Scots that they really did want their infant queen to be married to England's slightly less infant king. Meanwhile, many of the potential reformers in Scotland fled to England and built up a network of support there. In reality, it was the potential which England had for encouraging the Protestant cause in Scotland that reduced the long-standing enmity and distrust between the nations. The man given responsibility for guarding Queen Mary in Loch Leven Castle in 1567, William Douglas, admitted that it was only the prospect of success for the Reformation that won him over to the idea that England could be an ally and could be forgiven for the Battle of Pinkie which had killed his father in 1547.

Added to this, the Scots Protestant exiles were liberally scattered through other European countries as well as England, particularly Switzerland, the Low Countries and France. There was a constant interchange of news and ideas with them so that when the time was ripe for a major change in Scotland, it was the influence of the French Protestant, Jean Calvin, which John Knox and other exiles absorbed in Geneva that was critical.

Protestant Scotland was seen as 'Calvinist'; Calvinist theology is sometimes defined by five points which form the mnemonic 'TULIP':

'Total depravity'; the idea that every person is subject to original sin and needs to be brought to a new life.

'Unconditional election'; the idea that God will save some not because they deserve to be saved but because he has predestined them to be saved through his mercy.

'Limited atonement'; the idea that Christ suffered to pay the price for the sins only of the elect. This belief was to become a major reason for splits and disagreements in the nineteenth century.

'Irresistible grace'; the idea that God applies grace to those chosen to be saved, which they cannot resist and so brings them to faith.

'Perseverance of the saints'; the idea that the elect will continue in faith for the remainder of their lives; any falling away is seen as proof that they were not of the elect in the first place.

But if change was afoot in the upper reaches of Scottish society, how did it percolate down through society? By the time the Reformation was in full swing, it gave every impression of being a national movement supported by every class. There is no doubt that as the Protestant preachers, led by John Knox, permeated Scotland, they seized the imagination of the people. As elsewhere, the new technology of printing put the written word into people's hands. In Scotland, the technology was much newer than in most European countries, as it was only introduced in 1507. Books such as the *Guid and Godly Ballades* show the power of a popular song in stirring up the people as it combined songs of great religious fervour with scurrilous songs decrying the authors' papist targets. Existing copies only date from the 1560s, but there is no doubt that the songs themselves date from pre-Reformation years.

The change was largely free from the widespread bloodshed that accompanied the English Reformation or the religious turmoils in France and elsewhere in continental Europe. Prior to the Scottish Reformation, about twenty-four Protestant martyrs are believed to have paid for their faith with their lives; after the Reformation, Catholic martyrs were even more scarce. However, the Scots martyrs, though few, were influential; Patrick Hamilton, for example, was a great-grandson of King James II; John Knox wrote of his martyrdom in his *History of the Reformation* that 'the reek of Master Patrick Hamilton infected as many as it blew upon'. Hamilton, one of the many scions of the nobility who had acquired Church offices without any duties or qualifications, used his income as Abbot of Fearn to finance his studies in Paris where he came to accept Protestant, largely Lutheran, ideas. These were later reinforced during a period of exile in Germany. His martyrdom came at the age of twenty-four years, and in him Scotland lost a very talented composer of masses. Of the twenty-four martyrs, it is noteworthy that perhaps most were young and many were either priests or monks. This does actually characterize the early Protestant leaders; most had been part of the institution which they were trying to supplant.

One, Father Thomas Forrest of Dollar, broke with tradition and taught his flock from an English Bible. Forrest was somewhat of an anomaly; he was tainted by some of the ills which beset the Church being a prebendary of the Abbey of St Colm on the island of Inchcolm but was also awarded the vicarage of Dollar. Many priests in that situation would have pocketed the money from Dollar and used a fraction of it to pay one of the legions of barely educated priests to perform the duties. But Forrest did not do this. He declined to take advantage of the law which allowed him to take cattle as mortuary dues from those of his parish who had died and in fact used some of the money collected from the parish to build a bridge for the benefit of his parishioners. The bridge still survives: named 'Vicar's Bridge' in his honour, it is one of only a handful of Scottish place names with the word 'Vicar' surviving in it.

Another of the Protestant martyrs, Friar Killor, was executed for writing and having performed a play about the iniquities in the church of his time. As the play no longer exists, we cannot tell why Lindsay survived unchallenged while Killor and his play did not. All these small rebellions began to have an effect on the people in general and the Church became more and more unpopular. It is hard to gauge what ordinary people away from the court were thinking during this period owing to scanty evidence, but research on wills has shown that the standard 'Catholic' preamble of 'I leave my soul to God Almighty, the Blessed Virgin Mary and the glorious company of the saints' dwindled in the course of the sixteenth century and virtually disappeared after 1546. During the same period, the number of commemorative masses provided for in wills also fell sharply. In the nature of things, evidence from wills can only be taken as reflecting the changes in the views of those with money.

If Scottish society was changing, so too did the political situation. James V had died in 1542; the infant Queen Mary was under the tutelage of her mother Mary of Guise and Scotland was yet again immersed in a power struggle. At the time, it was a pawn in the power struggle between England and France; some of the Scots politicians, called the 'assurers' backed the English, and others, the French who were their traditional allies. Many of those in prominent positions backed the Protestants, but at the same time many of those Protestants were uncomfortable about being seen linked to the country which had done so much damage to Scotland. Repeated invasions by the English and the scorched earth policies that were pursued through the Borders, the Lothians and later in Angus and up the east coast had made the English thoroughly loathed by most Scots and only a greater dislike of Mary of Guise and her Catholic allies motivated many of the Protestants to look for English aid. The French supported the government of the Earl of Arran and

Cardinal Beaton did not manage to retain the loyalty of the Scottish people to Beaton's form of Christianity. Protestantism continued to spread.

One of the Protestant leaders, George Wishart returned to Scotland from first Swiss and then English exile and started preaching openly. In Ayrshire, he was able to preach within some of the Catholic parish churches under the protection of the landowners. In other places, he would preach in the open air. Violence was always in the offing but never quite broke out. Although the eventual leader of the reformed church, John Knox, came to prominence as the bearer of a two-handed sword carried to protect Wishart, he never actually wielded it. Wishart was eventually arrested, tried for treason and executed in St Andrews, but he had brought a style of religion heavily influenced by continental thinking about the absolute importance of the Bible and a much more restricted view of 'Sacraments' than prevailed in the Catholic Church.

Cardinal Beaton did not long survive Wishart's death. In May 1546, a group of eighteen men broke into St Andrews Castle where Beaton lived and assassinated him. Motives were certainly political but also religious; several of the assassins are said to have referred to the death of Wishart as they struck down Beaton. In the long term, though, none of the assassins became prominent in church affairs.

Perhaps unexpectedly, the death of Beaton did not trigger a bloodbath between the two factions. Before a successor to the archbishop was appointed, the sub-prior of St Andrews, John Winram, took control of the church in St Andrews. Winram was an interesting character; labelled as a time-server by some historians, he remained loyal to the Catholic Church when it was in charge, yet moved without qualm into the Protestant Church. He always was in the reforming wing prior to the Reformation and soon after Beaton's death, he allowed John Knox to preach in St Andrews Parish Church, much to the chagrin of the local friars. Few of his hearers agreed with Knox's views on Church of Rome being identified as the Anti-Christ or that only sacraments specifically sanctioned by scripture, that is, Communion and Baptism, should be used in Church. Winram and many others believed that reform could still be achieved within the existing structure but he did allow at least one radical 'new' practice, for, a communion service conducted with his permission gave the laity wine as well as bread (Communion in both kinds), a practice which was not common in the Roman Catholic Church until the late twentieth century. Soon after this event, the French captured St Andrews, and many of those with reforming views, including Knox, found themselves in French prisons or galleys. Winram was spared to carry on his quiet progress in St Andrews and later took prominence in the reformed Church, being instrumental in the placing of many former priests as Protestant ministers in post-Reformation Fife and further afield.

Despite England's military success in Scotland, the English realized that their plan of merging the two kingdoms with the marriage of Edward VI of England and his cousin Mary was not going to happen. They could prosecute raids and harry the land, but an occupation of a Scotland that did not support them was entirely another matter, particularly when French resources were also pitched against them. Surprisingly for the time, there was little recrimination against those who had backed the wrong side: the pro-English Protestants did reduce their profile somewhat but there was no wholesale campaign against them. A solitary Protestant martyr, Adam Wallace, was executed in 1550 but on the whole Protestants were quietly ignored. There was a distinct feeling of letting well alone as 1550s Scotland tried to recover from the ravages of the previous decade. That changed when Mary Tudor ascended the English throne and returned England to a doctrinaire and aggressive Catholicism. English Protestants fled to Scotland but the opportunity that existed for a concerted attack on Protestantism was not taken up because Scotland was firmly allied to France and England to Spain at the same time as France and Spain were in the throes of one of their perpetual dynastic squabbles.

In Europe as a whole the Council of Trent moulded the way in which the Catholic Church would defend itself. No Scot attended, but the decisions were transmitted back. Within Scotland, there were Councils of the Catholic Church held in 1549, 1552 and probably a couple more in the late 1550s. These could acknowledge and resolve the issues of clerical corruption and clerical ignorance that were so central to the Reformation but did not consider the theology of the Protestants. Issues such as using scripture in the vernacular, giving Communion in both kinds, reducing the number of sacraments and cleaning the churches of non-scriptural tradition, all issues at the heart of the Reformation in Scotland, were ignored. Nor did any reform movement within the Catholic Church ever give weight to the views of the laity; this was seen by one of the few Catholic priests remaining in Scotland after the Reformation, Ninian Winzet, as one of the most serious failings of his church.

As all these councils were meeting, the embryonic Scottish Protestant church was growing; supported by many of the lairds, 'privy kirks' grew in number, worshipping discreetly but regularly and encompassing not just sermons and prayers, but also discussions where those attending could contribute their ideas. One such debate was the question of the extent that it was acceptable to attend the 'papist' parish church while holding very different opinions secretly. John Knox condemned the practice, but many felt that an outward show of compliance kept them safe.

The tension between the Catholics and the Protestants grew more intense in the late 1550s. Events in France convinced the French powers in Scotland that the two faiths could not coexist. As theology took over from corrupt practices as the central issue, the two sides became irreconcilable. Vernacular prayers and sermons may have been acceptable, change to the sacraments and attacks on church ornamentation were not. Meanwhile, the Protestants were demanding communion in both kinds, whole services in the vernacular and the suspension of heresy laws.

The year 1559 opened with an attack on the friaries; documents pinned to their doors demanded that the friars should give up their wealth to the poor. More crises followed; the end of the council led to many of the reformers within the Catholic Church, such as John Winram, throwing in their lot with the Protestants. In some areas Protestant preachers had free access to parish churches; in some areas families long at each others' throats were able to cooperate through a shared faith.

The crisis point came in May; the recently returned John Knox preached in Perth on Christ's cleansing of the temple. His listeners immediately translated this into words and 'cleansed' the church and other churches and friaries in the town. The town itself was split between the two camps and the volatility of the Perth congregation perhaps reflected the tensions that existed there. Mary of Guise, who was by this stage ruling Scotland as Regent on behalf of her daughter, immediately sent troops to quell the town, but 2500 men from Protestant Ayrshire also arrived. The death of a young man led to the breakdown of a negotiated peace and two of those who had been the Regent's most influential allies despite their Protestant sympathies were persuaded to desert her.

Those 2500 men who had come from Ayr formed the 'Army of the Congregation', led by the 'Lords of the Congregation', and set out to 'reform' the Burghs of Scotland. With this process came the destruction of many of the church's treasures and indeed huge damage to the fabric of the churches themselves. A huge proportion of Scotland's heritage, buildings, statues, stained glass, books, paintings was destroyed. Only two of Scotland's cathedrals remained fully roofed, while only a handful of manuscripts survive of pre-Reformation music, almost no pre-Reformation glass. While from a today's perspective, almost all would condemn the material destruction, in terms of human life, there was only one fatality in the whole process, a friar in Aberdeen who tried to defy the mob. Meanwhile, the Catholic hierarchy hid what it could; they converted land to money and spirited as much as possible out of the country but, unlike twelve years previously, did not take up arms themselves.

The death of the King of France put Queen Mary's husband on the throne as Francis II when he was fifteen years old. Despite the regency in France being held by her uncles, French support for the Catholics in Scotland soon dwindled. Even Queen Mary seemed rather to lose interest in her own kingdom at the same time England was being convinced that the success of the Scottish Protestants served England's interests. As a result, a fleet was despatched to prevent French reinforcements landing on the banks of the Forth, while Queen Elizabeth's chief advisor, Sir Robert Cecil, worked to persuade the Army of the Congregation to concentrate less on a forcible conversion of the church than on resisting the French.

At this point, the health of Mary of Guise failed; she had ruled Scotland for eighteen years on behalf of her daughter and she was highly respected, if not loved. Even those who supported the Congregation attended her in her last few weeks to pay their respects and she died in June of 1560, with her daughter now an adult and safely, if absently, on her throne whatever turmoil ran through the kingdom.

It is easy to take the view that the Reformation in Scotland happened because the landowners wanted to share out the Church's property, but there is plenty of evidence to show that for many, the spiritual aspect of the Reformation was paramount. Even those who profited most were expressing strong religious beliefs and faith and showing an awareness of a religious kinship with their fellow men which reached across the classes.

In 1560, though, Scotland became officially Protestant virtually bloodlessly. Helped by the Army of the Congregation, Parliament accepted the new faith and told the people of Scotland to do the same. What then of those who wanted to remain with the old faith? The queen, the bishops, the clergy, the nobles, the people all had different options open, albeit limited ones. The queen quietly continued her own devotions with a Catholic confessor under her protection but did little otherwise to protect her Church. There is some evidence that, like most of the rest of the nobility, she was quietly happy to profit from the looting of ecclesiastical property. The revenue from the benefices was bestowed on her staff in time honoured fashion, and even vestments from St Machar's Cathedral in Aberdeen and taken to Huntly Castle for safe keeping were taken by her to be made into gauntlets for the Earl of Bothwell. Some of the bishops and clergy fled abroad, to Mary's re-Catholicized England or the continent, some went 'underground' in Scotland while many simply conformed quietly, retained their benefices and kept out of sight. It is one of the paradoxes of the Scottish Reformation that while churches were torn down and their contents destroyed in an orgy of iconoclasm, the former priests and monks were allowed to carry on living off their benefices so long as they did not visibly follow their old faith. For those who did want actively to follow Catholicism, the continent beckoned and both priests and laity emigrated. Just what proportion of the ordinary people remained with the old Catholic faith is unknown. According to Thomas Innes, a priest of the early eighteenth century, by 1580, 'the Catholics, tho not all publically declared, were yet as numerous as the Protestants'. This seems rather an overstatement and contrasts with a Scottish priest in 1689 who said that in 1650 there had been 'not more than 20 Catholic families in the whole kingdom, no secular missionaries, and only two or three regulars'. What is true is that the surviving Catholics were scattered, localized, dependent on protection on a few noblemen and with no way of presenting a united front. But, provided they were discreet, there was no deliberate persecution such as characterized other countries although there were periodic anti-Catholic riots.

Finally Mary's tumultuous personal life alienated her court and led to her abdication and a brief war at the end of which she fled to England, exile and finally execution. Although the small war that accompanied Queen Mary's abdication did have its casualties, they are not seen as religious 'martyrs', simply as casualties of war. Scotland probably had the most 'complete' Reformation in Europe in that there was almost no remnant of the old regime left visibly in the country afterwards. Almost all those who held to the ancient faith went into exile or kept a very low profile.

Mary's departure left the kingdom of Scotland to the rule of regents until her son James VI was able to take over at the age of twelve. James was brought up as a Protestant in a country where the political leaders had been asked to give up control of religious and moral matters to an institution which saw itself as equal partner of the state. Some of those leaders were happy to comply; others were not. In the eye of the Church the godly magistrate, the political leader who put principle ahead of profit, who supported the church for the welfare of the people, was a man to be praised and supported.

The state of course had seen the profit in supporting the Reformation; the old church lands made a tidy addition to the assets of the landowners and the new king; they recognized the need to support the church financially, but in no way was the church going to receive the full riches of its predecessor, despite the noble ideals of improving education that it needed the resources to promote.

The church was also not reluctant to take a moral stance on events which might be at odds with the interest of the king or his supporters. It was organized into a hierarchy of courts from the kirk session which governed the local parish church, through the synods which covered the area equivalent to the old bishops' dioceses to the national 'General Assembly' at the top. Clergy and laity sat on these courts but the higher the court, the higher was the social standing and the smaller was the proportion of the lay members. It is slightly ironic that the idea of the 'Presbytery', the court that administers the churches in a local area, the court that gives its name to the Presbyterian system of Scottish Church government was the last part of the system to be put in place in 1581.

On various occasions through 1580s and 1590s the church was seen to be meddling in political matters to the disadvantage of the king. The new court of presbytery gave particular offence to the king and was banned in 1584 then accepted again in 1592.

James did not like presbyteries; indeed James was trying to re-establish bishops in Parliament. Bishops had not been formally abolished and in fact the early reformers saw a place for 'Superintendents' who had some of the local functions of bishops, but this part of the system did not survive. By 1600, James had three in place which had risen to eleven by the time of the king's death in 1625. The one strength that James had was that he had the right to summon the General Assembly and to decide its place and date. This right he used cunningly, apparently paying expenses to those whose attendance he valued and leaving awkward discussions to the end of business when there was pressure on the commissioners to cut matters short and go home. Meanwhile, James was able to use the anti-Catholic riots in Edinburgh in 1596 as an excuse to punish the town and in so doing divided the civic authorities from the churches.

The departure of James for England in 1603 on his accession to the English throne changed the whole nature of Scotland; at its most simple, it changed Scotland from being the focus of the king's life to being a distraction which he wanted simply to control without any real involvement. Scotland as a whole was expected to lose its independent national identity and the continuing existence of a church that did not conform to his ideal was a continuing irritant.

Meanwhile, Presbyteries continued to develop. These were largely ministerial meetings, held at frequent intervals, weekly in summer, fortnightly in winter. Only rarely is it evident that elders were present in any other capacity than being involved in specific aspects of business. The first hour and a half was spent in the 'exercise and addition' where two of the ministers would preach on a given text, each covering different aspects. A critique then followed and it was not unknown for the preacher to be reprimanded for error. As a means of ensuring that the ministers were sticking to orthodox views, it was reasonably effective and it also gave Presbyteries the chance to assess students aspiring to become ministers.

Following this, the presbytery meeting would consider the cases sent to it; straightforward matters would be resolved by the kirk sessions but they might transmit upwards cases of adultery, repeated offences or refusal to submit to sentence. In addition, any cases involving ministers would come to presbytery first as did any cases that might lead to excommunication. In 1622, the Presbytery of Jedburgh heard eleven cases of adultery, nine of fornication, fifteen of profanation of the Sabbath, two irregular marriages, one each of neglect of duty by an elder, murder, desertion and violation of a Sabbath fast. Those found to have offended were normally sent back to their own church and kirk session to carry out the sentence. They might also be remitted to the magistrates if appropriate. The civil power had a legal obligation to back up the Church and enforce its decisions. Excommunication was the most severe sentence that a presbytery could recommend, but this had to be ratified by a higher court, Synod or General Assembly or, after 1610, by the diocesan bishop. The number of excommunications declined substantially after 1602 and became very rare.

The role of the elders had changed over the years. What prevailed was the pattern in which a number of men were elected to look after the affairs of the church, together with some lesser office-bearers called deacons who looked after topics such as poor relief. These were initially temporary elected appointments with new sessions being re-elected periodically, often by themselves. Elders were expected to be men of substance; they had to be able to commit to frequent daytime meetings and were likely to be at the very least established tradesmen in the towns, small farmers in the countryside. Those of real wealth and power were unlikely to take the time to attend their local kirk session though they might be members. Elders elected to attend presbytery were always men of higher standing within that session. Those elders elected from presbytery to attend the Synod or the General Assembly always came from the ranks of the aristocracy or the legal elite. The evidence is that in most cases, they had scant interest in the kirk sessions or presbyteries which commissioned them.

Brought up in the Reformed faith as he was, James VI remained committed to the Church in general and to his interpretation of how it should interact with his monarchy in particular. His backing for the 'Authorized Version' of the Bible was crucial to its success, not least because he had the power to prevent the dissemination of other versions. The 1611 'King James Version' as it often called became the standard translation for over three hundred years and there are still many who look on it as the supremely authoritative version. It was a version, not a fresh translation. Most of it, including some of the most lasting phrases in it, came from previous translations such as those by Wycliffe and Coverdale earlier in the sixteenth century.

His influence showed in a number of ways from the start. The favourite Bible of the presbyterians and English puritans was the 'Geneva Bible' produced first in 1560 and imported to Scotland and England before being printed in England and Scotland from 1575 and 1579 respectively. It too was heavily reliant on the previous translations but what marked it out was a very full set of marginal annotations to help the reader interpret scripture and to interpret it in the way that the reformers interpreted it. It was these notes that caused James's dislike of the translation and so the Authorized Version of 1611 did not have such things; footnotes were to be restricted to explaining particularly obscure Greek or Hebrew words. What really irked James about the Geneva Bible was that it did not support his opinions on the 'Divine Right of Kings' and even emphasized that unjust or ungodly kings could be deposed.

That said, the new version of 1611 ousted all previous versions remarkably quickly, not least because the previous ones were not allowed to be reprinted, and was never seriously challenged as the authoritative scripture. As a side issue, the fact that Scotland so readily and completely accepted English language translations of the Bible both in 1560 and after 1611 had much to do with the decline of Scots as a literary language.

As James grew older, his patience with Scotland's Church grew thinner, not least because he saw its love of spiritual independence as a dangerous precedent for England. He therefore worked to bring Scotland closer to English practice. The 'Five Articles of Perth' were the major tools for bringing this about. Passed by a somewhat unrepresentative meeting of the General Assembly in 1618, these decrees enforced kneeling during communion, confirmation of new communicants by a bishop, the observance of the old holy days including Christmas and Easter and allowed private baptism and private communion for the sick and infirm.

It is perhaps difficult for people today to understand the huge offence this caused but to many it augured a return to pre-Reformation practices. When it was passed by Parliament in 1621, there was still considerable resistance and only the bishops in parliament supported it wholeheartedly. The Five Articles did not finally disappear until 1690.

Meanwhile, popular piety in Scotland was on the increase; the passing of the Five Articles of Perth soon led to some of the ministers who felt most strongly about them being deprived of their livings. Some went to Ireland to take on churches there; others took to holding private services which became known as conventicles. This was a fairly radical step; despite Calvinism's view that only the elect would be saved, the Calvinist Church of Scotland saw itself as the church of all the people of Scotland and private services for whatever reason were frowned upon. Imprisonment for attending conventicles therefore started in 1620. A conventicle, defined in 1624, was 'a private meeting of men and women to a private religious exercise in time of public sermon'. Later, it became more attached in the popular mind to services held in the open air, remote from human habitation.

King James died in 1625, to be succeeded by Charles I. Charles' views on the Church went much further than his father's and he was determined that it should be subordinate to his will. He immediately claimed to the crown all the land that had belonged to the Church in 1542. This was later explained to be a device to let the king review what had happened in the intervening eighty-three years and tidy up the system, but people did not quite see it that way. The King's Coronation brought him to Scotland ten years after he succeeded to the throne; it also brought the Archbishop of Canterbury. Archbishop Laud did not claim jurisdiction over the now episcopal Church of Scotland but he had a great influence on the king and was asked to prepare a prayer-book for Scotland, a book of church law and regulations for the Church. The former was widely known as 'Laud's Liturgy' when it appeared in 1637 and it gave great offence. Where time had to a great extent removed the sting from the Five Articles, Laud's Liturgy acted as a fresh spur to concerted opposition. The result was the National Covenant, drawn up by order of a group of nobles but signed by thousands of men in churches and churchyards around most of the country except the Highlands and Aberdeenshire. Women were to swear their allegiance to it but were not allowed to sign. Many copies still survive though many more have been lost, and they show the extent to which opposition to the King had crystallized. The document detailed the history of action against the Church of Rome including all the acts of parliament passed and quoted previous documents. It promised to resist evils and innovations introduced into the Kirk 'to the ruin of true reformed religion' and finished by vowing loyalty to the monarch.

In the face of this opposition, the king hesitated for three months before he finally gave in. He withdrew Laud's Liturgy and allowed a General Assembly to be called for the first time since 1618. It met in Glasgow in 1638 and proceeded to undo everything that every Assembly had passed since 1600. It even produced records of older assemblies which were believed to have been destroyed. The bishops were not present; indeed several had fled to England for safety. Nonetheless, the Assembly affirmed its support for the king and blamed his advisors for all that had gone wrong.

Charles was not impressed; he saw the actions of the 1638 Glasgow Assembly as an act of rebellion and sent an army to deal with the 'rebels', the 'Covenanters', as they were called for the first time. They raised an army too and a brief war ensued, before the king, lacking support from an increasingly unhappy English Parliament settled with his enemies; he agreed to call a new Assembly the following year, without even inviting the bishops. This was a far less radical gathering, but the king's Commissioner agreed to its Acts. The Scottish Parliament, which had been dissolved by Charles, met again and ratified the Acts of Assembly also deciding that bishops had no place in Parliament.

A few months later, a covenanting army set out to challenge the king's authority in the north of England; this was seen as supporting the stance that the English Parliament was taking in their dispute with the king. A treaty was soon signed and in its wake came the second document that underlies the later Covenanters' beliefs, the 'Solemn League and Covenant'. English opposition to Charles was growing ever more resentful of the power of the king over the church through bishops. Many believed in a Presbyterian system of church government while others followed different agendas, but particularly in the Parliamentarian Army, Scottish ideas were seen as acceptable. The 'Solemn League and Covenant' was written to consolidate these views, eradicate episcopacy in England and papacy in Ireland and bring all three countries to a uniformity in religion under one king under 'the example of the best reformed churches'. So far as the Scots were concerned, this document, as widely signed in Scotland as its predecessor, pledged England to pursue Presbyterianism and invited the king to do so too.

As part of this whole process, the English Parliament had summoned its own assembly of 121 ministers and thirty laymen to reform the worship, doctrine and government of the Church of England to which the Church of Scotland sent a team of learned and respected ministers as observers. One of several documents which came out of this was the 'Westminster Confession of Faith' of 1647. The Scottish Church recognized it as the principal subordinate standard of belief of the Presbyterian churches in Scotland. It remains as such today, defining the, generally accepted interpretation of Scripture and summarizing the orthodox theology of the Church. Ministers and elders are still obliged to subscribe their belief in it although now in most churches liberty of conscience is allowed on details that are not central to faith.

The Westminster Confession and the other three documents, the Directory of Worship and the Larger and Shorter Catechisms all became part of the fabric of Scottish Presbyterianism, despite being designed for English use. In England, however, they were never endorsed. Circumstances changed; Presbyterianism was superseded by Independency in the Parliamentary Army and any likelihood of its being accepted generally in England disappeared as did any influence that the Solemn League and Covenant might have had.

A number of previous Covenanters, led by the Earl (later Marquis) of Montrose thought that the Solemn League and Covenant went too far. He transferred his allegiance to the King and raised an army on his behalf; Scotland was once again suffering Civil War with religion at its heart. The failure of the English Parliament to agree to the Solemn League and Covenant led to a wave of sympathy for the king; Charles agreed to the Covenants and promised to do his best to bring England into line with Scotland. The Covenanters and Parliament split; many Scots supported the King now that England had failed them, but when the King joined the Scottish army at Newark after his defeat at Naseby in 1645, nine months of negotiation led to the retreat of the Scottish army and the king's captivity by the Parliamentarian forces. The Scots, to the shame of many, received a substantial reward for their actions. Meanwhile, the success of these earlier Covenanters led to a period when Edinburgh was effectively ruled by the church. Even the most powerful nobles could be held to account for their misdeeds and the town was ruled with a strictness that seems extreme to most modern eyes. On the other hand, matters such as poor relief were also taken in hand and run more effectively than was the case either before or after. For those on the radical side of Presbyterianism, it was a golden age.

From his captivity, Charles tried to play opposing factions off against each other and create an 'Engagement' to try to satisfy everyone who might possibly support him. It did not; it split the nation yet again; the Scottish army raised in Charles's support on the promise that England would be made Presbyterian for three years, marched to destruction at Preston in 1648. The Scottish forces were further split by the 'Act of Classes' which excluded from any public office all who had supported the 'Engagement' or for Montrose. Early the following year, Charles was executed.

This caused outrage in Scotland and his son was proclaimed King as Charles II; he was invited to Scotland on condition that he accepted the Covenant with all its implications; he duly signed up among jubilant crowds in Edinburgh. This proclamation was seen as a declaration of war by the English Parliamentarians and Cromwell's armies headed north where they roundly defeated the still weakened Scottish army.

Cromwell then ruled Scotland with a rigour and effectiveness which Charles I might have envied. The Privy Council, the courts and even Parliament were suppressed. The church was bitterly split between two parties known as Resolutioners and Protesters and in any case the General Assembly itself was dissolved by Cromwell's government in 1653. The Commonwealth insisted that all forms of religion excepting Catholicism and prelacy (rule by bishops) were to be tolerated and that none had primacy. Even Catholicism was tolerated provided its followers kept out of politics. As a result Scotland played host to a large number of opposing beliefs and sects imported form south of the border and promoted largely by the soldiers who ruled Scotland. To some extent, even Scotland's Roman Catholics looked back on Cromwell's reign as a time of peace in a way that their Irish and English counterparts could not.

Reflecting on 1650 when Cromwell's army arrived, the diarist John Nicoll commented that the names of Protestant and Papist were no longer in use and reeled off a list of sixteen names to define the religious loyalties that now held sway; some of these are familiar: Covenanters, Puritans, Quakers, others less so: Babarters, Brownists, Malignants. The Church of Scotland found itself in a dilemma; 230 ministers had been deposed in the previous decade and there were all sorts of ideas gaining ground with some Scots being converted to the ideas of the invaders. Meetings of the 'Protester' party discussed all sorts of ideas that would never have been considered publicly ten years earlier and even the Covenants were under scrutiny, largely because they supported the idea of kingship. There was a real push for 'Independency' the rights of congregations to worship in their own way without supervision from Presbytery or bishop or any external human authority and a few congregations did break away. Meanwhile, another group of men were advocating 'believers' baptism' rather than the infant baptism that was conventional in

Presbyterianism, Episcopacy and Catholicism. Baptist congregations sprang up in at least eight towns and probably there were Baptist groups in almost all the sixty or so garrisons in Scotland. Brought in by the army, these ideas initially proved attractive to many Scots but by the end of the 1650s, it seems that most of the adherents were once more English soldiers and that particular variety of faith disappeared from Scotland with the restoration of the monarchy in 1660. Of all these imported sects, only the Quakers remained in Scotland after 1660. Meanwhile, even the two parties that dominated the Presbyterians were deeply riven and antagonistic to each other; what the ordinary people thought is harder to gauge but it is clear that feelings ran high. As one symptom of social stress, this was a period when witchcraft trials were at their height.

When Charles II returned to Britain to reign in 1660, he was not the fugitive who had been 'encouraged' to subscribe to the two Covenants in 1651. By the time he arrived back in London to an ecstatic welcome, the Church of Scotland had an emissary there to press the case for Scotland. James Sharp, Minister of Crail in Fife and one of the leaders of the Resolutioners, reported on what he saw unfolding. He quickly saw that there was no hope of England following the Presbyterian line; Episcopalianism was in the ascendency and nothing else would prosper. Very quickly leaders of the Protester party were arrested after writing a letter to the King reminding him that he had signed his name to the Covenants. It was soon clear that Charles was as unsympathetic to Presbyterianism as his father had been. As might be expected, all those who had suffered on behalf of Charles I were rewarded; those who had stood in his way punished. Sharp himself saw which way the wind was blowing and made sure he was on the right side.

Among the first of the executions was James Guthrie, a leader of those Protesters who had written to Charles, and he is seen as the first of the martyrs of the later covenanting times. At the same time the Resolutioners, led by Sharp, supervised the deposition of other Protester ministers from their churches. The Rescissory Act of 1661 swept away all the acts of Parliament from 1633, including the one that restored Presbyterian Church government and it was clear that episcopacy was now likely to return. Return it did; by the end of 1661 every bishopric was filled, all but one with new men. Only two were life-long Episcopalians, the rest were former Presbyterians of the Resolutioner party, with James Sharp, now Archbishop Sharp, at their head.

The arrival of bishops once again meant another huge change in the character of the church. All ministers who did not accept the new regime were deposed, 200 in the western counties of Scotland alone, although some 560 conformed throughout the nation.

In the churches themselves, little changed; the form of services barely altered and there was no attempt to bring back the hated prayer book. Nor did episcopally controlled ministers look or sound much different from their Presbyterian counterparts. Indeed, the theology of belief hardly changed except in this one major area of church governance. In particular, Robert Leighton, the new Archbishop of Glasgow, did his best to incorporate the Presbyterian courts of the church into the new system; bishops were to preside over synods and kirk sessions were to continue. Some Presbyterian ministers who had accepted rule by bishops were allowed to be reinstated after 1669 and forty were even allowed to remain in their parishes on submitting directly to the King's direct jurisdiction bypassing the bishops. The latter were rather disparagingly referred to as the 'king's curates' but were joined by a further fifty in 1672. In 1674, a proclamation of indemnity offered pardon for previous opposition but was accompanied by ever more stringent penalties for future transgression, including the death penalty for those convicted of holding conventicles.

The dispute became more and more bitter. Attempts to find a middle way failed; Archbishop Leighton had tried his utmost to find a peaceful solution but he recognized his failure and retired to England. The Presbyterian opposition itself split as the supporters of the Covenants became more radicalized and more adamant in their opposition in the face of greater threats. As a 'turncoat', Archbishop Sharp was particularly hated and has been demonized by many of the more doctrinaire Presbyterian historians; to Episcopalian historians, he is a martyr as a result of his death in 1679, being murdered on Magus Moor not far from St Andrews.

Sharp's death ushered in that most unhappy period of Scottish history, the 'Killing Times' where those Covenanters who opposed Charles and his brother James VII, who succeeded him in 1685, were pursued with extreme cruelty, a cruelty which they reciprocated whenever they had the chance. Pitched battles at Drumclog and Bothwell Bridge in 1679 gave success first to the Covenanters and then to the government forces. Most Covenanters were Royalist; Scotland's experience under Cromwell showed that republicanism was even less in their interests than a king believing in his 'divine right' to rule. However, led by their fiery young preacher, Richard Cameron, one section of the Covenanters renounced the rule of King Charles altogether in 1680. This ushered in the worst of the 'killing times'.

It has to be said that these later Covenanters were a small proportion of presbyterians in Scotland and were largely, though not entirely, restricted to the south west of the country. Various estimates of those killed are quoted and vary wildly, although even the smallest numbers are horrifying. The figure of 18,000 is quoted on the most famous of the Covenanter Memorials in Greyfriars Kirkyard in Edinburgh where hundreds were imprisoned after the Battle of Bothwell Bridge. Over the period, many of the Covenanters leaders were killed, some in battle, some murdered, some executed. Many of their followers were killed after capture despite the promise of their lives; those spared suffered cruel tortures and imprisonment in vile conditions. Many were transported as slaves to the New World, hundreds dying on the way. Covenanter memorials have sprung up in many of the places associated with particular incidents and form a focus for those tracing back either their bloodline or their beliefs to them.

This contemporary description is of the torture inflicted is chilling in its very matter-of-factness:

> On Friday, the 25th of July last, Mr. Wilham Spens, sometime Argyle's Secretary, was put in the boots, and received many strokes till his leg was quite crushed. ... Having as yet discovered nothing, he was taken from the Council to the Canongate, and there put in the Guard hall, and set upon a form where he had nothing to lean on, the soldiers being commanded to keep him from sleep, which they did till Saturday the 2d August, so as, holding his hat before his face designing to seek a blessing to his meat, his head fell into his hat. [....] The council then fearing he would not be able to subsist, caused take him to Edinburgh Tolbooth, where he got sleep, and on Tuesday thereafter he was called before the council, and his leg being booted, he received two or three strokes. Now they had another torturing instrument prepared, which they called thumbkins, which they fastned upon his thumbs till the broken bone was appearing thro' the skin.

(The 'boots' were made of iron or wood with wedges put in around the ankle and hammered down, thus crushing the bones with excruciating pain: William Spense survived the killing times to become the Minister of Fossoway in Kinross-shire after the accession of William.)

The history of the covenanting struggles was to be drawn on by the Free Church when it seceded in 1843. The young church, often forced to worship in the open air was keen to draw parallels with the way the Covenanters had suffered 160 years earlier. It is perhaps not surprising that the Covenanters still polarize opinion 300 years later; for many, they are heroes who stood up to oppression against terrifying force; to others, they were fanatics whose own activities were as cruel and violent as those of their opponents.

Paradoxically, for most Presbyterians, relaxation of the laws they suffered under came as a result of James VII's conversion to Catholicism. In his enthusiasm for easing the path of his Roman Catholic supporters, he removed all the penalties against them but disguised the fact by giving freedom of religion to all in 1687. Moderate Presbyterians were once again able worship freely in meeting houses, as were Roman Catholics. The Presbyterians began to organize themselves once more and gradually those in exile in Ireland, England or the Netherlands started to trickle home.

The trickle became a flood when James was deposed in England after the invasion of William of Orange. William and his wife Mary, oldest child of James VII & II then reigned jointly as dual monarchs. In Scotland, news of William's success led to Roman Catholic chapels being attacked, and in the south-west in particular, episcopally appointed ministers were 'rabbled', driven from their homes and parishes, although without loss of life. The remnants of the Covenanters meanwhile were split over supporting William as king since he was prepared to accept episcopacy in England. A substantial number of them however formed into a regiment to fight for his position in Scotland. William already knew many of the Dutch exiles and although there can be little doubt that he would have preferred to continue episcopacy as the mode of church government in Scotland, the loyalty of the Scottish bishops to the Stuart family made that impossible. That said, William himself was in favour of a system that allowed loyal Episcopalians to worship in Scotland in the same was as loyal non-Episcopalians were to be allowed to worship in England.

In the event, the returned exiles were able to dominate the first General Assembly of the newly re-established Presbyterian Church of Scotland by inviting only those who shared their views. This made sure that the future lay with Presbyteries and the other courts of the church, not with bishops or those who supported them. No episcopally placed minister could be sure of keeping his church and manse and many were put out very quickly before and after the Assembly. The Church of Scotland was finally Presbyterian in its governance.

2

Dissenting Voices Backing Bishops; Roman Catholics and Episcopalians

The (Roman) Catholic Church

By 1567, Scotland's Catholicism had gone, or at least gone underground. There was no hierarchy of bishops; although the last Scottish bishop, James Beaton, did not die until 1603 and lived to welcome the accession of James VI to the throne of England with fireworks. His last effort to reverse the Reformation was to ask the Pope to send Jesuits, preferably of Scottish birth, into Scotland to minister to those who remained and attempt to wind back time.

For the next two hundred years, there were probably never more than two dozen Roman priests in Scotland at any one time and usually far fewer. Indeed in 1623 it was reported that there were only four Jesuits in Scotland, two in the north and two in the south. Ten years earlier, it had been reported that there were a hundred young men who wanted to go abroad for training and return. The lack of interest in Scotland by the papacy came into play, for although there were colleges in Paris and in Rome for the Scottish students, they were largely sent to combat Protestantism elsewhere in Europe and few came back to Scotland. Scotland's few remaining Catholics came under the theoretical authority of English archpriests. Many of these seventeenth-century priests were in fact converts from Protestantism whether Episcopalian or Presbyterianism, but the conversion was a two-way traffic with several instances of Catholic priests becoming Protestant ministers and at least one becoming a prominent Covenanter.

By 1622, all Scottish pre-reformation priests were dead; sixty-two years after the Reformation, most pre-Reformation Catholics were dead and

Scotland had lost all semblance of ever having been a Catholic country. That year, the papacy created a new Sacred Congregation 'de Propaganda Fide' (for the propagation of the Faith) which was charged with converting all the world not under Catholic rulers, whether hitherto pagan, fallen into Protestantism or Eastern Orthodox. One of the consequences in Scotland was to place all Roman Catholics under the authority of what was essentially a civil service rather than of a bishop specifically responsible for the land and its people. More specifically, it was the responsibility of the 'vicar apostolic', the first was William Bishop, nominal Bishop of Chalcedon, who had England as his territory and probably never visited Scotland; he was followed by Richard Smith, about whom exactly the same can be said. On a more positive note, what the Congregation did achieve was the recruitment of a small number of Irish Franciscan priests who were able to work with the Gaelic speakers of the north-west Highlands and the Western Isles. However, under Smith there was considerable tension between the 'secular' clergy (clergy who were not members of monastic orders) and 'regular' clergy (members of either monastic or preaching orders such as Franciscans or Jesuits), a situation not helped by Smith's early exile from England. By 1653, the secular priests in Scotland were petitioning for their own representative of the Sacred Congregation and it came with the appointment of William Ballentine or 'Ballenden' as 'prefect-apostolic for Scotland'. Ballentine was a convert, the son of a Presbyterian minister, no less. He became a priest in 1649 and so was early in receiving preferment. He had a short career in Scotland though, being arrested in London in 1656, imprisoned for two years and then exiled to France for a further two before returning to Scotland for the last year of his life in 1660.

The dislike that secular and regular priests felt for each others' efforts was a feature of Catholic life in seventeenth-century Scotland and certainly did not help its cause. One of the points at issue was that the secular priests were accused of allowing their charges to attend Presbyterian worship, and even sign the National Covenant, in order to preserve their own safety and that of their families. On the other hand, they were also accused of being more likely to cause trouble for the faithful. Jesuit priest said of the 'Irish' priests that 'none such are fit for our Loulandes bot to giue euil example and cause (as it said) persequutions'.

The story of the resurgence of Roman Catholicism is one of slow development in the first instance. One of the difficulties, though, is in gauging the numbers involved. One estimate for 1680 puts the figure as high as 14,000, not much different from the number at the beginning of the century, but one feature of the surviving records of the seventeenth-century church is their concentration on the upper echelons of society. A manuscript of 1654 lists about 150 Scottish Catholics, some of whom represented whole households; most of them were landowners, with the exception of a handful of merchants in Lothian and Aberdeen. Only in the northeast, Moray and Banffshire, is a reference to 'very many whose names are not known' and in the northwest 'very many of the name of Stuart or Robertson'. The year 1694 brought the next step towards re-establishment of a hierarchy in Scotland with the appointment not of a 'prefect-apostolic' but of a 'vicar-apostolic' with the status of bishop. This was not a bishop of any Scottish diocese, however, but the titular bishop of the rather medical sounding 'Peristasis', Thomas Nicholson, another convert, this time from the Episcopalian wing of the Church of Scotland, who had been ordained at the age of forty-one and consecrated as a bishop nine years later. His consecration was abroad and in secret, as was that of his successor, James Gordon, and that secrecy still typified the role. If any Catholic was seen as a political threat, any priest, and even more so a bishop claiming local authority, was seen as a serious threat to the Protestant realm. Under Bishop Nicholson, the missionary work in Scotland prospered, helped by the foundation of seminaries actually in Scotland, although these had a rather precarious existence at times.

So, at what point did normal relations begin to develop between the Scottish Catholics and the other Christian churches? In the smallest of ways, it began with the universities, Glasgow University in particular, for, in 1738 the Principal wrote to the Superiors of the Scots College in Paris regretting the long silence between the two institutions and requesting copies of various documents in their archives. The Scots College replied favourably and the copies were made at the College's expense as a gesture of reconciliation. From this time, there are clear indications that, at least on a personal level, the loathing of Scots Protestants for anything associated with Catholicism was beginning to weaken in some areas. By the 1770s, the Aberdeenshire priest, Alexander Geddes, moved comfortably among the professors and ministers of Aberdeen, even to the extent of being accused of occasionally attending Presbyterian services. As a scholar of renown, his life's work lay in his attempt to produce a new translation of the Bible with commentary. This caused consternation among both Protestants and Catholics by being among the earliest works of scholarship to suggest that the concept of a six-day creation was in fact a myth. Nonetheless, he became the first Roman Catholic since the Reformation to be awarded an honorary degree by a Scottish, or indeed a British university, becoming a Doctor of Laws of Aberdeen University in 1780. Perhaps not surprisingly given this history, he was not popular with his superiors and was finally deposed from his charge and forbidden from officiating in Scotland. Thereafter, he moved to London to pursue his translation. Apart from his scholarship, he was clearly well-loved as a pastor by his small and struggling flock for they are said to have competed to buy his possessions at extravagant prices when he sold his belongings to move south.

Where there were Catholic enclaves, they were largely Gaelic-speaking. Despite Protestantism's avowed intent of having worship in the vernacular, the national church always struggled with Gaelic and never did give any standing to the Scots language. English, which was the only language that most ministers spoke, was therefore as foreign to the average Gaelic-speaker as Latin had been, with the further difficulty that while priests in the Highlands used Latin for worship, they were able to converse with their flocks in a form of Gaelic which though foreign, was intelligible. This was recognized belatedly by the Protestants, but there never were enough Gaelic-speaking ministers to make inroads in the Highlands. The Parish of Crathie and Braemar, for example, was ministered to for thirty years till 1701 by the same priest, Father Forsyth. Little is known about him, but during his time, he increased the number of Catholics in the area, building chapels and even erecting crucifixes in prominent places. By this time, of course, the Toleration Acts of Charles and James had begun to give them public confidence.

By 1700, the Presbytery was worried about the increase in converts that Father Forsyth had achieved. The Church did belatedly recognize that the solution was to recruit Gaelic-speaking ministers to replace the Episcopalians who had been chased out in the wake of the re-establishment of Presbyterianism in the Church of Scotland. One such was Adam Fergusson. He had been a probationer for seven years: a tutor in the Borders who had never been called to a church. So, in 1700, at the age of twenty-eight, he was duly ordained and inducted into the united Parish of Crathie and Braemar, a church to acquire much greater prominence in modern times as the Parish Church that ministers to Balmoral Castle. Fergusson was a native of Moulin in Perthshire and before his acceptance for ordination had to conduct the usual 'exercises' before Presbytery to show that he was competent. He had to produce a 'homiletic', an 'exegesis' and a 'thesis' on topics the Presbytery assigned to him. His exegesis subject was 'The Roman Pope as Anti-Christ' and his thesis was on 'the cult of images' both a clear indicator of where the Presbytery's priorities lay for the parish and what they wanted him to do. After the Presbytery was satisfied with his orthodoxy, he then had to preach in Gaelic for his parishioners, for at this point the elders and heritors had the right to call a minister. They were duly satisfied and in September 1700, Fergusson became their minister. His task was clear: travelling the parish from house to house, preaching in Gaelic and dealing with the various issues that every minister of his day had deal to with. He started the process of excommunicating a Catholic convert and recorded a list of Catholic children. He failed. In 1698, the Privy Council had recorded sixty Catholics as living around Braemar. In 1709, Fergusson listed 409 'Papists' in his parish, of whom 148 had apostatized since his arrival nine years previously. He had three explanations for this; the size of his parish that allowed priests to sneak in unseen to administer last rites, a sacrament not recognized by the church but much valued by the sick, the 'lightness of temper of the people' which led them to hanker after the old ways, and the lack of schools to address the profound ignorance of the people. Fergusson was acute enough to know that a 'hearts and minds' campaign was needed, not the big stick of the law. He tried, but without much success; he got funding for two teachers from the SSPCK, but one did not speak Gaelic and declined to sign the Confession of Faith, so was himself suspect. Finally, Fergusson had had enough and tried to find another church; three years later, in 1714 he was 'presented', since Patronage had now come back in, to the Parish of Logierait in Perthshire, still Gaelic-speaking, but with only Episcopalians to bring back into the fold, not Catholics. With the new Catholic seminary at Scalan near Glenlivet producing home-grown priests, the Roman Catholic Church was in a strong position by 1712.

Then came the Jacobites. From the earliest times, the Church in Scotland has been immersed in politics; the same can be true of the Church anywhere if truth be told, but that special relationship that made Scotland at times the most church-guided nation in Europe made the politics of religion particularly powerful. When Bishop Rose declined to allow his Episcopalian version of the Church of Scotland to support the new King William, he gave an unmistakeable message that he expected his followers to be loyal to their oath of allegiance to King James VII. As a result, a substantial proportion of Scottish Episcopalians nailed their colours firmly and disastrously to the Jacobite mast. If that were true of the Episcopalians, how much more was it true of the Roman Catholics who saw in James the one monarch to give hope of a return to Catholicism as the national church of Scotland and the one man to release them from the crippling legal disabilities from which they suffered? The few gains they had begun to make in the years from 1680 to 1712 were lost pretty much at a stroke when they supported the campaign of the aspirant James VIII in 1715. The triumphant Whigs used the failure of the rebellion as the perfect excuse to step up the campaign to make Catholicism as difficult and unattractive a cause to espouse as it could, especially in the north of England. In Scotland though, the Catholic communities were to some extent protected by their remoteness and in the years immediately following 1715, they were able to make small gains in forming the seminary at Scalan, although another one on an island in Loch Morar had been quietly closed in 1715. These early seminaries had a very tenuous existence, but by 1725, the first priests to be trained totally in Scotland were ordained.

The Jacobite risings and the loyalty of most Roman Catholics to the old regime did nothing to aid the acceptance of the community; a strong popular anti-Catholicism remained which was bolstered by immigration from Ireland to the industrial areas of Scotland from the late eighteenth century onwards. This immigration had two side issues; the first was that it brought a Catholicism that was almost as alien to Scotland's traditional Catholic families as to the rest of the country. In fact, it brought two traditions, one from the south of Ireland was very much parish-based and largely ignored anything beyond the parish and the second prominent in the north, brought a clergy used to negotiating with a Protestant ascendancy. Neither sat well with the native Scottish Catholicism, which was more conscious of the authority of the pope and suspicious of the preachings of Jesuits and Dominicans. Immigration also brought a much less visible group of Irish protestant immigrants with their own traditions, albeit arising from a Scottish heritage a century and a half previously.

A Catholic population estimated at 30,000 by 1800 had risen to 150,000 and more than doubled again by 1878. The bulk of this number was of Irish origin and imported Irish-born priests, but until well into the twentieth century, the Scottish Catholic tradition held authority in the Church. Many of the early histories of Catholicism in Scotland were very aware of this tension and depending on the writers' own origins largely ignored the history of the other faction. In society at large, periodic anti-Catholic rioting occurred; Roman Catholics were prevented from playing any part in the running of the country; they were very much the second-class citizens and the vast majority of the population were happy for this to be so. Gradually things changed.

This was not without opposition; the attempt to remove some of the anti-Catholic legislation in 1778 in the 'Papists Act' led to widespread rioting in London, the 'Gordon Riots'. That they did not spread to Scotland was because prior opposition to the terms of the Act, and indeed earlier riots, had already led to Scotland being exempt from it. The outbreak of the French Revolution further complicated the situation; the Revolution was very much anti-clerical in France, but it also gave hope to Irish nationalists and so made Roman Catholics' political loyalty suspect yet again. At that time, Irish nationalism also had a strong Protestant following; so, it is not a clear argument. There was much damage to British property as a result of the French wars; among this was property belonging to the Roman Catholics of Britain, so when compensation was organized as part of the peace process after the fall of Napoleon, there was outrage that the British Government was seen to be giving money to the Roman Catholic Church. More outrage came with the Catholic Emancipation Act of 1829 which for the first time allowed Roman Catholics to take up seats in Parliament and opened the way for their participation in local politics. Petition after petition came to Parliament against emancipation, while a few were in its favour. The Established Church was particularly exercised against it; the United Secession and Relief Churches tended to be in favour, although one Relief minister was ejected bodily from his pulpit when he spoke in favour of it during a sermon. Throughout the country anti-Catholic feelings gave rise to demonstrations and occasionally, in Inverness for example, to the burning of a chapel. From a distance of nearly two centuries it is easy to consider that the Church of Scotland ministers who were so against Catholic emancipation were actually fighting their own war in trying to show that their particular brand of Protestantism was 'purer' than those of their opponents within the church. The Act duly went through against the wishes of many Scottish Protestants.

One of the issues was undoubtedly the matter of poor relief and the fact that so many of the Irish immigrants were close to destitute was a complicating factor. They were so desperate for work that they were accused of driving down wages by being willing to work for less than the indigenous population. Their willingness to work in place of striking workers also did not win them much local support, although in these pre-union days it was not seen as the heinous offence that it became later. The potato famine of the late 1840s added significantly to this problem with the exodus of many from Ireland; it was noticeable though that for the first time the Catholic Church was officially included in the efforts to mitigate its effects in the north-west of Scotland which was also seriously affected. By mid-century, the numbers of Roman Catholics had risen substantially and a pattern of their spread had begun to be apparent (see Figure 3, Roman Catholics in 1851, see page 215).

All this time, the Roman Catholic Church in Scotland was being governed by a series of Vicars-Apostolic from Rome. Unlike England which had its own hierarchy restored in 1850 (amid considerable opposition), Scotland had to wait until 1878 primarily because of the tensions between those of Irish and those of Scottish ancestry within the church. Even some of the Scottish Catholics vilified their Irish brethren as rabble-rousers, undermining the position of the traditional Roman Catholics. However, by the 1870s, the Irish hierarchy had begun to distance themselves from the Fenians and the more extreme elements of Irish nationalism which in turn made the Scottish church seem slightly less threatening.

When it did come, though, the restoration of bishops brought back the two archbishoprics and four bishoprics of pre-Reformation Scotland, unlike in England where the new bishops took a different set of titles from the ones taken over by the Church of England. Partly, this action of appointing Scottish bishops was a reaction to a new confidence caused by a series of high profile conversions to the church, particularly among the peerage. They had little affinity to the industrial Irish of Glasgow and Lanarkshire but instead valued the idea of community and the mediaeval aspects of the papacy. One of the results was a love of all things Gothic and an antiquarianism which had nothing to do either with the Irish immigrants or the traditional Catholic families, but their conversion added to the status of the church and to its social acceptability.

Like most of the other churches, the Roman Catholics opened schools; in truth there always had been small schools hidden around the country, and periodic references to them appear in Church of Scotland records, but by 1848 they were brought under government inspection, accepted by the Church because it opened the way to the receipt of government grants. Apart from schools, other institutions followed, specifically religious communities such as convents appeared from about 1830 but also temperance societies and many other societies, not least football clubs intended to keep men out of public houses. Even more than most other churches, the Roman Catholic Church had a greater attraction for women than for men and congregations were weighted accordingly. The missions that the Protestant churches sent into the slums of Glasgow targeted those of Catholic origins as much as anyone else, but the hierarchy also targeted them and sent in their own missionaries. Urban sectarianism flourished, both religious in terms of deeply committed people believing theirs was the only way to salvation and secular in a form that reflected more tribalism and a distrust of the 'different' and had little to do with any real religious belief. This sectarianism still exists although at lesser levels.

By the end of the nineteenth century, the Irish Catholics were also being supplemented by Italian and Lithuanian immigration, to be followed by the post-war Polish community. The Italian presence in the chip shop and ice-cream trade made them seem particularly disquieting as they were able to operate on Sundays and thereby evade and undermine Sabbath restrictions. Through this time there was a constant but small series of 'triumphs' as a priest or a minister was persuaded to change his allegiance to the other side. One minister even became a bishop, while the conversion of a former priest at the turn of the century became the focus for wild celebration on Glasgow Green (see Figure 4, Roman Catholics in 1891, see page 216). Meanwhile, the Roman Catholic community gradually assimilated into a kind of parallel culture with its own class system and its own education system. It did not join the other churches in handing its schools into state control in 1872. But in 1918, the government garnered them into the national system, somewhat against the will of the hierarchy itself. For some there was outrage at Catholic education being paid for out of the rates and 'Rome on the Rates' became a slogan in the campaign. Sixty-six former Episcopalian schools were brought into the national system at the same time. Of course the parents paid rates too and had previously been paying for schools that they did not use. Nonetheless, the 1918 act enshrined separate education for much of Scotland and therefore perpetuated the situation that meant that people rarely had contact with those of the other community. On the other hand, the municipalization of education meant that the 8.5 per cent of Roman Catholic children that received a post elementary education in 1919 had increased to thirteen per cent by 1939.

Perhaps the two aspects that began to break down barriers were the Great War where men fought and died beside each other regardless of faith and the growth of the Labour movement which led many from the Catholic community into local politics or simply into voting for those known to be more tolerant. Against that came Protestant Action in the 1930s standing for Edinburgh Town Council on a sectarian manifesto and winning several seats.

Regarding relationships with other churches, even John White, one of the outstanding Church of Scotland ministers of his day sponsored a deliverance to the General Assembly in 1923 on 'the menace of the Irish race to our Scottish nationality', while a decade later the Rev. George MacLeod, that most consciously social of Presbyterian ministers, was deeply suspicious of the concept of 'confession and clerical control'. It was only in 1961 that for the first time a Moderator of the General Assembly met the pope and they embraced as fellow Christians.

Episcopal Church

With one sentence in 1690, Alexander Rose, Bishop of Edinburgh, condemned the Episcopal Church of Scotland to a future as a dissenting church. When asked if the Scottish bishops would follow their English counterparts in supporting the new regime, he told the newly arrived King William that 'I will serve you as far as law, reason or conscience shall allow me.' The king took that as a refusal and turned his back on Rose and the episcopal regime that had ruled Scotland's national church since 1660.

The Scottish Church had been episcopal (that is, ruled by bishops in a hierarchy) before, and there are still many in the Episcopal Church of Scotland who regard it as the historical Church of Scotland. After the Reformation, the original reformers were not doctrinaire about bishops and appointed 'superintendents' in several areas who had some of the powers of bishops. Indeed some of the pre-Reformation bishops converted to Protestantism and held on to their dioceses but were not replaced when they died. Queen Mary also attempted to appoint a bishop or two without much success. In 1581, the General Assembly decided that bishops should no longer be appointed or hold any power beyond their own parish.

James VI was keen to have power over the Church via bishops whom he could appoint, a keenness which grew when he became King of England and Head of the Church of England. In 1610, he prevailed and appointed a new bench of bishops for Scotland and for some years the national church toed the episcopal line. James's efforts and still more those of his successor Charles I, created considerable offence, especially the introduction of the Prayer Book, and the National Covenant was signed in Scotland in 1638 in protest against innovations in the worship or organization of the Church without the approval of a free General Assembly. The General Assembly called in Glasgow in 1638 deposed all the bishops and declared null the six Assemblies that had taken place since they were appointed.

A war followed and the armies of the first Covenanters were largely victorious and joined the English Parliamentarian forces in the Civil War. The Solemn League and Covenant was signed in 1643 and committed Scotland and England to pursuing Presbyterian Church government. Not all agreed with these developments and a royalist army was raised in Scotland which was however defeated. Charles was captured and executed and Scotland fell under the rule of Cromwell through his henchman General Monk who ruled Scotland with a grip far tighter than Charles had ever achieved. Despite the Covenants, the Church of Scotland was sidelined and it was made clear that any system of reformed church government was equally acceptable. Under Monk's rule, the presbyterians were split into many factions and the English soldiers brought in many forms of English non-conformity previously unknown in Scotland.

When Charles II regained the throne in 1660, he promptly restored the Church to government by bishops. There was resentment against this in the lowlands but Aberdeenshire in particular showed a distinct preference for the episcopal way. Among the new bishops appointed, for only one remained of those appointed by Charles I, the most senior was James Sharp, Archbishop of St Andrews. Among the others consecrated though was Robert Leighton who was widely respected by all sides and was largely indifferent to the religious politics of his time while maintaining a saintly way of life. Those opposed to episcopacy left, for exile in England, Ireland or the Netherlands, took to the life of an itinerant covenanting preacher or left the Church. Finally, only those ministers prepared to accept rule by bishops remained.

Then, as now, there must have been many who simply wished to serve God in their chosen community and ignore the politics of the age, although it was much harder to do so then than now. Throughout the country, church-life carried on despite the turmoil of the covenanting troubles. Even Archbishop Sharp realized that there were limits to what could be expected. Existing ministers were not expected to be re-ordained by their new bishops, there was no insistence on the use of prayer-books and indeed Knox's *Book of Common Order* returned to use. There was little difference in the conduct of church services except the regular use of the Lord's Prayer was compulsory, but then Knox had recommended that too. kirk sessions continued to govern individual churches in much the same way and it would be difficult to tell the difference from the records.

With the accession of William and Bishop Rose's response to him, everything changed. The Episcopalians found themselves out of power. The old regime was back in control and those who had served under the bishops were without a voice. They were immediately excluded from the General Assembly. In the most Presbyterian areas, especially those with a covenanting history, they were 'rabbled' from their parishes, and every pre-Restoration Presbyterian minister who had been deposed from his parish during the reign of Charles II was entitled to be reinstated and would help form the nucleus of the new presbytery.

In the event, not all Episcopalian ministers, 'curates' as they were disparagingly called, were deposed; largely with the complicity of sympathetic landlords, many continued for years and presbytery minutes show a slow process by presbyteries of gaining control over every parish in their bounds. It has been estimated that by 1706 there were still 165 Episcopal priests still in possession of their parishes. This was particularly true of the north-east which was particularly sympathetic to Episcopalianism but the last parish to fall under the sway of Presbytery was in Aberfoyle, a scant twenty-seven miles from Glasgow, where the last Episcopal 'intrusion' took place several years after the Revolution and where the priest remained in splendid isolation with no reference to the Presbytery until his death in the 1720s. Perhaps his predecessor's fate, supposedly kidnapped by the fairies, was sufficient warning to Presbytery not to become too involved in the life of the parish.

However, gradually Presbyterian control of parishes intensified and, with few exceptions, even those episcopal clergy loyal to William found themselves unable to continue. In the years from 1690 to 1695 some forty previously episcopal ministers were accepted into the Church of Scotland with a further 116 subsequently swearing oaths of loyalty and putting themselves under the rule of presbytery by the end of the seventeenth century.

Those who did not sign the oath found themselves out in the cold; if the landowner did not protect them, and sometimes even if he did, they would be driven from their churches and had to make a choice whether to remain trying to maintain services in a meeting house or to leave. Again presbytery minutes show the efforts made to close down meeting-houses and prevent the priests from functioning. Services of marriage and baptism could only legally be performed by the parish minister, so any deposed minister was breaking the law if they continued the practice. As a result, a thriving industry arose in Edinburgh particularly where deposed Episcopalians offered their services (literally) in performing irregular marriages without asking too many questions. These were often arranged through agents in country parishes facilitating communications.

Meanwhile the existing bishops in Scotland, tainted with Jacobitism as they were, followed a variety of paths; one transferred to an Irish bishopric, others moved to England or abroad. Rose himself stayed in Edinburgh as *de facto* leader of the remaining Episcopalian clergy in Scotland, ultimately and perhaps ironically receiving a royal pension. Their next move though was to secure the succession of bishops for the future; by 1704 only five remained to cover fourteen dioceses and several of them were elderly. Two new bishops were appointed and consecrated the following year with a further four by 1711. At least one of these never visited Scotland at all and it was clear that those appointed were in alliance with the English churchmen who did not recognize King William (non-jurors) rather than with the now Williamite Church of England. By 1712, Queen Anne had come to the throne and the now united Parliament of Great Britain passed the Toleration Act which allowed Episcopalians in Scotland to worship freely provided they took oaths of allegiance to the monarch. Many of them decided that the time was ripe for the acceptance of the Revolution that had happened twenty-five years previously, but the death of Anne changed everything back again; the Jacobite Rising of 1715 was heavily supported by the Episcopalians and they paid a heavy price.

Many of the surviving Episcopal priests were ejected from such parish churches as they retained and from their meeting-houses. Where they were allowed to carry on they had to take the Oath of Abjuration and pray for King George. If they did not, they were restricted to congregations of less than nine people on pain of imprisonment. Some were indeed imprisoned but those who took the oath and conformed were effectively outside the jurisdiction of the Scottish bishops and so two parallel Episcopal churches came into being. Such bishops as survived by 1720 had been appointed without specific responsibility for any dioceses as they felt the right of appointment lay with the exiled Jacobite prince, but the new bishops they consecrated gradually took on dioceses. With no archbishop to wield authority, bishops were just as prone to serious disagreement as their Presbyterian counterparts and the presence of diocesan bishops alongside the older men appointed to the whole of Scotland made for a very fraught situation. This effectively resulted in a stagnation within the Church until it was resolved in 1743. By that stage, numbers had diminished substantially and there were probably fewer than 150 clergy in the country. The resolution of 1743 might have improved matters but, just as in 1712, external politics came into play with the 1745 Jacobite Rising.

Once more the Episcopalians were in general support of the losing side; once more they paid the price in the suppression of their meeting-houses. Those unwilling to take the oaths of allegiance and keeping a meeting-house were liable to imprisonment and even transportation to the American colonies, usually Barbados. A meeting-house was defined as holding a congregation of five or more people and punishments were visited on those attending services as well. Attempts to get round this act included the design of buildings so that several group of five people in different parts of the building could the preacher positioned at a central point, each claiming to be in a meeting-house of five. Additionally, it was decreed that only priests who had been ordained by English or Irish bishops could function legally as 'Qualified' priests. Initially this allowed Scottish ordained priests to be re-ordained in England or Ireland but after 1748 this route too was closed to them. On top of this no Scottish Episcopal priests were allowed to take up appointments as priests beyond Scotland

A growing number of Episcopalians went south or west to be ordained and again two parallel churches evolved, 'English Episcopal' with 'qualified' priests and 'Scottish Episcopal' largely underground. With the passage of time and the diminishing threat of Jacobitism, though, the Scottish church began to emerge from its obscurity, although still afflicted by penal laws. By 1784 they were down to forty clergy under five bishops. The event that increased their public profile was the independence of the United States. Up until the American Revolution all Americans who wanted to become Episcopalian priests had to travel to England to be ordained; as one of the ways of keeping the colonies dependent, there was no bishop appointed to the Americas. On American independence, the English hierarchy still declined to consecrate a bishop for the former colonials but the man sent across to seek consecration, Samuel Seabury, approached the Scottish bishops who were only too happy to oblige in 1784. As a result, the American Episcopal Church traces its ancestry to the Scottish Bishops.

The Penal Laws finally were abolished in 1792 on condition that the Episcopalians subscribe to the Oath of Abjuration and pray for King George and his family. They were however still barred from accepting posts or officiating in England without re-ordination there, and the Scottish bishops still had no jurisdiction over the 'English' chapels. Attempts were made to draw the English congregations into the native church and with the consecration of the one of their leaders, Daniel Sandford as Bishop of Edinburgh in 1806, the Episcopalians in Scotland gradually united. At the same time they adopted the white robes of their English counterparts and within a few years were receiving governmental help in paying stipends.

Meanwhile the Scottish Episcopal Church also received a new lease of life among the laity. Many Scottish landowners now sent their children south to be educated and with the general anglification of the gentry, the services of the Episcopal Church were seen as normal. Attendance there also took the landowners out from under the potential discipline of their local kirk sessions. Less understandable was the fashion for Edinburgh lawyers to adhere to Episcopalianism but many did, not least the lawyer, novelist and poet, Sir Walter Scott. As well as these, though, there were simply far more English people in Scotland who wished to worship in the way they were accustomed to. New churches began to be built; replacing the tiny meeting-houses which were often little more than cottages or tenement flats.

Through the middle years of the nineteenth century the Scottish Episcopal Church grew, as did many churches, although the numbers of members were never large (see Figure 5, Scottish Episcopal Church, see p 217).

In England, the Church of England was re-invigorated, and then split, by the Oxford Movement. This movement re-introduced many of the practices of the mediaeval Roman Catholic Church back into the Church of England, especially in the conduct of services, concentration on the rite of Communion, revival of church music. This was a tendency known as 'Anglo-Catholicism' or 'the high church movement' Additionally, due to way in which members were marginalized by the reluctance of bishops to appoint them to livings, many became priests in urban slum areas and in so doing acquired a more active social conscience than those in more sheltered livings. The views of the Oxford Movement chimed with the Scottish Episcopal Church and it gradually became generally more 'high church' than the Church of England, where a part of the Oxford Movement had gone the whole way and moved back to the Church of Rome. In Scotland, it was opponents of the 'high church' movement who left the main body of the Scottish Episcopal Church and for a while a number of Episcopal churches accepted the authority of the Church of England; the last two congregations which are still much more evangelical in tone rejoined the Scottish Episcopal Church in the late twentieth century.

The Episcopal Church of Scotland had 150 churches by 1858, with 163 very ill-paid clergy. The final restrictions on them were finally lifted in 1864 when at last they were put on an equal footing with English priests.

Like other small churches, the Episcopal Church made considerable use of prefabricated iron or timber halls, some of which can still be seen but other more substantial buildings also appeared. Like the other churches, mission work among Scottish communities was a priority. Not all churches had a middle or upper class congregation; churches were erected for railway workers in Edinburgh and for slate workers in Aberfoyle. By the end of the century it was prospering with 315 congregations representing an estimated national membership of about 46,000 communicants. It had developed its own naming system, with the incumbents of churches being referred to as 'rector' ('vicar' was never found in post-Reformation Scotland) and the ruling College of Bishops being chaired by the 'Primus', elected from among their number. There has been no Episcopal archbishop in Scotland since the death of Archbishop Paterson of Glasgow in 1708.

Membership peaked shortly after the Great War at nearly 60,000 communicants but had dropped to below the 1900 figure by 1950. Individual congregations though prospered; in 1900 one Glasgow congregation was worshipping in a rented shop; a hall was built in 1908, the nave of a church followed in 1912, the chancel in 1924 and the tower finished off the building in 1935. In the early years of the twentieth century the Church pursued several money raising campaigns aimed at church building mainly in urban areas. The first built six churches around Glasgow from 1914; the following decade saw a further campaign which built ten mainly in the four major cities with a further five following after the Second World War. Later activities concentrated more on mission initiatives in areas of deprivation than on bricks and mortar. Meanwhile, the Episcopalians also supported church schools in Scotland, although most disappeared or were absorbed into the state system in the following decades.

The Episcopal Church of Scotland, although often referred to as the 'English Church' is as Scottish in its roots as any of the Presbyterian churches and is rightly proud of its national heritage. It is also proud of its independence and despite its 'high church' leanings was ahead of the Church of England in allowing communion to members of other churches. It began ordaining women as priests in 1994 and was well ahead of the Church of England in approving the principle of women as bishops, although none have as yet been appointed.

3

Overview 1688–1843;
After the Revolution

The arrival of William and Mary onto the throne of Scotland changed the course of all the Scottish churches at a stroke. William was a moderate Calvinist brought up in the Dutch church. He knew many of the exiled Scottish Presbyterians who had flocked to the Low Countries as a result of the policies of Charles II in 1661 and the exile of a large number of those who refused to submit themselves to Charles' newly appointed bishops. There is no doubt that William too would have preferred to run the Scottish church through bishops, but the loyalty of the Scottish bishops to the Stuart regime made that impossible and he was left with no alternative to the Presbyterian system which Charles had dismantled but which many, though not all, Scots hankered after.

William's original intention was to leave most of the existing clergy in their churches so long as they would swear allegiance to him. Several things conspired against this; firstly the people themselves drove unpopular episcopally appointed ministers from their parishes in large numbers, particularly in the south-west of the country. This was a process known as 'rabbling'. Almost entirely bloodless, it must nonetheless have been a thoroughly unpleasant experience for the victim and rather a satisfying one for their persecutors. Secondly, the exiled ministers from 1661, although reduced by old age and death to about sixty, expected and were given the right to be reinstated in the parishes of which they had been deprived. Further, there was a similar number of younger ministers who had been ordained in exile; some of these had remained in the Low Countries while some had quietly come back and after the Indulgence Act of 1687 were operating meeting-houses around Scotland. These men felt they had a right to be the minister of the parish that contained their meeting-house and in many cases were accepted as such. As well as this, there was a group of Covenanters who had remained in Scotland.

The three surviving Covenanter ministers all applied to be accepted by the new national church, but many of their followers rejected their actions and remained outside. The final complication to William's intention, though, was the first General Assembly of the Church of Scotland. When it first met, its members could in no way be described as representative of the church in Scotland, for it comprised only the sixty pre-1661 ministers who had returned together with a lesser number of like-minded ministers and a still smaller number of elders most of whom were of similar opinions. The episcopally ordained ministers who had agreed to conform to Presbyterianism had no voice; their loyalty to the new regime was still suspect. These ministers had been largely appointed by patrons, usually the major landowner in the area, and in the case of Burghs, by the Town Council.

Meanwhile, there was a growing number of parishes which were vacant either as a result of the rabbling of the previous minister or because the newly re-established church deposed the previous minister. As a result, the church nationally, not for the first time and not for the last, found itself with a significant shortage of ministers.

By 1695, the Scottish Parliament finally regularized the situation and allowed those episcopal ministers who were to take an Oath of Allegiance to William to remain in their parishes without becoming members of presbyteries. Fifteen years later, there were still 113 of them in place, nine of whom were without even taking the oath. These were largely to be found in the north-east of the country which was always more episcopally minded than the rest of Scotland.

But if newly re-established Presbyterian Church lacked ministers, it also lacked elders. Such kirk sessions as existed in the late seventeenth century were fairly moribund with few powers; they seemed to spend most of their time pursuing fornicators. Again the sessions were likely to comprise those with Episcopalian sympathies and therefore potentially Jacobite sympathies. Under new arrangements, patrons no longer appointed ministers; that was now the right of a combination of heritors (all landowners of a certain standing in the parish), elders and (male) heads of families. Presbytery had a right to veto anyone whose doctrine did not accord with the opinions of the national church. In the case of a parish which took too long to appoint a minister, Presbytery had a right to appoint someone, subject to the congregation's approval. This right still exists today, although it is rarely enforced.

There were distinct regional variations in how the shortfalls were made up. Some north-eastern presbyteries barely functioned for the first quarter century after the Revolution and ministers had to be drafted in for several months at a time to provide any Presbyterian preaching.

When they did function, they might have to take on a fairly pragmatic approach. Dunblane Presbytery covering eleven parishes joined with Stirling which had twelve parishes together with a section of the Presbytery of Auchterarder comprising three parishes. Initially, the combined presbytery had twelve ministers and only added another four in their first three years. Of the remainder of the parishes, some seemed to have previous ministers still 'lurking'. Other parishes were being educated into Presbyterianism by the provision of preaching by neighbouring ministers. To these last could be added more sustained visits of students and probationers who would preach around the area while the Presbytery decided whether they were suitable for ordination and while congregations decided whether they were acceptable. The probationers would also have to preach and lecture to the Presbytery and have their work criticized minutely as part of their 'trials for licence'. Once deemed ready, individual churches might seek to call them to be their minister, sometimes more than one church at the same time in which case the candidate tended to ask the Presbytery to make the choice for him. Sometimes, though, students were recommended to submit themselves to substantial further study before contemplating seeking a church. The whole process was then, as now, lengthy

But if recruiting ministers was a time-consuming process, for a parish with no active Presbyterian minded elders, there was the further hurdle of re-establishing a kirk session. In the towns, this might be done by the Town Council giving a list to the Presbytery which would then examine each for religious and political orthodoxy. In 1693, Stirling Town Council nominated a list of potential elders; '*it having been the constant and undoubted right of the magistrates to give in the list of the elders*'; the Presbytery thought differently and a different list was finally accepted. In the country parishes, a visiting minister would ask for nominations of appropriate men, covering all the geographical areas of the parish. They would be examined and the whole congregation was given the opportunity to object to any or all of the names. It is difficult to identify the general standing of these early elders, although their names are to be found in the records.

Elders were generally men of substance and influence in their communities but inevitably it is easier to identify the rich than the poor and it is likely that the names that cannot be positively identified were those of less substance. The elders who attended presbytery or synod were very often land-owners or of that class. Aside from anything else, attendance implied travel to the venue of the meeting and giving up a complete day and sometimes even more to transact business and ordinary people could not afford the commitment. Even in kirk sessions, the lowest court of all, the elders were likely to be men of substance and authority, merchants, even magistrates in the Burghs, land-owners or substantial farmers in the country. It was recommended that they shouldn't be 'menial servants', and in many cases they were selected from specific communities to give a geographical coverage of the parish and to be responsible for the people of their own community

Part of the disagreement over Stirling's new elders in 1693 arose from the presence of the Castle within the Parish, but beyond the Burgh boundary leading to Presbytery's insistence that there should be elders from the Castle. Three army officers served on the Session, among them, a former covenanting exile and the son of an exile. Due to his connections, the first of these, Lieut-Col Erskine, Lieutenant Governor of Stirling Castle, by his presence at the session, and even more so, at presbytery meetings carried considerable weight. On the other hand, one of the Burgh's nominees was suspended for wife-beating; his defence was that she was drunk at the time and attacked him.

Once a new session was installed, it became possible for the parish to call its own minister. The patron had lost power, but as a compromise, the right was given to the heritors and elders, with the heads of family (male) also having some right to be consulted and with the presbytery having the right of veto on doctrinal grounds as it still has to this day. Occasionally there are traces of a nod to the old system such as when a neighbouring minister is told by presbytery to write to the previous patron to make sure that the new nominee was acceptable to him, or even her.

So why were the heritors given the power? Quite simply because they paid the bills. The traditional pattern of the Church of Scotland was that the stipend of the minister together with the upkeep of church and manse were the responsibility of the heritors. Of course, the heritors themselves raised the money from their rents, and rental agreements often contained payments described as being for the teinds. The congregations were asked for money for poor relief and not much else. Those who could pay would also pay for their desks or pews in the church but that also tended to go to poor relief. Unfortunately the records of heritors' actions are very sketchy in the archives of Scotland.

However, while it was one thing for the heritors to be responsible for those costs, it was quite another to get the money out of them when the church changed in 1690. Many heritors who lived far from the parishes where they owned property were not interested; some still supported the previous regime while some disliked the new minister who had been foisted on them. Periodically, presbytery had to take up the issue of persuading heritors to face their responsibilities. In extreme cases, the minister could be driven out by sheer poverty, merely lodging several miles from the church, with his stipend years in arrears, with no manse and with no land allocated for the upkeep of his horse. It was not unknown for the kirk session or even the minister to put up the money for essential repairs and then it was up to them to try to get the money back.

But if presbyteries were spending much of their time in pursuing financial and property matters, they had other roles too which they had never lost through the episcopal times. The records are full of discipline cases where individual kirk sessions were out of their depth, cases with one accused party adamant in their insistence of innocence, cases which involved the possible murder of a newborn child or cases of habitual re-offending. Often, the people involved were sent back to the individual churches to do penance in the community where they lived, but sometimes they flouted the greater authority and then the presbytery were able to summon the town's officers to imprison the offender or send them to the Justice of the Peace to be dealt with in country areas. On the more pastoral side though, it was the presbytery that sometimes arranged for special collections to be made over several parishes for people whose needs were greater than their own parish could cope with.

The lack of ministers in the 1690s leads to the question of what happened in those parishes where there was no minister. Family worship was expected to be observed in every household but how prevalent it was is unknown. It is quite clear though that some churches only had services every second Sunday or once a month. Indeed, those services created a gap in the church which provided the minister. Account books for churches show many gaps where it was clear that there had been no service because the minister was away preaching elsewhere, attending the General Assembly or attending one of the Commissions of the Assembly involved in rooting out dangerous Jacobite preachers in the northeast. Even when there were ministers available, then as now, ministers could become discouraged: Hugh Whyte, minister of Larbert and Dunipace,

being interrogat if he had sermon weekly answered that he had so ordinarily but not always being discouraged through his people's not resorting frequently to the weekdays sermon, the most of them living at so great a distance from both Kirks.

Gradually, though, pulpits were filled by new ministers. The old incumbents or their representatives were usually persuaded to give up the parish records, the Communion utensils and the Poor-boxes, although sometimes more easily than at other times. If the church was vacant for a while, and the vacancies in Scottish churches could be long, such money as was forthcoming for the stipend was generally put to repairing churches or often bridges in the parish. In at least one case though, the money was passed to the deposed episcopal minister, 'he being insufferably poor'.

The records show that the re-established presbyteries worked slowly to bring parishes under their oversight, perhaps concentrating or only one or two per year; the process seems to have followed the same pattern: obtain control of the keys to the building followed by the possession of the records, the Communion plate, the Poor-box and sometimes the mortcloths. The householders would then ask for 'supply of sermon' which would be done by a variety of people including probationer ministers looking for a church. After that, a neighbouring minister would look for potential new elders; once they were identified and approved by presbytery, the church would be declared vacant. Vacant churches were not advertised (that is a modern feature); instead, various men would be sounded out, perhaps invited to preach especially if they were probationers, and finally a call presented to presbytery to approve, or 'sustain' as it is still referred to. After that things might move reasonably quickly for a brand new minister, but if the sought-after minister was already in a charge, his existing presbytery had to give permission and it or the minister could obstruct the process. In that case, the whole affair could be protracted for several years as the case went all the way to the General Assembly to be decided. It was not unknown for the minister involved to have died before the process of translating him to a new charge could be completed.

Finally, by the end of the seventeenth century, the Presbyterian Church of Scotland was established and largely settled. A few 'outed' Episcopalians were still making a nuisance of themselves by conducting irregular marriages and keeping meeting-houses but it seemed unlikely that the Episcopalian regime would come back while King William or Queen Anne held the throne. William had also enacted that Episcopalian ministers who signed an Oath of Allegiance to him could retain their parishes without interference from presbytery or the compulsion to join a presbytery. William Carstares, King William's main Presbyterian adviser reported in a letter that there were 649 Presbyterian ministers, 154 Episcopalian ministers who continued under the protection of the law, 124 churches vacant and ten churches into which Episcopalian ministers have intruded themselves, while at the same time there were 150 Presbyterian preachers available to fill the vacancies. Finally, the Treaty of Union of 1707 made Presbyterianism permanently the mode of government for the Church of Scotland.

However, although Queen Anne was tied to a Presbyterian Church in her northern kingdom, she could still influence matters and create unrest. In 1712, the Parliament of Great Britain passed the 'Patronage Act' which put the privilege of calling a parish minister back to the 'patrons' who had had the right in King Charles's time, just as in England. The General Assembly objected strongly at first and then later more as a yearly ritual. Meanwhile, splits began to appear in the church at a national level; a tension arose between those who looked back to the Covenanters and Puritans as heroes and those who saw Scotland developing into a different kind of society in the eighteenth century, where the church had far less influence on people's lives. Probably, this split was more apparent in the attitudes of ministers than in those of the people. The old-fashioned powerful preachers were still popular, but there was a feeling that many of the younger ministers in particular were more worldly and more interested in their social standing. The splits became more obvious in 1721 when a group of ministers, nicknamed 'The Marrowmen', were censured for promoting the republication of a puritan book from the 1640s called *The Marrow of Modern Divinity*. This was seen as promoting an outmoded theology. Meanwhile a divinity Professor in Glasgow, John Simson, was cleared of a charge of heresy for promoting a new reason-based theology to his students. Part of his defence was that his students did not understand the Latin in which he lectured. However, although he was warned to be more careful in what he said to his students, no real action was taken against him, while the Marrowmen were formally rebuked.

It is hard to know how much impact these controversies had on ordinary people. It would depend very much on the ministers reporting back, for the elders in the General Assembly in general had little connection with the presbyteries which commissioned them.

In the mid-eighteenth century, for example, the General Assembly comprised 364 members; 201 ministers and 89 elders appointed by presbyteries, 57 elders appointed by the royal Burghs, five from the universities (either ministers or laymen) and two from the church in the Netherlands. The 201 ministers represented approximately one in four, but the effort required to attend made it so much more difficult for those in remote areas, that attendance might require an absence from the parish of many weeks. Rev. John Mill of the parishes of Dunrossness, Sandwick and Cunningsburgh in Shetland took between six and ten days each way for the trip to Edinburgh but often combined his trip with visits elsewhere lasting up to ten weeks. Incidentally, he was able to use the Assembly period as a time to select a wife three times, although one of his fiancées decided, upon reflection, to marry a minister who had a parish closer to her friends.

The elders attending the General Assembly were not the regular members of local kirk sessions or presbyteries. They were men of substance and social standing. In the early years of the eighteenth century, some peers and major landowners took on the role, particularly after the loss of the Scottish Parliament removed one forum where they could exercise their energies. Over time, this practice reduced. This was partly because so many went over to the Episcopalian church when it ceased to be seen as a hot-bed of Jacobitism and partly because the Assembly itself became less important in the life of the nation. The magnates' places were taken by lawyers, mainly Edinburgh lawyers. In 1820, there were 133 elders attending the General Assembly; seventy-two of them were lawyers nine judges and 98 per cent of them Edinburgh-based. It was seen as a suitable forum for young lawyers to become well known and to practice their skills of oratory. They were even less inclined to report back to the presbyteries which sent them, although there were honourable exceptions to this.

However, the rights of the people were gradually eroded by the Assembly. When they made it harder to veto an unpopular choice of minister and finally appointed 'riding committees' to induct ministers whom the local clergy had refused to accept, a group of ministers objected strongly. The terms of the objection, centred on a sermon given in Perth in 1734 by Rev. Ebenezer Erskine, led to his deposition and the setting up of the Secession Church by him and three other ministers. The rise of the Secession Church is covered in Chapter 4 but its effect on the national church was to polarize opinion and then remove from it a large number of ministers and people with a loyalty to the old-fashioned style of Presbyterianism and allow the 'modern' 'Moderate' party to take a control of it which lasted about ninety years.

So what did an elder do in the eighteenth century? He was allocated a part of the parish and was to visit the families frequently, looking for the results of the minister's preaching to be shown in their lives. He was to join the minister in assessing the people's religious knowledge and in visiting the sick. He had to tell people their duty and report scandal to the kirk session. As part of the kirk session, he had also to administer discipline to those who failed to live up the required standard. He would also be responsible for administering poor relief, although some parishes had deacons to do that part of the work, and look out for those in difficulties. As a kirk session, elders decided when special services and fast days would be, they would decide who was worthy of taking Communion, handing out tiny tokens which signified acceptance to those who deserved them. These tokens were usually of lead or pewter, often crudely cast or struck, but can be identified to individual churches and even occasions. The regulations at the beginning of the century give a great list of sins that the session was to look out for and deal with, although the most heinous of them were dealt with by the higher courts of presbytery or synod. Of course, elders and ministers were human too and from time to time appear before the church courts for their own misdemeanours, and it has to be said that they were treated no more leniently than anyone else, rather the opposite, as expectations were higher.

Once the Secession Church came into being, the Established Church quietened down: there were frequent losses to the Secession, almost all because of the attempt to impose a minister whom the people did not like. This took from the Church of Scotland most of the conservative element, and what was left became much more liberal in its views (although perhaps not to modern eyes). It also became more rigorous in dealing with those who rocked the boat politically. It was not just the theologically conservative who disliked the imposition of ministers; in 1752, the Rev. Thomas Gillespie, a mild-mannered gentle liberal preacher was instructed to induct an unpopular choice of minister in Inverkeithing in Fife and declined to do so. He was disciplined, deposed, out of his church and homeless in a week. Others followed him and the 'Presbytery of Relief' came into existence in 1761 as a Second Secession, accommodating those who did not agree with the backward looking stance of the Seceders or the Reformed Presbytery and who would happily go back into the establishment if they could simply be allowed to call their own ministers. The Relief Church is dealt with elsewhere in Chapter 4, but it is worth mentioning that the Relief Church was the only Scottish secession which was more liberal theologically than the church it came out of and the only Presbyterian one that did not suffer its own split.

So, having said the Church of Scotland was becoming more liberal; then what? Traditionally the Church of Scotland has had two camps, 'Evangelical' and 'Moderate'. The first has always been seen as conservative and old-fashioned, the second as liberal and modernizing. Over the last three centuries, even if the labels survive, they actually stand for quite different positions so the 'Moderate' of the early eighteenth century would have far more in common with an 'Evangelical' of the early nineteenth century than the latter might have with an evangelical of the late nineteenth century. Today 'moderate' has disappeared, but 'evangelical' remains as a label meaning lots of different things to different people.

So once the first Secession had removed the most notable evangelicals into the Secession Church, the Established Church settled down into a relatively comfortable humdrum existence for a few decades with the 'Moderates' holding power and not making any waves against the encroaching power of the government and the landed patrons. Individual congregations and people fought patronage bitterly but the result tended to be the rebellious segment of those churches joining one of the Secession presbyteries while the patron's man took over ministering to a church depleted to a greater or lesser extent by the walk out.

The Church of Scotland as a whole stagnated; ministers were chosen for gifts other than their theological insights or inspiring preaching. But although in some parishes the minister might have been chosen for his ability to make a fourth hand at whist, there were many able and brilliant figures even if they didn't shine at being ministers. The Scottish Enlightenment involved many ministers; historians, philosophers, agricultural improvers, mathematicians, scientists and even playwrights, all represented in the ranks of the clergy. This was helped by the virtual monopoly the clergy had of university posts, but equally it was helped by the breadth of the education of ministers which allowed the gifted ones to build up expertise in subjects that would leave most ministers today utterly lost. The enlightenment figures were centred round the universities, but just as the judges, also widely involved in the Enlightenment, moved to their country estates when courts weren't sitting, the ministers they had put in place in their local parishes reflected their interests even if those interests did not include the state of their souls. The width of parish ministers' interests and knowledge can be seen from the contributions many of them made to the *Statistical Account of Scotland* in the last decade of the eighteenth century.

Much as that contributed to the intellectual life of Scotland, it did not render much benefit to the church or the people. An Edinburgh bookseller, William Creech, one of the publishers of the works of Robert Burns, contrasted the Edinburgh of his youth with the Edinburgh as it was in the 1790s:

> In 1763 it was fashionable to go to church and people were interested about religion.... Families attended church, with their children and servants; and family worship was frequent. The collections at the church doors, for the poor, amounted yearly to £1500, and upwards.
>
> In 1783, Attendance on church was greatly neglected, and particularly by the men: Sunday was by many made a day of relaxation; and young people were allowed to stroll about at all hours.... The collections at the church doors for the poor had fallen to £1000.
>
> In 1763 the clergy visited, catechised, and instructed the families within their respective parishes in the principles of morality, Christianity, and the relative duties of life.
>
> In 1783, visiting and catechising were disused (except by a very few) and since continue to be so; nor, perhaps, would the clergy now be received with welcome on such an occasion.... Religion is the only tie that can restrain in any degree, the licentiousness either of the rich or of the lower ranks, when that is lost, ferocity of manners, and every breach of morality may be expected.

Traditionally, people in the church have always harkèd back to a golden age when 'everybody went to church' and it is perhaps reassuring to know that such attitudes were as prevalent two hundred years ago as they are now. One comment though does characterize the trend of the eighteenth century and that is the order of priorities: '*the principles of morality, Christianity, and the relative duties of life*'. It does seem that the Established Church sermon of the later eighteenth century was becoming fixated on morals in the present life rather than the questions of salvation and spiritual life that dominated the more conservative Secession and Reformed Presbyterian Churches. Hand in hand with this was a falling off in behaviour: the celebrations for New Year's Eve in 1783 were '*devoted to drunkenness, folly and riot, which in 1763 were attended with peace and harmony*'.

To some extent this was a side-issue of the Enlightenment, in full swing in Edinburgh as also in the rest of Scotland. People began to be able to make a living from writing, even from writing sermons. Creech commented that Dr

Hugh Blair received £200 per year for his sermons so if the church seemed to be diluted in its message some message was still being bought if not widely lived.

The national church clearly changed during the eighteenth century; the availability of alternative churches that were not going to lead to court appearances was part of this. There was a steady dribble of both ministers and people away from it from the 1720s onwards. It was largely the conservative elements at first, motivated both by a dislike of the dilution in traditional theology, but so far as the people were concerned, by the attack on their rights to have a minister of their choice. The four original churches of the 1734 Secession had become several dozen by 1770 while those who wanted to leave the establishment because of the patronage issue without returning to seventeenth century theology had an outlet in the Presbytery of Relief, founded in 1761 and also with an increasing number of congregations in the lowlands. Meanwhile many of the rich and fashionable were deserting the national church for the newly respectable and acceptable Episcopal Church.

As a church, it was as though the establishment wanted to disassociate itself from the excesses of the previous century. Its central tenet was to make people respectable and peaceable citizens. By later in the century the most influential member of this establishment was William Robertson who combined being Principal of Edinburgh University, a prominent and prolific historian, Historiographer Royal for Scotland, founder member of the Royal Society of Edinburgh and a chaplain to King George III with being one of the ministers of Greyfriars Church in Edinburgh. Despite this range of interests that would fill the life of three normal people, most of Robertson's efforts went into managing the Church of Scotland in such a way as to make the least trouble for those who ran Scotland. Robertson was the consummate politician; as leader of the 'Moderate' party in the church, he managed to persuade the General Assembly to follow his lead in almost every case, even when he was outnumbered by members of the 'Popular' party. Part of this was due to a knack of retaining friendship and respect even when disagreeing with people. He was seen as having integrity and recognized integrity in his opponents and he made a point of befriending the young ministers coming into the church so that even where they disagreed, the young ministers felt a loyalty and obligation to him. Finally he was skilled in debate and foreseeing difficulties and he knew when he was beaten and needed to cede ground. His chief aim was to preserve the peace of the church and of the nation rather than preaching the Gospel to the people, and by all accounts he was an ineffectual parish minister however skilled he was in his other roles. There is a fair argument for suggesting that, under his guidance, the church gathered into itself educated men who had no particularly vocation for ministry but saw it as a safe steady employment that allowed them time to do the things that really interested them and one which was financially very much' better than being a schoolmaster. Times have changed.

This was particularly true of Edinburgh and the surrounding area, where 'influence' was at its most influential. The autobiography of Alexander 'Jupiter' Carlyle, minister of Inveresk just outside Edinburgh showed that he and his clerical friends led a very comfortable life, drinking large quantities of claret and burgundy and rubbing shoulders with high society. At the same time, the views of this group of ministers were getting further and further away from those officially accepted by the church and by the ministers at their ordination. Robert Wallace for example openly advised ministers whose views had changed since ordination to keep quiet and be discreet; another unpublished piece of writing by him found in a manuscript in Edinburgh University Library had this surprising statement:

> It would be much better if fornication gave less scandal & there was less jealousy of wives and mistresses. I dare say there is no foundation in nature for placing so much happiness in the sole enjoyment of a woman.

Robert Wallace, it might be noted, was Moderator of the General Assembly in 1743.

Of course the urbane, polished moderate minister of the Enlightenment was not the only kind of minister in the later eighteenth century. With the departure of so many evangelicals into the Secession, a new breed of evangelical developed in those left behind. The works of Burns lampoon some of them, the fire and brimstone preachers of the day. Yet these were the ones who were beginning to develop a social conscience. John Russell, caricatured by Burns as a hellfire preacher in *The Holy Fair* as 'Black Russell' was among the earliest of Scots to campaign against slavery in the New World and was well enough thought of by the people of Stirling to be invited to go there as their minister without the influence of any patron.

By the end of the eighteenth century, Scotland produced a written work that gave virtually every minister in the Established Church his place in the written history of the country. Sir John Sinclair of Ulbster started on his great enterprise, *'The Statistical Account of Scotland'*. *'The Old Statistical Account'*, as it is known to distinguish it from its successor fifty years later, has an account of every parish in the country mostly written by the parish minister. Each was given a stock list of headings to consider but the treasure trove of local lore, agricultural history, descriptions of industry and natural history shows the catholicity of the interests of those contributing to it. On the other hand, while the contributors were asked for population numbers of the various churches in their parishes, it is clear that most of them had no idea how many of their parishioners did not attend the parish church, nor did they seem to care. Of course it was also written with an eye to the landowners who paid the stipend, provided the glebe and the upkeep of church and manse.

To place the minister entirely in the pocket of the landowner is somewhat simplistic. It is true that the patron selected the minister whether in accordance with the wishes of the congregation or not, once appointed though, the minister could not be legally ousted by the patron. He was appointed *aut vitam aut culpam*, for life or until found guilty of a fault. What the patron could do, though, was make life very uncomfortable by failing to pay stipend on time, or at all, by letting the manse moulder into a ruin or any of a number of petty irritations. In contrast, the minister paid directly by the members of his Seceder congregation was actually in a far more vulnerable position: if he stepped out of line the offerings which paid his stipend disappeared with the congregation. For this reason there is an argument for suggesting that patronage gave a minister more freedom to speak his mind to his congregation without fear of losing his source of income. Meanwhile the 1647 *Westminster Confession* was losing its universal influence. It was still a requirement that ministers and elders had to subscribe to it, indeed it still is in 2014 (with a conscience clause added to the subscription and one paragraph in it amended) but more and more ministers, especially moderates, were quietly ignoring what it actually said. In addition the old moderates who had steered the church through the threat of Jacobitism, and hence of papacy and who had been such a prominent part of the flowering of the Enlightenment were dying off and the leaders of the new generation were generally undistinguished.

The time was therefore ripe for a renewal in the evangelical wing of the party. Attempts in the 1780s to have another onslaught on patronage failed but gradually a new party arose, partly influenced by revivalism in the fledgling United States, partly triggered by a realization that industrialization was changing Scotland radically, partly by the recognition that the various alternatives to the main churches, Presbyterian and otherwise, were gaining considerable support.

One of the worries for all the institutional churches was the spread of independent preaching laymen and of churches which did not have an ordained ministry. Prime among these were the Haldane brothers, Robert and James. Their conversion in the 1790s led them on a career of preaching around Scotland and the foundation of many new independent meeting-houses. The biggest of these was James Haldane's 'Tabernacle' in Leith which was built to hold 3000 worshippers. The Established Church responded by banning the preaching of laymen in 1799, as did some of the Secession ones, but the forces that led to the Haldanes' conversion were at work on others too and many who remained in the institutional churches were led down an evangelical path.

One of the problems faced by the church from the Reformation on, but particularly during the headlong industrialization of Scotland, was that organization into parishes could lead to unbalanced results as population moved. One solution was to build 'chapels of ease'. These were churches built to ease the problems of distance and lack of accommodation. There were two main kinds of these, and on the whole they began to be erected in the 1790s. There were earlier ones; Gorbals Chapel of Ease, for example was founded in 1730, but was 'promoted' to a full parish in 1771. Some were erected in the towns and cities to accommodate the inhabitants of newly built up areas; others were built in huge country parishes to accommodate those who could not reasonably be expected to travel to a church which might be many miles away. Even where action had been taken it was often inadequate; the new Parish of Gorbals, already erected in 1771 to serve the influx of people there, saw its population grow from 500 to 35,000 between 1793 and 1833. Incidentally the 2011 Census shows the range in modern-day parish populations being from 61 to 17,866 and at least one mainland parish with a population of under 100 had its own minister at that time, so it's a problem which has never been satisfactorily tackled.

These new 'chapels of ease' were not however churches in the legal sense. Their ministers, although they had the same training as parish ministers, had no seat in presbytery. Nor did the chapels have elders and kirk sessions of their own; they came entirely under the jurisdiction of the parish minister and kirk session. What they might have was a group of managers who were responsible for the building and the collections taken on behalf of the poor. Perhaps inevitably, ministers who felt called to serve in such chapels had an evangelical mind-set and perhaps more of a social conscience than those more conventionally placed. Equally inevitably the new ministers of such charges tended to be young and newly ordained and tended to move into parish churches in the course of time, building up a core of evangelical ministers who helped to turn the tide against moderatism.

The process of erecting chapels of ease was slow: it had to be done with the consent of the local minister and kirk session; it then required the backing of presbytery and in the late 1790s, the approval of the General Assembly was made compulsory. This was a reaction to the suspicion in some minds that these new churches took money away from poor relief and could be used as a means to avoid unpopular ministers. Meanwhile the Secession Churches were able to build up new congregations without any hindrance from anyone. For twenty-three years in the late eighteenth century the Relief Church in Anderston in Glasgow had the whole of that growing area to itself with no other church in easy walking distance; a century later the area had fifteen churches of seven different denominations.

By the beginning of the nineteenth century change was in the air for the Established Church and indeed for all the churches. The French Revolution had brought a challenge for the established order; the long wars ultimately brought economic misery. The original ideas that spurred the Revolution led to changes in all parts of Scottish society, whether it was the growing taste for democracy, an increasing tendency to question the social order or a growing consciousness of human rights. As the Revolution unfolded though, revulsion against its excesses also led to a movement against some of the eighteenth century thought that primed it. The anti-clericalism and rejection of religious institutions in France helped to promote a more orthodox religion in Scotland and the more philosophical musings of the moderates came to by seen by some as tainted by the events in France.

Meanwhile the Secession Churches in Scotland, split in 1747 into Burgher and Anti-burgher factions, were successively rent by schisms with the same cause, the 'New Light' controversy. In the wider context this controversy led a majority in each group to question among other topics, the relationship of government to the church, leading to what became known as 'voluntarism'.

The war itself and the economic changes associated with it also led to a diminution in religious zeal. One, Doctor Lucas, writing his diary in 1813 wrote;

The Kirk, the Old and New light seceders, the Anti-burghers, the Cameronians all held their Sacraments about this time. The crowds of people who used to attend them are much diminished. Their respective Churches and Meetinghouses contains them now with ease but bigotry is not yet extinguished.

Once the immediate sparks of the 'New Light' controversy had died down, it became clear that little separated the two 'New Light' churches except their mutual distrust and bitterness over the past and that union between the two was likely if not inevitable. This concentrated the minds of the Established Church for it did not take a mathematician to see that the combined 'New Light' churches would be a significant rival to the Church of Scotland in the lowlands with the common cause of voluntarism to make it potentially attractive for many. At the same time the independent churches of the Haldanes and their disciples were growing in number to about 200 while the Scottish Episcopal Church had emerged from its long association with Jacobitism and was proving popular with the landed classes and Edinburgh lawyers. Those committed to the Established Church as a national church knew that it had to change. Moderatism had had its day and the evangelical wing took over.

Some of the battles that were fought to allow the change may seem unlikely today. The first real victory for the evangelicals was when their candidate for the Chair of Mathematics in 1805, was appointed over the candidate of the moderates. The significance for the evangelicals was that they were supporting a mathematician while the moderates were supporting a churchman who would combine teaching mathematics with being a parish minister. The evangelical view was that being a parish minister was and should be a full-time job and university teaching should be done by others, preferably those that specialized in their subject. The whole battle against pluralism was not won for many years though and even in the 1840s King's College, Aberdeen had professors whose knowledge of their subject was not much ahead of their students.

The early results of the French Revolution on the church were to prompt some stirrings of democracy in Scotland. 'The Society of the Friends of the People' was seen variously as a great movement devoted to social and political improvement or a deeply dangerous revolutionary movement devoted to overthrowing the government and society as a whole. Robert Burns' flirtation with it is well known, but among those who suffered for their devotion to that cause were those who were attached to both Church of Scotland and Secession Churches. Thomas Muir was the best known of these political martyrs. An elder of the Church of Scotland, he had successfully fought against attempts by mill owners to impose their choice of minister in his own parish. Allied to him was William Skirving who had started to study for the ministry the Burgher branch of the Secession Church before becoming a farmer. They both paid the price and were transported to Australia for their political, rather than their religious, beliefs. At least some in the churches saw these changes abroad as having significance for Scotland and as signifying potential changes at home.

For some though the changes were more religious than political. Robert Haldane became one of the great evangelical figures of his day, honoured as a heroic figure by the Baptist and Congregationalist traditions. He said he was 'awakened from the sleep of spiritual death' by the French Revolution and his example fired a new spirit of evangelism. Although Robert and James Haldane started their work within the Established Church, they soon parted company with it and began to promote a form of independent church, complete with a college for training new pastors, before splitting again from that group, repudiating infant baptism and instituting one of the founding branches of the Scottish Baptist tradition.

With the end of the French wars in 1815, though, further change was in the air. The two main Secession churches, 'New Light' Burghers and 'New Light' Anti-burghers, were on their way to a union in 1820 that would make them a serious rival to the establishment and it was also seen that the Secession Churches and the Relief Churches had a substantial presence in the new areas of built up cities. Finally the Established Church woke from its torpor, or at least a portion did, and began to try to reach that portion of the population that had been neglected in the previous few decades. This took two routes: on the one hand there were fresh efforts to provide churches that the people of the Highlands could attend without walking miles. This probably was a reaction to the efforts of the Haldanes and others outside the Kirk to evangelize the Highlands. The other route, as previously alluded to, was to increase the numbers of 'chapels of ease' in the areas that were experiencing substantial population growth. The 'evangelical' party in the church began to grow in numbers and in influence.

The way that the evangelical party had put the needs of ministry to the fore began the process that pulled many to the evangelical point of view even within the Established Church; Praying Societies again flourished for the laity, individual and personal religion took on a new lease of life. Into all of this came the figure of Thomas Chalmers.

Chalmers is still looked on as one of the giants of the Scottish church even if his reputation has been revised much in the two centuries since his ordination. Many church buildings throughout the country have been named after him in the course of the last 150 years.

As a young minister in Kilmany in Fife he had ambitions to become Professor of Mathematics at St Andrews University and when that ambition was baulked gave rival lectures in the town to show the University what their students were missing. This did not make him many friends in high places in Fife, but was part of a process that showed that he was equally at home in the sciences as in theology. This led him to the study of economics and the publication of a book whose title still chimes with modern ecological concerns, *Extent and Stability of Natural Resources* in 1808. It also coincided with the time in which he moved from the 'moderate' camp in the church into the 'evangelical' camp. The early attempts to make an academic name for himself were deferred in 1815 when he moved from his Fife village church with a parish of about 800 people to Glasgow, first of all to the Tron Church with a parish of about 11,000. Once in Glasgow he tried for a while to concentrate purely on his parish and ignoring the other city-wide duties that fell to the lot of the ministers, committee meetings, charitable foundations and the rest. When that attempt failed he took a different direction by galvanizing his active church members to take on the role of visiting the parish, all 11,000 of them. After four years, Chalmers persuaded the Council to appoint him to the newly erected parish of St John's in the east end of the city where he was intent on conducting a great experiment. This experiment was the product of a combination of a Tory mind and evangelical faith; he wanted to make this large and poverty stricken area of Glasgow both Christian and self-supporting in poor relief; equally he wanted to make sure that political radicalism would not gain a foothold. In a wider context he believed that this could be the model of social care throughout the nation. It was adapting what was the general rural way of life of neighbour looking after neighbour to an urban context where the social bonds needed to be built up for the first time. By the time he left . four years later the scheme was running, but it was never viable in the long term and it is tempting to suggest that he left just before the bubble burst. Among the reasons for its failure was that it relied totally on organization and resources from outside. The people of the parish were too busy scraping their meagre living to devote time to organized visitation. All those who did the work in relieving the poor were in fact brought in from Chalmers' old parish of the Tron; it was essentially a paternalistic experiment where the better-off worked to bring benefit to the poor who in turn were meant to be duly grateful.

One result of this, in fact, was that the Tron Church was so denuded of elders and active church workers that it struggled to survive in the year or two after Chalmers' departure; his successor there did not share the widespread admiration of him.

After eight years in Glasgow, Chalmers had a huge reputation. Despite not being a particularly good public speaker technically, the intensity of his oratory carried his listeners. One writer said that if he had only learned to speak without notes 'he might have been king of Scotland'.

In 1823, Chalmers achieved his ambition of a professorship at St Andrews University; it is said that he had been offered no fewer than seven professorships during his time in Glasgow. This was not in Mathematics as he had hoped twenty years previously, but in Moral Philosophy. From this time he became more and more a national figure and a leader of the evangelical wing of the church. In 1828 he was appointed as Professor of Divinity at Edinburgh University. It was reported that his first lecture in Edinburgh was punctuated with rapturous applause. He even became a national figure in England; although English ears needed to be attuned to his Fife accent and rapid delivery.

In an attempt to strengthen the evangelical party in the courts of the church, the General Assembly voted to give ministers of chapels of ease the same rights of membership of presbyteries, synods and the General Assembly as parish ministers. By 1826 there twenty-seven chapels of ease, with forty or so 'Parliamentary Churches' planned in the Highlands and Islands, to be built with government money; six years later there were eighty-two. The General Assembly of 1833 decided that the Parliamentary Churches should be given the same status as parish churches. The remainder had their status changed the following year. For the first time the evangelical party had a majority in the national church and they intended to mould the church to their views. The admission of the ministers of the chapels of ease gave them a safe majority.

With that done the Assembly turned its attention back to patronage and the rights of congregations to have a say in choosing their minister. The Assembly voted by 184 to 139 to pass the Veto Act which laid down that if a majority of male heads of families in the congregation disapproved of the minister nominated by the patron, then presbytery had to refuse to sustain the call (allow the minister to be inducted). While this did not address the principle of patronage itself, it did restore an element of choice to the congregations. These two acts were the first shots in what became known as the 'Ten Years' Conflict' leading to the Disruption of 1843 and the founding of the Free Church. Although now remembered as a conflict over patronage as the earlier secessions of 1734 and 1761 had been, it was not quite as simple as that. For one thing, until the Veto Act was passed and challenged in the courts, imposing ministers against the will of the parish had largely become a thing of the past, and even some of those against patronage itself did not feel comfortable in passing an act which seemed tacitly to accept the principle. It was actually a means to reduce the likelihood of civil disorder at a time when the people were getting increasingly restive both politically and in terms of their faith.

As well as the 'Ten Years' Conflict', the 1830s saw a great deal of activity in the other churches of Scotland. New churches were springing up with no reference to the tradition of Presbyterianism. Some of these were trying to reproduce practice in early church by working without governing institutions, Primitive Methodists, Brethren, Baptists all started to make significant inroads into Scotland in this decade, aiming largely at the unchurched urban poor. But other less conventional churches such as the Catholic Apostolic Church and the Mormons were coming along behind and again attracting a population ready for change. Political radicalism and the faith even made common cause in Chartism which managed both to found Chartist Churches and be one of the earlier outlets for atheism. The growth of personal faith among the people of Scotland during the years from 1820 largely found the national church wanting. Meanwhile the United Secession Church of 1820, having bitten the bullet of union, found its numbers increasing and began regarding a further union, this time with the Relief Church, as a prospect worth pursuing. As if all this was not enough, a number of independently minded ministers began to preach a faith that was seen as incompatible with the *Westminster Confession* of 1647 and were deposed for heresy. In retrospect, two of them, John McLeod Campbell and Edward Irving are now regarded as among the most original and influential thinkers of their time.

Irving died young, but Campbell's importance was acknowledged by his being honoured by Glasgow University a few years before his death in 1872.

So Scotland of the 1830s was in somewhat of a ferment. The law took a hand, well backed up by the government of the day and found that the new status of chapels of ease was illegal as it beyond the powers of the church to redesignate them.

At the same time, however the church asked the government to fund endowments for the stipends of the ministers of twenty new churches erected to serve the newly arrived residents of the rapidly expanding Glasgow. As the various Seceder churches had been active in these areas for some time this seemed a direct challenge to them, and worse, a challenge backed up with financial resources to which the Seceders could not get access. Relations between the Church of Scotland and the Seceder churches quickly degenerated into acrimony and this was followed by the disagreements between moderates and evangelicals within the Church of Scotland becoming equally acrimonious in language and feeling. As a result virtually all the contemporary writing about the years leading up to the Disruption of 1843 has an unashamedly partisan flavour that may well reinforce the modern reader's view that Christians of the early Victorian period were a fairly unlikeable bunch.

The Veto Act in particular was speedily tested by a number of high-profile cases of ministers being presented and the presbytery refusing to induct them. In Auchterarder only two parishioners signed the call to the nominee, one Robert Young. Disapproval was recorded by 286 out of 330 heads of families. When the presbytery refused to induct him, Young took the presbytery to court. The Court of Session found in his favour by eight to five; the judge who had originally proposed the Veto Act as an elder in the General Assembly ironically had to sit in judgement on it as a lawyer. He was, not surprisingly, one of the five in the minority. According to the judgement, the Church of Scotland only had such power as Parliament gave it and was not the independent spiritual community that it claimed to be. Furthermore the right of patronage was a property right and therefore an attack on patronage was an attack on property which could not be countenanced. The Church took the case to the House of Lords which backed the Court of Session. The case carried on for years and it was not until after the Disruption that Robert Young was inducted to Auchterarder. The principle that the Church of Scotland only had such power as Parliament gave it was not overturned until the 1920s when it was recognized that the Church of Scotland is in fact and in law an independent spiritual community in no way subject to Parliament.

Other cases rumbled on too; there were parliamentary attempts to change the law which failed largely through lack of interest in Parliament and there were more disputed presentations referred to the civil courts. As a result the seven ministers who had inducted the unwanted nominee to the Church of

Strathbogie in Aberdeenshire were deposed by the General Assembly of 1842 which was itself interrupted by an attempt by the Civil Courts to serve an interdict on the Moderator. Not unnaturally the Assembly took huge offence at this 'violent intrusion of the secular arm into the ecclesiastical province'. The evangelicals began to increase their demands: patronage was to go completely and a 'Claim of Right' was adopted which summarized the grievances that the evangelicals held regarding the position of the church as they saw it. It accused the Court of Session of controverting the oath that successive sovereigns had taken; it claimed breaches in the Treaty of Union and declared it to be an essential doctrine of the church that it had no Head but Christ. The role of the state was to protect the church, not to try to govern it.

In amongst all this controversy came another. Although the majority of the Seceders had joined into the United Secession Church, the remnants of the two 'Old Light' churches still survived, strengthened by gathering in those New Light ministers who didn't like the union. One of those groups, the 'Old Light Burghers' decided to rejoin the national church on the grounds that it was now agitating in support of the stand that their predecessors had taken over a century previously. This brought thirty-eight evangelical ministers into the church and their churches were given the status of chapels of ease. There were many within the church who believed that the Assembly did not have the power to give these churches parochial status or admit a new group of ministers and elders into presbyteries and higher courts and there was strenuous opposition from the moderates. Aside from the 'political' aspect of the reunion, they also claimed a dilution of the intellectual standing of ministers by accepting these Seceders whose training, they said, was inferior to their own and had no compulsory university education in it.

Meanwhile it began to be clear that a major change in the ecclesiastical landscape of Scotland was being planned. The combination of the hardening of evangelical attitudes, the unwillingness of Parliament to change its policy towards the Scottish church, the increasingly bitter and personal war of words between the different factions in the church all meant that some sort of crisis-point was inevitable.

In November 1842, 465 ministers gathered in Edinburgh and started planning the Disruption in earnest; 423 of them signed a Statement of Grievance, with 354 signing a further paper promising to resign their charges and stipends if the grievances were not addressed. From there, actions moved to congregations and minute books exist showing the plans for raising money for stipends, manses and church buildings. These being separate from the official minutes of those churches, the records went with those who left and often became the first records of the infant Free Church congregations. Not all the evangelical party joined the Convention. One group, a middle party of about forty-five, held a separate meeting and ultimately remained in the

Established Church, being known disparagingly as 'The Forty Thieves' for their pains. Meanwhile the evangelical majority was threatened by Parliament's decision that ministers of former chapels of ease, now redesignated as *quoad sacra parishes*, did not have a vote on the Assembly. As a result some presbyteries found their choice of commissioners to the Assembly challenged and the evangelical party found that what they had expected to be a firm majority on any partisan matter was likely to be a slim minority. This played havoc with what had been intended to be a carefully constructed strategy. The original idea had been that the Assembly would vote for disassociating itself from the establishment as a whole and then carry on as the Assembly without moving. Those who disagreed would then have had the dilemma of whether to walk out and hence secede from the majority, or stay put and acquiesce in the decision. The lack of a sure majority meant this could not happen.

Finally in May 1843, the General Assembly met in St Andrews Church in Edinburgh. The Moderator from the previous year opened proceedings but immediately protested against the meeting proceeding further and invited those of like mind to withdraw and meet in another place. This avoided the need for a vote which might not have given the desired result. He delivered his protest, signed by 203 commissioners to the Assembly, and left the Church of Scotland followed by 120 ministers and 72 elders and watched by large crowds. They processed down to the Tanfield Hall in Canonmills and there constituted themselves the first General Assembly of 'The Church of Scotland, Free and Protesting', the Free Church of Scotland as it became known. (Confusingly, some early newspaper reports refer to them as 'Free Presbyterians', a name that came to refer to an offshoot church some fifty years later.)

Meanwhile, back in St Andrews Church, the remaining two-thirds of Assembly carried on with the work including continuing to lobby parliament to give the Church of Scotland and its people the freedoms that they and those they had just lost wanted. A couple of days later the Assembly deposed those who had walked out and started the long process of rebuilding the undoubtedly weakened national church.

4

Dissenting Voices; The Covenanter and Seceder Traditions

Many people when they think of the varieties of churches that Scotland can offer will think primarily of the Free Church, colloquially known as the 'Wee Frees', or perhaps the Free Presbyterian Church, colloquially known as the 'Wee, Wee Frees'. There were, however, a number of other splits within Presbyterianism over the last 325 years and this chapter attempts to show the variety of denominations that have arisen and in many cases disappeared as a result of unions.

Reformed Presbyterians

After the establishment of Presbyterianism as the structure for the Church of Scotland in 1690, two groups were immediately 'dissenters' but with completely opposite views, and largely at opposite ends of the country.

One group, that we saw in Chapter 2, was made up of those who wished to remain Episcopalians, largely in the north-east of the country. The other group were the successors to the Covenanters, mainly in the south-west. This latter group were often referred to as Cameronians but also as the Hill People, the Society People, the Corresponding Societies, among others. In due course, many of them formed into the 'Reformed Presbyterian Church' and there are still churches in Scotland which take their descent from them and form a presbytery.

When William and Mary took the throne and established Presbyterianism, many hoped that it would end the turmoil the killing times had brought; some of the Covenanters immediately offered their services to the new king and were incorporated into the army as the twenty-sixth Regiment of Foot, or as 'Cameronians'. One of the toughest regiments in the army, the Cameronians retained some of their covenanting traditions until the day of their disbandment in 1967, posting armed guards at their services (still called conventicles) and having a regimental Kirk Session.

However, a substantial part of the Hill People actually disapproved this, for they were pledged to support only a 'covenanted' monarch who would promise to make their brand of Christianity the national and compulsory church. As a result, they cut themselves off from the rest of the church and formed instead 'Praying Societies' which became the central core of their religious observance. This was in a sense inevitable for they had no minister for the first sixteen years of their existence after the Revolution. They met in small, mainly rural groups comprising tenant farmers, cottars and the like. They maintained a proud separation and in secular matters would not recognize any of the crown institutions as having any authority; they would not use the courts, would not take oaths, would not vote or take any official position. In cutting themselves off from the Established Church, however, they also lost all their ministers, for the three covenanting ministers still operating in Scotland at the time of the Revolution of 1688 rejoined the establishment, to the disgust of many of their followers.

The remaining Covenanters were therefore left in a quandary. They could hold prayer meetings and services for they had a religious knowledge and background that would put most modern ministers to shame. While the various societies could meet together (or correspond) to decide on what was the accepted doctrine or on what to do about back-sliders, they could not celebrate the Sacraments of Baptism and Communion or perform marriage ceremonies. So, for sixteen years, the remnants of the Covenanters had to find other ways to resolve this issue. Therefore, some quietly went to their local parish minister to perform marriage ceremonies, while some went to Ireland to find ministers to baptize their children and yet others looked for ministers as close to their own views as possible. Ironically, all these routes they took were wrong and quite likely to lead to penance being required.

Given their firm view that they represented the only true Church and any deviation from their views was heresy, it is not surprising that the various groups of covenanting views which remained after the accession of William split into various factions. In addition to the Reformed Presbyterians, who survive to this day, several groups were active until well into the eighteenth century. One of the last survivors of the strictest group, John Calderwood, who survived into the nineteenth century, died unmarried because 'only a lawful Minister of the Gospel could perform the ceremony and there was not such a minister to be found on earth'.

Though largely based in the south-west, the Praying Societies stretched as far as Perthshire, Stirlingshire and Fife. An event in their heartland that settled the long-term future of the biggest of the groups was when John MacMillan, minister of Balmaghie church, in Galloway, left the establishment in 1706 to join the Hill People. MacMillan gave his name to yet another nickname for the group 'MacMillanites' and worked unceasingly, travelling from one Praying Society to another, baptizing children, performing marriages and celebrating the Sacrament of Communion. His baptismal roll which has been preserved and published shows how far his responsibilities covered. Judging from the number of baptisms listed, it seems likely though that his followers numbered fewer than 1500 at any one time.

However, the existence of one minister did not guarantee a Presbyterian future in itself, for a single minister could not ordain anyone else as a minister; that savoured of bishops, nor could he form a presbytery without other ministers. The Praying Societies discussed the possibility of working with a minister from beyond the group but that was not a practical proposition given their strict stance. Finally, another disaffected minister, Thomas Nairne, joined them and in 1742, fifty-two years after the split, they were finally able to form the 'Reformed Presbytery'. Nairne himself disappeared into obscurity, deposed from the ministry for 'scandal' but not before the young presbytery had ordained four more ministers and assured the succession.

It was not always a comfortable church. MacMillan himself was given a testing time by his flock who looked upon him as a bit too liberal (to this day, in many churches, the members tend to be more conservative than the clergy). In particular, he barely escaped censure for being married by a minister of the establishment. The early ministers were peripatetic and church buildings were not necessary, the groups meeting in farmhouses and barns as was convenient. A directory of worship from Praying Societies dating from the 1780s directs that the proper number for a society was between twelve and fourteen adults. If numbers reached twenty-nine, it was time to split into separate societies. Sunday worship had to be five hours long in the summer and four in winter. The prayer meeting should always be opened and closed by a man, but women could lead worship within the meeting. (A fairly revolutionary concept; in eighteenth-century Britain only Methodists allowed women to speak.)

Only men could vote in the election of a minister except in the unlikely case of a congregation entirely made up of women where the heads of households would have the vote.

Gradually, the presbytery became settled. With four ministers by 1775, all called 'John', they had fixed areas of interest but there was a gradual expansion. In the north for example, Stirling and Linlithgow was a single charge for a few years and then split into two. Stirling received as its first minister John MacMillan, grandson of the original John, preached into his new charge by his father, also John.

Separate as they kept themselves, it is interesting to note that the Stirling congregation received a loan of £120 from the Rev. John Muschet, one of the local ministers of the Established Church, covering a third of the cost of the church they built in 1784, so relations cannot have been that bad, especially as they seem to have worshipped in the unused part of the parish church for several years before that.

As their dislike of government institutions still gave some problems, a workaround was sometimes found. For example, the Militia Act of 1797 called up a random selection of men by ballot to serve in the Militia and defend Britain against France. Reformed Presbyterians would not serve in the armed forces, so they had to find substitutes even to take part in the ballot.

Because of the type of people who formed the greater part of the membership, they had little need for contact with officialdom, but with the passing of the Reform Act of 1832, some became eligible to vote and this gave rise to a crisis of conscience as to whether a member of the church was allowed vote for an uncovenanted government. It was judged a disciplinary offence to vote and the separation continued.

Strict as they were, the members were fallible, like anyone else, and discipline cases occurred regularly. In the Stirling congregation for example, two brothers were nominated for the eldership, they demurred on account of their economic circumstances, but within a couple of years, one of them was charged with drunkenness and keeping the company of women of ill-fame, although it was not proven. At about the same time, the wife of one elder was rebuked for drunkenness while another elder was asked to resign because he never attended services.

Against that were the anecdotes of members who walked eight miles every Sunday to Stirling from Dunblane regularly while one walked in from Gartmore each week, a round trip of forty miles (see Figure 6, Reformed Presbyterians 1851, see page 218).

The 'Praying Society' ethos persisted in theory too; but the church records that contain the minutes of the prayer meetings show that only a couple of elders attended on a regular basis. In the early 1860s, a majority of the Reformed Presbyterians finally decided that voting in parliamentary elections was acceptable. As a result, the Church was split with a small group continuing its opposition to all matters official. It was this group which gave rise to the RP church which continues to exist. The greater part of the church spent a year or two in discussions with the United Presbyterians and the Free Church to form a three-way union but when the UP Church and the Free Kirk stepped back from union, the RP decided to join with the Free Church and this came through in 1876. For a while they retained the identity of a separate presbytery primarily to deal with property matters but finally were absorbed and joined the later unions with the majority of the Free Church.

That minority group remained as one of the smaller Presbyterian denominations. A slow decline left them with only two churches by 2000, in Stranraer and Airdrie, but since then a small number of other churches have joined them as a result of splits in other conservative denominations.

The RPs were not just a Scottish denomination; emigrants took the sect to the United States where it flourished. Again it went through various splits and unions and has several descendant bodies such as the Associate Reformed Presbyterian Church which is based in South Carolina. The church also played its part in the Victorian expansion of missionary endeavour. It sent a significant number of its ministers and their families to the New Hebrides. As a final sidelight, however, it is to the Reformed Presbyterians' abiding credit that one of its American daughters was the first church formally to condemn slavery in the United States in 1802 and enacted that no one who kept slaves could receive the sacrament of Communion.

Other former covenanting groups; The Hebronites and others

Not all Covenanters were united. Various groups, all believing that they had the one true faith, proliferated among the Covenanters, so there were Adamites, Harlites, Hebronites and Howdenites, not to mention Russelites and Wilsonites. There were also Gibbites but they had died out prior to the revolution of 1688 and therefore are dealt with elsewhere. There is not much contemporary written record from these groups, although pamphlets promoting their particular theologies and squabbles exist.

Of these groups, the largest was probably the Hebronites led by John Hepburn. Hepburn, unusually for a Covenanter, had been an Episcopalian and was educated at King's College, Aberdeen. Ordained in London by Scots exiles, he preached before the Battle of Bothwell Brig in 1679, and in the following year he was asked by the parishioners in Urr (Galloway) to 'preach the Gospel occasionally among them as his conveniency and safety doth allow'. He was periodically imprisoned but amazingly seems to have been in little real danger during the 'killing times'. He had a reputation for looking after his own skin; as one contemporary remarked, 'he aye joucked to the leeside'. That said, after the Revolution of 1688, he found himself the leader of a party which didn't want to accept the newly defined Established Church but equally did not want to reject it out of hand. This party was then described as Hebronite in an allusion to the biblical land of Hebron.

In 1690, the Hebronites took their grievances to the General Assembly, grievances largely to do with the attitudes towards those who had toed the episcopal line prior to the Revolution. Hepburn, as a minister of the church, had the opportunity to present his case and the petition was handed over to a committee to deal with, in the time-honoured fashion of the church. As he gradually became more outspoken, he was summoned by the Synod of Dumfries and then to the General Assembly. Another committee of the Assembly ruled that he should confine himself to preaching within his own parish with the permission of presbytery or synod, a restriction which he declined to accept, and was therefore suspended. Shortly after, he was imprisoned for a brief period for his apparently treasonable comments when invited to take the Oath of Allegiance.

He soon returned to Urr and continued to lead the opposition to a church which supported an uncovenanted king. Another attempt at reconciliation took place in 1705 at Sanquhar, where a new committee which included several former Covenanters met with Hepburn. According to the son of an eyewitness, three or four thousand attended the meeting and it appears to have been a somewhat tumultuous occasion. Finally, instead of the desired reconciliation, the process led to Hepburn's deposition. That was the theory; in practice, he remained in full possession of the church, manse and the parish. His followers then formalized their existence into 'societies' especially in Galloway and Nithsdale but also in Ayrshire and Lanarkshire. Attempts were made to reconcile them with the Cameronians but to no avail.

The Hebronites were emphatically against the Union of 1707 and attempts were made to raise an army to march on to Edinburgh. John Ker of Kersland was sent from Edinburgh to negotiate with the potential rebels though, and apparently persuaded the 'army' of about 300, horse and foot, to confine themselves to a public burning of the Articles of Union at the market cross of Dumfries. In fact, at least two contemporary commentators, including Daniel Defoe, believed that Hepburn was actually acting as a government agent at the time. The Hebronites took to arms again in 1715, marching on Dumfries in defence of their religious rights. In the event, they gradually dispersed without violence and it is hard to see any of them throwing in their lot with the Jacobites.

The Hebronites seemed rather to have suffered a seven-year itch, for in 1722, the 'Levellers' hit Galloway, demolishing the dykes that were newly built to enclose common land. Whether all the Levellers were from Hepburn's party is not known, but a substantial number were, and they were certainly publicly blamed. Some modern left-wing historians look on the Levellers as one of the earliest heroic working-class associations fighting for the common man. It is doubtful whether the Hebronites themselves would accept that description.

When Hepburn died in 1724, many of his followers accepted that their cause was lost and came back into the national church, but fifteen years later, some of his Praying Societies petitioned the newly formed Secession Church for supply of sermon, and in due course, Sanquhar became the home of the first Secession Church in the south of Scotland, with another following soon after in Hepburn's former parish of Urr. With these moves, the Hebronites came to an end as a distinctive body within Scotland and the Church. Nationally, their influence and their legacy were small and localized, but within the southwest of the country, they had their fifteen minutes of fame.

Of the other groups listed, the Adamites are so obscure that it is uncertain whether they were a group following William Adams, Minister of Humbie in East Lothian, or John Adamson, Minister of Sorn in Perthshire. The Harlites followed the lead of John and Andrew Harley. One early eighteenth-century author, Patrick Walker, attended a service that Andrew Harley conducted in Edinburgh; his congregation consisted of his brother, five women, a girl and a boy. Walker described the service in these terms: *'He rambled through the whole 58th Chapter of Isaiah, but his sermon had neither top, tail or mane; he had not one material sentence.'* To this, Harley responded by accusing Walker of *'sotting and sleeping like one intoxicate with drink'*.

The Russelites were one of these groups to predate the Revolution; they were the followers of James Russel who had been implicated in the murder of Archbishop Sharp in 1679. Following the Covenanter rule of not contributing to an uncovenanted government, the Russelites would have no truck with anyone who paid tax; therefore ale and tobacco were both banned. They also objected to the idea that the days of the week and the months of the year should be called after heathen gods. Russel himself seems to have spent the remainder of his life in exile and his party faded into obscurity.

The Howdenites were perhaps the most aggressive of the eighteenth-century covenanting groups. Again there is some doubt about what they actually believed, but after the death of Queen Anne in 1714, they seem to have considered both the Jacobite and the Hanoverian claimants of the throne to be usurpers. John Howden, who had been an upholsterer to trade, was even accused of being a Jacobite by one contemporary, who also claimed that the Howdenites had never exceeded 100 in number. At the Jacobite Rising of 1745–1746, the Howdenites to all intents and purposes declared war on both sides, referring to both Prince Charles and the Duke of Cumberland as 'pretenders' and referring to the redcoat army as a 'hellish crew', thus being amongst the first to condemn the barbarous reprisals the redcoats carried out after Culloden in 1746. Prior to that, in 1739, they had proclaimed that they were against all Acts and Laws not founded upon the common equity of the Word of God.

Finally, in this group of dissident extreme Protestants come the Wilsonites, named after a teacher called William Wilson in Dumfries, who had left the United Societies led by John MacMillan, reputedly because MacMillan had accused him of drunkenness. The Wilsonites again were small in number and much of the evidence for their existence is restricted to a few copies of pamphlets that survived. Like the Howdenites, they were against the accession of the Hanoverian dynasty, but to be fair they were against almost everything else; the evangelist George Whitefield was referred to as an 'emissary of Satan', a description with which few would agree. The Wilsonites largely died out after the death of Wilson, but it is to them that the last survivor, John Calderwood, owed his allegiance.

The Secession Churches; 1733–1901

One of the aspects of the church in Scotland and its history is the strange names that are attached to some of the groups that appeared and disappeared over the years. 'Burghers' and 'Anti-burghers' rub shoulders with 'New Lights' and 'Old Lights' or even worse, 'Auld Lichts'. Worse still is both New Light Burghers and New Light Anti-burghers disagreeing with each other as well as with New Light Anti-burghers and Old Light Anti-burghers. It's very tempting to say at that point 'enough!', leave them all to their own devices and look for some light relief. Then the realization comes that there was a Relief Church as well and despair sets in. Nonetheless, all these groups were part of Scotland's lowland heritage and were individually of importance to many of our ancestors and however irrelevant their disagreements may seem now, they helped to form Scottish society and indeed the modern Church of Scotland.

All these churches take their origins from one particular event in Scottish history, the Patronage Act of 1712. Although the Act of Union in 1707 had enshrined in its principles the independence of the church and the legal system, it was not long before both were under scrutiny. In 1712, the Patronage Act (an Act to restore the patrons to their ancient rights of presenting ministers to the churches vacant in that part of Great Britain called Scotland) was passed, which saw the right of presentation of a minister to a parish given (or restored, depending on your point of view) to any of a variety of bodies including the crown, town councils, the universities or individual landowners. The General Assembly protested that the right to call a minister lay with the parishioners or, to be accurate, with the male heads of households in the parish; the local gentry had the same rights as any other members. The local gentry, as heritors, might have the burden of the upkeep of the church and the obligation to pay the minister but that obligation went with their privileges as landowners.

The new act claimed to restore the situation as it had been before the accession of William and Mary; it excluded known Roman Catholics from the right of patronage but not Episcopalians and others out of sympathy with the Established Presbyterian Church. Parishes where the right of patronage had lain with bishops or archbishops fell to the crown. The Church of Scotland protested vociferously but to no avail; indeed it continued to protest for many years, but gradually the protests became more a matter of habit than of conviction and for many in the church, patronage was an accepted fact of ecclesiastical life.

However, there was a body of men in the Church of Scotland who did look at the church and saw it backsliding from the principles established in 1690. They first came to notice in 1718 when they supported a reprint of a puritan book dating from the 1640s, *The Marrow of Modern Divinity*. This reprint created a fair amount of fluttering in the ministerial dovecots and was condemned by the General Assembly of 1719. Those who supported it were called to give an account of themselves on heresy charges at the General Assembly of 1722 and were rebuked for their views. The twelve who had been rebuked became known as the 'Marrowmen' and as a result took on an identity as a party in opposition to those whose views moulded the church as a whole. Among the twelve were Thomas Boston, a Borders minister known for his piety, principles and his authorship of various theological classics, and the slightly younger Ebenezer Erskine. Also a borderer, Erskine was altogether more fiery, obstreperous and was seen as the leader of the group. Erskine's younger brother Ralph was also one of the Marrowmen. The Marrow controversy rumbled on. Other controversies came and went; John Simson, the Professor of Theology in Glasgow University, was charged with heresy twice, in 1717 and in 1727 and his escape from serious censure at the earlier trial and his deposition while still keeping hold of his salary at the later trial enraged his opponents and were a symptom of a deep split with the church as a whole.

In 1731, the General Assembly decided that the pragmatic approach to the patronage controversy was to bow to the inevitable and stop complaining. Ebenezer Erskine, who was then ministering in Stirling and serving as Moderator of the Synod of Perth and Stirling, was so enraged that he preached to the Synod about the iniquity of wealth having undue influence in the church. This sermon was preached from Psalm 118. In this sermon he said:

> I can find no warrant from the word of God, to confer the spiritual privileges of his House upon the rich beyond the poor: Whereas, by this act, the man with the gold ring and gay clothing is preferred unto the man with the vile raiment and poor attire.

He then went on to condemn the General Assembly for insisting that a minister presented to a congregation needed to be acceptable only to the heritors and elders rather than all the (male) parishioners. The offence caused by this sermon, followed by Erskine's own intransigence when the General Assembly offered a compromise, led to his deposition and joining with another three ministers in setting up the 'Associate Presbytery', a grouping of those in opposition to the way the national church was developing. The Associate Presbytery gathered adherents from all over southern Scotland and soon had a significant number of churches.

But if ministers were sufficiently troubled by the developments in the national church, what of their parishioners? There is a good deal of evidence to show that Erskine's church, the Burgh church of Stirling was split down the middle. Of the three ministers who shared responsibility for the Burgh, Erskine was the most recently called. One of his colleagues, Alexander Hamilton, was elderly and in poor health; the other, Charles Moore, was a government placeman. The third charge, which Erskine occupied, was a new appointment created, so it would appear, because the townspeople wanted to call an evangelical minister and Erskine, who had family ties with Stirling, in particular. The church building had been split into two during the rule of Cromwell; Hamilton and Moore shared the west half of the church and Erskine preached in the east.

After his deposition, Erskine held onto his half of the church for seven years and it was only when his supporters lost control of the Town Council that he was barred from the church. The Kirk Session records show that Erskine had the support of twelve of the seventeen elders and Town Council records show which parties were in power at each set of annual elections, with elders on both sides being in positions of power in the town.

So, if Erskine had the support of a majority of his elders, the support of congregation members as a whole can be gauged from baptism records. These show that in 1742, for example, the Established Church had sixty-seven baptisms of local people, while Erskine's new breakaway church had fifty baptisms of Stirling children but also large numbers from neighbouring parishes.

The picture in Stirling was echoed in other communities. The young Secession Church spread through the lowlands: by 1745, the initial four churches had become forty-two, organized first into the 'Associate Presbytery' and then into the 'Associate Synod' comprising three presbyteries totalling twenty-five congregations with ministers and a further seventeen congregations as yet without ministers.

As 'rebels' from the national church, the Seceders were also considered to be potential political rebels. Experience of the Covenanters implied to those who ran Scotland that Seceders were not friends of the government.

To an extent this was true. There is considerable evidence to suggest that the birth of the Secession Church was aided by the opposition party of the 1730s Scotland looking for any way to embarrass the government of Robert Walpole and his Scottish henchmen, the Duke of Argyll and his brother Earl Ilay.

This suspicion changed with the onset of the Jacobite rising of 1745. Both in Stirling and Edinburgh, Seceders were in the vanguard of opposition to Charles Edward Stuart. Both Erskine in Stirling and Adam Gib in Edinburgh formed regiments to oppose the Jacobites. In the event, neither regiment fought, but their loyalty did not go unnoticed and official suspicion of the Seceders subsided.

Dissent was on the horizon for the fledgling church. Even before the Jacobite rebellion, several Secession ministers were troubled by the imposition of the Burgess Oath, to be taken by anyone who wished to become a burgess of one of the Royal Burghs. Each Burgh had its own oath and some of them made allusion to the church and religious matters, mainly to prevent Roman Catholics becoming burgesses. In 1744, the Secession Synod first took note of this and debated as to whether taking such an oath was permissible especially when it referred to loyalty to the Church as established. A long and increasingly bitter debate ranged over the question of whether any civic oath that included a religious element was acceptable and whether allegiance to the church as established meant allegiance to the ideal church as established in 1690 or specifically to the national church as it was when they seceded from it. Unlike most splits in Scottish churches, there doesn't seem to have been any other real issue other than the Burgess Oath. In fact, the form of the oath that caused the problem was only used in three Burghs, so it affected relatively few members of the church. However, the three year debate which led to 'The Breach', as it was thereafter called, became increasingly personal and in April 1747, the Associate Synod now with thirty-two ministers, split into the Associate and General Associate Synods, popularly known as Burgher and Anti-burgher Churches. The bitterness caused by the Breach lasted for over seventy years. John Erskine, Secession minister in Falkirk, became an Anti-burgher, his uncle Ebenezer Erskine in Stirling remained a Burgher, and the younger man was party to the decision of the new Anti-burgher Presbytery to excommunicate his Burgher uncle. In Ebenezer's own church, while most members followed the lead of their minister, there was a handful who followed the Anti-burgher line. Ironically, the baptismal roll shows that few of the original members were burgesses of Stirling, most coming rather from the neighbouring parish of St Ninians, but one member, up before the session accused of that favourite misdemeanour of 'antenuptial fornication', was further accused of '*dishonouring the Lord by hearing Mr. Ebenezer Erskine*', a sad reflection on the way relationships could break down. It is hard not to sympathize with the notable historian who wrote that, 'The fissiparous nature of holier than thou Presbyterianism was shown in the tendency of dissenting congregations to find further principles on which new divisions could take place.'

Erskine's congregation in Stirling was very large. As well as the townspeople, the records show that substantial numbers of people from surrounding parishes were drawn to his ministry; in that year of 1742, Erskine actually baptized 213 children including some from parishes twenty miles away such as Balfron, Killearn and Cumbernauld. An ever-widening circle in those first few years can be seen in the baptismal roll of the new church and the figures used to gauge the relative sizes of the Secession and Parish churches, and in due course the Burgher and Anti-burgher churches.

The Burgess Oath controversy made it less likely the burgesses in Perth, Glasgow or Edinburgh would be Seceders. The original group who supported Ebenezer Erskine did include many burgesses, but a few years later it was commented that the social class of the congregation tended to be lower than that of the Parish Church. However, that does not tell the whole story; those who remained with the Established Church had a church provided for them, whether by the heritors or by the town council. They had a minister provided for them. Even if they didn't like him and had no say in his appointment, at least they didn't have to pay his stipend, that too was provided by heritors or Burgh council. All they had to pay was a contribution to poor relief as they went into the church. In return they had the expectation that if the worst came to the worst they would have access to those same poor funds for their own support. By contrast, in following the Secession, people were committing themselves to building and financing a church building, to paying a minister and funding their own poor relief. It was a brave step to take.

Some of the new congregations physically built their own churches; an account of Ebenezer Erskine's congregation shows how the land was given by one of his richer supporters, but the church was built physically by its members, colliers and labourers giving their skills free. This in its turn led to further issues, stemming from the awkward legal position of 'meeting-houses'. The solution was to appoint a small body of trustees who then tied up possession into such a legal tangle that it would have been very difficult to establish who had legal right to the building. The board of management appointed was thus the first example of a management system that became common in many Scottish churches where one group, the Kirk Session look after the spiritual interests of the congregation, and another group, called variously 'Board of Managers', 'Deacons' Court' or 'Congregational Board' look after the financial and property interests of the congregation.

So although the legal beginnings of the Secession churches stem from the actions of the handful of ministers the Secession appealed strongly to many lay people in southern Scotland who were ready to support an alternative church.

As well as the disaffected throughout the Established Church, there were also the Praying Societies. Many of those joined the Reformed Presbyterian Church but the young Seceder church soon had links with the groups nearby. Among its earliest acts was a reasserting of the values of the National Covenant and of course this chimed with the beliefs of the surviving Covenanters. However, many of the covenanting groups declined the association because the Seceders had betrayed the Covenants by siding with the establishment between 1690 and 1733; memories and grudges lasted long.

That said, some of the Praying Societies did join the Seceders and the early records of Bridge of Teith Church at Doune show how this worked. A group of old elders, possibly of covenanting stock, petitioned the Associate Presbytery to constitute a kirk session. Ebenezer Erskine was sent out from Stirling to constitute it. Those elders, together with two who had recently left the parish church became the first Kirk Session of the new congregation. One of the first moves was to find additional elders and so the Societies in the surrounding parishes brought forward a list of men to be ordained, with people specifically nominated to work in individual small areas. So here existing informal church structures were used to formalize the new structure. The new elders included two wrights, two weavers, a gardener, a farmer and others. The new church was not expected simply to serve the parish of Kilmadock where it was situated; in 1745 the area defined as being served by the church was described as 'all the Dissenters in the following parishes; Kilmadock, Callander, a part of Port, Kincardine, Dunblane and Lecropt'.

This in itself raises several issues. The first point to make is that, like the financial commitment already mentioned, the distances involved imply a significant commitment simply to attend, or in the case of office bearers, to take their part in the governance of the congregation. The habit of appointing elders by district however may imply that the local Praying Societies continued in place and small scale worship continued in individual localities.

Secondly, the discipline of the parish churches still remained a factor. Seceder churches were old-fashioned in their outlook and therefore no less likely to take moral shortcomings seriously. While contemporary writers may have been hostile to their independence of mind, they often pay tribute to their moral standing. This is not to say that Seceders never transgressed, they were as human as anyone else as the records show.

The church at Bridge of Teith continued without a minister for several years. From its start in 1740 it took until March 1745 before elders were instructed 'to visit quarters and sound the mind of every particular member anent their ripeness for a moderation'. It then took a further two years until their first minister was ordained and inducted.

This kind of pattern is found throughout southern Scotland, leading to the fact that in 1745 the church had twenty-five ministers but forty-two congregations, and demonstrates that the early lay Seceders were not simply following popular ministers as they left the church, but rather laymen were leading the increase in the Secession. This point of view is further strengthened by the decision of the Bridge of Teith Session at the time of the Breach; rather than split the congregation just as it was about to call its first minister, the elders voted that the decision of Synod should not be made a condition of communion but that everyone should be at liberty to enjoy their private judgement and opinion. This view sat awkwardly with the polarized views of those who had attended the Synod as it split.

After the Breach of 1747, both Seceder churches grew as increasing numbers of people took offence at the ministers who were being imposed on them. However not all those who objected to patronage were in sympathy with the other views of the Seceders, there were many who thought the constant recalling of the Covenanters and the golden days of old fashioned Presbyterianism had little relevance to modern eighteenth-century Scotland.

Among these was a minister called Thomas Gillespie in Fife. In 1751 he was deposed from the Established Church for refusing to induct a minister appointed by the patron. Unlike Erskine and MacMillan before him who managed to hang on to church and manse for seven years after deposition, Gillespie was homeless within the week. His congregation supported him though and they worshipped in the open air to begin with. The patronage issue was the only thing keeping them from the Established Church. They didn't look back to the 'golden years' of covenanting or try to take their church back to a previous century, so they had little in common with the Secession Church. As others joined however, they too made themselves into the Relief Presbytery, an association of those seeking relief from the ills of patronage, and hence the 'Relief Church'. There are still two churches in Scotland which have 'Relief' in their name. As they developed though, they took the forefront of the liberal thought in Scottish churches. From an early stage, they decided that any Christian should be allowed to receive the Sacrament of Communion, not just those whose beliefs chimed with their own. They were the first Presbyterian Church to sings hymns as well as psalms and were among the earliest churches in Scotland to use organs to support the singing. They also appointed Boards of Managers to deal with the business affairs of the congregation, leaving the elders to deal with the spiritual matters. In many ways the Church of Scotland today owes more to the Relief Church tradition than any other single denomination.

The Relief Church was always lowland in nature and it attracted a particular kind of person, self-employed artisans such as weavers and tradesmen. A broadside published in Edinburgh in the 1820s describing the argument over introducing a church organ in a Relief Church, took great pains to point out that the protagonists were people like dyers, glaziers or plumbers and poked fun at their accents. The broadside ends;

> Is it not absurd for such illiterate and vulgar speaking men to be rulers of a church 'Wha's that talkin' there WILLIE SMITH! gi'e him a daud i' the lug the daft brute, what right has he to set up his chat'.

While the Relief Church was growing in numbers though, the other Secession churches were also growing and changing. Despite being founded as a church looking back to its past, both Burgher and Anti-burgher elements began to be influenced by more modern thought. This was partly influenced by what was happening across the Atlantic, for there was a constant flow of ministers to and from the American churches in the late eighteenth century. As a result the 'New Light' controversy took hold and brought fresh thought to the two denominations. It also incidentally affected the Established Church but didn't split it, whereas the Burghers and Anti-burghers did, one in 1799 and the other in 1806. Without going into the theology, the result was that in the 'New Lights' were to be found people challenging the role of the church and its relationship with the state and challenging some of the traditional beliefs of Calvinism while the 'Old Lights' were preserving what they thought the church had always stood for. The 'New Light Burghers' and the 'New Light Anti-burghers' decided fairly speedily that there was little real difference between their views and worked towards a union in 1820, when the United Secession Church was formed. Of course, being Scotland, it left remnants of unhappy un-united people behind and spawned another denomination but it was absorbed into the Old Light Anti-burghers in a very few years. The sticking point in the union which meant that it took ten years to achieve was the insistence by both parties that their opposite numbers had to admit their ancestors were wrong in their stance over the Breach, some seventy years previously.

With United Secession Church now the biggest of the Secession Churches, its leaders began to recognize that their views were not so different from those of the Relief Church, and gradually they came round to the idea of reuniting with them. One of the difficulties in pushing this union through was that some of the United Secession divinity students claimed that they couldn't forge links with the Relief Church students because they couldn't actually work out what if anything they actually believed in. However in 1847, the two groups came together to form the United Presbyterian Church and for the next fifty years that was, with the Established Church and the Free Church one of the three denominations that dominated Scottish life. Incidentally, on going into the union of 1847 without leaving a rump of congregations and ministers behind, the Relief Church achieved the unique achievement of being the only

Scottish Presbyterian denomination never to suffer a schism, although one or two congregations hived off to join other denominations individually.

The United Secession Church could not claim the same achievement, for in its twenty-seven year history it managed to have its own schism shortly before the Union of 1847. This was a split on theological grounds, the 'atonement controversy' and concerned one of the fundamental tenets of Scottish Calvinism, the question of whom Christ died for. Was it only the 'elect', predestined for heaven from birth, or was it all believers? This argument raged throughout the nineteenth century in many churches. For one thing the growth of mission work made people realize that they could not promote a Gospel of Salvation and at the same time say to converts *even if you believe and live good lives you may still be predestined to go to hell when you die*. The controversy in the United Secession Church led to the formation of the 'Evangelical Union' which will be described in Chapter 6.

At its formation in 1847, the United Presbyterians, drawn from these reuniting denominations, became one of the three biggest groups in Presbyterian Scotland (see Figure 7, United Presbyterians, see p 219).

Meanwhile as the majority of the Seceders reunited, what of the others? The Old Light Burghers decided in 1838 that their chief difference from the New Lights was their conviction that there should be a national church, so they rejoined it, only to leave again five years later at the Disruption to be part of the Free Church. The Old Light Anti-burghers decided to throw in their lot with the Free Church too, but not until 1851 and a remnant continued as the 'Original Secession Church' for a further century before being absorbed back into the Church of Scotland in 1956. Like the other surviving small dissenting Presbyterian churches they were very conservative in outlook and it is hard to see just how they differed from the Reformed Presbyterians for example.

So in the centenary of the Breach that fragmented the eighteenth-century Seceders, there was once again a single major Secession Church, the United Presbyterians. It was perhaps symbolic that this reunion took place in the exact same hall, the Tanfield Hall, where the Free Church, the last of the major splits from the Church of Scotland had held its first meeting three years earlier. In many ways the ideas that propelled the UP Church were much the same as the other two major Presbyterian churches. As mentioned elsewhere there were the beginnings of an impetus to re-unite Presbyterian dissent as soon as it became evident that the Established Church was not going to shrivel and die after the Disruption of 1843. However the Free Church and the UP Church had widely different views on the relationship between church and state and this proved a barrier until the end of the nineteenth century.

The UP Church developed its own ethos; its predecessor churches had already been seen as attractive to the emergent industrial middle class, the manufacturers, the merchants, the craftsmen, the owners of small businesses and this continued. It was particularly strong in Glasgow. It had been quick to recognize the need for mission in the parts of the city that the Established Church was finding it hard to reach, but a fair degree of upward mobility affected many of its members. These members moved to the suburbs of Glasgow and re-founded their churches there while the older ones in poorer areas were left to look after themselves. As a result a series of very affluent churches rose which acquired wealthy and influential members. At the same time this group were active politically and some have suggested they effectively ran Glasgow as a pressure group in the late nineteenth century. A growing tension, though, grew between the older-established congregations and the wealthy upstarts.

One of the reasons for this growing confidence in the UP Church lay in its roots. The Secession churches had a long tradition of self-reliance financially. If they were not supported, they closed. They had a long tradition of lay 'managers' dealing with all the temporal matters without reference to the minister. Long after the UP Church disappeared as a body, old UP congregations still insisted that the minister was not entitled to attend congregational meetings let alone managers' meetings. The managers were men of financial awareness and skill and had a confidence in their own judgement which led them to act without feeling they had to consult others beyond the bounds of the room they met in. The UP Church had a tradition of high congregational giving; the tiny UP congregation in Stitchel in the borders was known locally as the 'penny kirk' while the Established Church was known as the 'halfpenny kirk' in recognition of the different demands on the congregation. Tables of giving per head of membership in every presbytery in Scotland were published in Howie's 'The Churches and the Churchless in Scotland; Facts and Figures' in 1893 and they show just how big the contrast was.

Overall an ethos of 'keeping the minister in his place' was found as shown by the case of Viewfield Church in Stirling. Their minister suffered ill health and was allowed to go on an extended trip on full pay while another was brought in. When the first returned to take up his charge, the second remained and relations were cool. One Sunday when the senior minister was away preaching elsewhere, a congregational meeting was called which sacked him. Not surprisingly he appealed and the Synod agreed this was entirely illegal. The upshot was that many of the congregation left and founded a new church with the other minister 400 yards away. It was said that the new congregation took with it 40 per cent of the people and 60 per cent of the income. UP congregations had an independence of mind that could be quite challenging for their ministers.

The main topic that set the UP Church apart from the other two main Presbyterian churches was voluntarism, the view that the churches should have no relationship with the state; finally this view began to be found in the Free Church too and the result was the Union of 1900 when the whole UP

Church joined the great majority in forming the United Free Church. Many of the old UP churches, though, kept their own constitutions and title deeds into further unions and some congregations to this day have a slightly different legal status from the norm. This can lead to interesting situations if the congregation decides to leave its denomination for any reason.

5

Governing Lives; The Churches' Impact on Personal Life

Mr John Watson reports that he supplied St Ninians as appointed and after sermon did publicly warn the congregation concerning George Williamson in Airth and Janet Richardson in St Ninians guilty of relapse in adultery aggravated with dreadful circumstances and that for the third time in order to their excommunication and that he publicly prayed for them. Compeared the said George Williamson and Janet Richardson and they seeming to be hardened and obdurate creatures they were removed. And the Presbytery taking their case to their serious consideration and finding that the said George is guilty of trilapse in the horrid sin of adultery, he being a married person and that the said Janet being a single person is guilty of relapse in adultery with the said George and that their horrid guilt hath been attended with very aggravating circumstances. The said presbytery out of zeal to the glory of God and for clearing the Church of such a dreadful scandal do excommunicate the said George Williamson and Janet Richardson out of the society of the Church of Christ and do deliver them over to Satan for the destruction of the flesh that their souls may be saved. And appointed the Moderator to intimate the said sentence unto the said persons. Who being called, the same was intimate accordingly. Also the presbytery appoints this sentence to be publicly intimate to the congregation of St Ninians by the minister that shall be appointed first to supply them and also to the congregation of Airth by the minister that shall first preach there and to require the people to look upon them as pagans and to keep no company or society with them and they would not incur the comfort of the Church so long as the said persons shall not be absolved from the said sentence.

(Stirling Presbytery, 3 April 1695 Stirling Archives: CH2/722/8, reproduced by permission.)

Two of the enduring preconceptions about the Scottish churches are that they were obsessed with sin, especially sex, and that they ruled the country with a heavy and joyless hand. The truth though is not as simple.

From the Reformation onwards, the Reformed Church had a responsibility for the moral welfare of the people; however, this was not a new development. Even before the Reformation, the Church had oversight of many of the courts of Scotland as it had in many other countries. Bishops were judges over ecclesiastical matters in their dioceses and including other matters deemed as ecclesiastical then. Anything to do with marriage came under canon law as marriage was a sacrament celebrated by priests. But so did anything to do with wills and executry of estates, any question of the legitimacy of children, of defamation and slander and the provision of curators (guardians) for children.

One of the biggest parts of this work was in administering oaths. Being taken under God, oaths were religious in nature and hence the responsibility of the church courts: this gave the courts a place in commercial law. In each diocese, the bishop delegated responsibility to a court presided over by an official imaginatively called 'the Official', and they in turn appointed judges of lower status. These local courts, staffed with church trained lawyers, probably had a higher competence in law than the local civil courts run by Burgh councils or local lairds. A tiny fraction of the records of these pre-Reformation ecclesiastical courts have survived, perhaps half a dozen volumes in all.

With the acceptance of the Reformation by the Scottish Parliament in 1560, the authority of the courts which owed allegiance to the Pope disappeared, and there was a resulting vacuum. In some cases, this authority was taken up immediately by the new church. In August 1560, the Archbishop of St Andrews had complained to the Bishop of Glasgow that kirk sessions in every town were taking over ecclesiastical cases. For instance, even in early 1559, the Kirk Session of St Andrews had taken it upon itself to adjudicate on a divorce case with the result being read out to the congregation on Sunday 23 March 1559, the Kirk Session having sat as 'judges judicially' on the previous Thursday.

Only St Andrews has kirk session records as early as this, but sufficient references in other sources show that the pattern was repeated elsewhere. There was however a period of two or three years when it was unclear whether divorce in particular came under the jurisdiction of ecclesiastical or civil courts. So much so that in 1562, the General Assembly petitioned the 'Secret Council' (Privy Council) asking it to decide once and for all where the responsibility should lie. The result was the erection in 1564 of new 'Commissary Courts', entirely non-ecclesiastical, with the responsibility for divorce proceedings, confirmation of wills and other such matters.

This still left the kirk sessions with a many legal matters to occupy themselves with; they regarded a 'good and godly people' as a symbol of the true church. So, they considered sexual behaviour, breaches of the Sabbath, family discord, marital bad relations, strife within the community whether physical or verbal and a general catch-all category of 'scandalous carriage'. On the social side, the churches under their kirk sessions provided for poor relief, education, even the repair of bridges as well as extending help to Christians outside Scotland who were enslaved by North African pirates or were trying to establish churches abroad. The kirk session records show the extent that poor relief was required and events such as the 'seven lean years' of bad harvests in the 1690s, or the potato famine of the 1840s can be evidenced in church records. This was accompanied by help at a smaller level, such as supporting a poor father of new-born triplets or the widow of disgraced minister.

Perhaps, the most significant aspect of church records for modern researchers, especially those interested in family history is their recording of 'Rites of Passage', the hatches, matches and despatches of our ancestors. These and the other church records reflect the life of their communities as well as provide evidence for ancestry, but the records are not of marriages, births and deaths but usually of proclamations of banns, baptisms and burials.

Marriage

Many of the historic 'marriage' records kept by the churches refer to the 'proclamation of banns' a few weeks before the wedding. Proclamation of banns was a pre-condition of marriage in Scotland right up until the late 1970s. In theory, the intention of a couple to marry had to be read to the congregation on three Sundays, although this later dwindled to one. Where the two lived in different parishes, the banns would be read in both churches and recorded in both. This gave people who knew them the chance to draw attention to impediments to marriage such as kinship or potential bigamy; this was later replaced by the registrar posting a notice of intent to marry in a public place. A request for a proclamation of banns however could still be made to solemnize the marriage of a Scot in England.

Marriages ceremonies themselves were traditionally low key in Scotland and rarely conducted in churches before the Second World War. Prior to about 1900, they were conducted at the manse with the minimum of fuss. George Taylor, a gardener in the Borders described his marriage thus:

Our marriage was fixed on the 19th of January, 1837. We arranged to make a trip to Edinburgh, and so early in the morning of that day, we were united at the Presbyterian Manse in Kelso by the Reverend Henry Benton. We then had breakfast and took the stagecoach at 9 o'clock for Edinburgh.

Incidentally, although the bride was from East Lothian and they were both living there at the time, they went back to the groom's home parish to be married. An example of a slightly later time refers to the practice of a UP minister in the 1850s. George Gilfillan was a minister in Dundee who habitually performed marriages in his manse on a Friday night, apparently even as many as twenty on the same evening. Reflecting his efforts to ensure that the poorer sections of the city were legally married, he sometimes went by the nickname 'Buckle the Beggars'. Naturally, the ceremony was extremely brief, but one of those he married recorded that the address at the service started with the words 'Marriage is an ordinance of God, established in Eden, for taming the ferocity of man, for contributing to the happiness of both sexes, and for securing the continuance of the species.'

Civil marriage was virtually unknown in Scotland prior to 1875, with the vast majority of ceremonies being conducted by Presbyterian ministers. Even for regular church members, it was common to be married in a hotel well into the 1950s. After a few decades, when church marriages had become the norm, weddings in hotels, castles, tents, hot air balloons or anywhere else the bridal couple fancy, have become dominant. It is worth noting that, unlike in England, the place of a wedding does not need to be licenced or approved, only the celebrants.

From a marrying point of view, Scotland was of course famed for its 'irregular marriages'. Gretna Green, just over the border from England, managed to transform marriage into a minor local industry because eloping couples found it convenient to marry under the less strict laws of Scotland. These particularly related to the differing ages at which parental approval was required in Scotland and England. English marriages required such consent till the age of twenty-one, while Scottish ones allowed marriage without parental consent from the age of sixteen. Obviously, other border villages were able to provide the same service, but only Gretna continues to provide it on an industrial scale, having no longer any relationship with different marriage laws. There is also something absurd about Scottish couples travelling south to Gretna for the same purpose, but then, few of the English brides coming north to Gretna show any sign of being under the age of twenty-one.

The point of Gretna was its handiness for 'irregular marriage'. Scotland, despite its greater religious control for many centuries, had various non-religious versions of marriage. Other forms of marriage included the exchange of vows before witnesses, 'betrothal and consummation' and 'cohabitation and repute'. These were forms of marriage recognized by Scots Law but they are unlikely to make their way into church marriage records. Some did though and cast light on the practices.

Soldiers in particular had difficulty in complying with the regular practice of marriage due to their being liable to move at short notice. In Leith in 1749, Janet MacAuley married a soldier, courtesy of one of his friends in the regiment acting as the celebrant. He,

> having on a black coat, and asked the parties if they were free persons, who answering in the affirmative, the said Smith made a fashion of marrying them; upon which the said Janet MacAuley gave the said celebrator Smith three shillings sterling, after which they had a supper.

Such a marriage was fully legal but there were clearly huge opportunities for fraud or bigamy, and there were many cases where afterwards the groom denied the marriage or was killed in action without having acknowledged the marriage. The widow in such a case would have great difficulty in proving her right to a pension or even receiving confirmation of his death to allow her to remarry.

Such irregular marriages tended to be a feature of the eighteenth century. Prior to this they were much rarer being tied to religious ceremonies beyond the established church. In 1661, an act of Parliament imposed stringent fines on those marrying irregularly, but these were people being married either by covert Roman Catholic priests or by equally covert Presbyterian covenanting ministers. In either case, banishment could be invoked against the offending cleric. The revolution of 1688 put the Presbyterians back into power, and it was the ousted Episcopalian 'curates' who were conducting marriage services. By this time there were no real effective sanctions against them, despite the attempts to force the couples to identify both celebrants and witnesses on pain of a fine of up to £2000. According to the 1694 hearth tax records for Edinburgh, although there were fifteen positions for ministers in the town, there were, however, eighty-two men describing themselves as 'ministers', most of the remainder having been ousted from their parishes elsewhere. Even without the threat of fines, irregular marriage was not cheap, and probably no cheaper than regular marriage, especially as agents were used to make the links between the couple and their celebrant. In 1730, a Leith man paid a crown (five shillings or twenty-five pence) to the minister, two shillings to the man he called his 'beadle' and afterwards spent fourteen to sixteen pence on drink with the minister and company.

Nonetheless, irregular marriages were common, particularly, in Leith. In the 1750s, North Leith had an average of 11.8 irregular marriages (only those that were known of) each year compared to 8.5 regular ones. In 1754, there was only one regular for nine irregular marriages. The Jacobite rebellions forced many non-juring Episcopalian preachers to go underground and it is likely that they made a living out of this. In the Session records for Leith in the eighteenth century, about 150 celebrators of irregular marriages were identified, with three of them being recorded as responsible for over 120 each. The same names appear in the records for other places; so clearly, they had lucrative small businesses running. One minister, David Strange, who was imprisoned for his habitual offences in this regard, nevertheless, continued to marry people even in his prison cell.

Having said that, however, on many occasions irregularly married couples would be called before the kirk session or indeed voluntarily appear before the kirk session and do the appropriate penance for their irregularity. The Scottish equivalent of running away to Gretna was colloquially known as the 'Ru'glen Marriage'; couples would go to Rutherglen, near Glasgow, to be married irregularly and then a friend of the couple would report them to the civil authorities who would impose a small fine. The receipt for the fine would then serve as evidence that the marriage had occurred and that the two were legally man and wife. The official penalty for an irregular marriage tended to reflect the fees that an official wedding would have incurred in calling the banns and recording the marriage, and for the sake of having their children recognized as legitimate and domiciled in their home parish, it was often felt worth the expense.

The rise of the Secession churches added another complication; technically marriages conducted by Secession ministers were 'irregular' but in reality they were not normally treated as such. This reflects both the greater numbers involved, but also that Secession ministers were not seen as a threat to the civil establishment in the same way as Presbyterians were between 1660 and 1688 or non-juring Episcopalians were between 1688 and 1760. Finally, in 1784, thirty years after a similar act had been passed in England, it was recognized that marriages conducted by recognized ministers of dissenting churches were to be deemed as 'regular'. Thereafter irregular marriages became much less common as people were much less inclined to go looking for ministers of dubious history when they had 'respectable' alternatives in their own community.

After about 1800 kirk sessions simply ceased recording irregular marriages especially in the rapidly growing industrial towns; records of them simply do not exist nor is it possibly to estimate their numbers after this time.

The other form of marriage which does not figure frequently in church records is that of 'hand-fasting'. This was a practice which long predated the Reformation and is found elsewhere in Europe. A form of betrothal took place outside the church sometimes at the church door, sometimes elsewhere. It was then tacitly accepted that any children born to the union were legitimate despite there being no 'official' marriage. Scottish oral tradition takes this further and converts the practice into a trial marriage which could be easily broken up until a year and a day after the betrothal provided no live children were born, but there seems very little actual evidence for this happening. Generally it is said that the practice of hand-fasting died out in the late sixteenth century, shortly after the Reformation.

It should be noted that although the various forms of irregular marriage were against church law, whatever penalties were put upon bride, groom, celebrant or witnesses, they were legal and binding marriages and accepted as such by the church whether pre- or post-Reformation. The 'sin' involved lay in disobedience to the rules the church put around marriage, not in the fact of the marriage.

The facility for alternative forms of marriage finally was stopped in 2006 with most alternatives being banned on 1940. No longer by living together for a year and a day as man and wife and being assumed to be married, were people legally married, nor was a declaration of marriage before witnesses accepted as sufficient.

Divorce

Of course where there is marriage there is the scope for marriage to go wrong. Divorce and separation is largely a matter for civil law but the traditional legal basis of divorce in Scotland lies in the attitude of the church from Reformation times and so a summary is needed, especially as this was so unlike the position in England.

Prior to the Reformation, 'divorce' was allowed on the grounds of adultery or extreme cruelty. An alternative outcome, 'nullity', the statement that the marriage was never a marriage, was allowed for lack of consent; for the bride and groom being within the forbidden degrees of relationship; or for lack of the ability to consummate the marriage. Remarriage after divorce was not, however, allowed at that point. When the authority of the old church courts came to an end in 1560, new arrangements had to be found. For the first three years, kirk sessions took it upon themselves to grant divorces to men and women whose spouses were guilty of adultery. This is a major point of difference from England, where only men could sue for divorce on the grounds of adultery. It was a direct acceptance of Calvin's stated view that 'in bed, man and wife are equal'. A second major difference was that in reformed Scotland, remarriage was permissible after divorce. The law treated an adulterer as legally 'dead' in relation to the former spouse and so the 'surviving' spouse was entitled to their legal share of the estate and was free to marry again. The adulterer could also legally remarry but remarriage to the person with whom he or she had been adulterous was specifically forbidden by an act of Parliament in 1600. The reorganization of the Commissary Courts as civil rather than as ecclesiastical courts in 1563, together with the Court of Session conducting oversight, removed the Church's immediate power over divorce proceedings, it being the responsibility of the Commissary Court of Edinburgh until 1830.

One odd area of the Church's involvement did remain; when Parliament added desertion as grounds for divorce in the 1570s, the procedure included the pursuant petitioning the local presbytery to have the absent party admonished and excommunicated. This would be formally put to presbytery which would equally formally refuse to have anything to do with the matter and the civil court case would run its course.

If it had lost its power, the church had not lost its influence. Adultery was a heinous sin in the eyes of the church, whether or not legal divorce followed. Adulterers were regularly called before kirk sessions to answer for their misdeeds. Until the later eighteenth century, the penance might be twenty-six weekly appearances in sackcloth before the congregation after which the sinner was absolved. If legal proceedings for divorce were instigated the church would normally suspend its proceedings.

There are records of 904 actions for divorce being brought between 1684 and 1830; so it was never common, particularly earlier in that period. In 1783, one correspondent was complaining that 'church censure is disused and separations, divorces, recriminations, collusions, separate maintenances are becoming almost as frequent as marriages'. Though clearly exaggerated, this complaint does show a perception that standards had changed. In fact, of the 904 actions only 118 were instigated in the period from 1684 to 1770; the remaining fifty years of the Commissary Court involvement accounted for 786 actions.

The other change which seems to have occurred in the later eighteenth century was that actions by women increased at a greater rate. Of the earlier 118 actions, only forty-two were pursued by women; after 1771, however, the equivalent figures were 370 out of that total of 786.

If Scotland was more equable than England in its attitude to women and divorce, that is not to imply that gender was not an issue. Double standards did still come into play, though perhaps to a lesser degree. But there was another radical difference from England: that was the accessibility and affordability of the process to ordinary people. In England, divorce was ruinously expensive. A full divorce in England by Act of Parliament cost about £700 whereas in Scotland, a full divorce might cost anything from £5 to £30, depending largely on the cost of bringing witnesses to Edinburgh and the amount of property to be redistributed. This was still considered expensive in the days when a working man's annual income was in the region of £50 per year, but the cost was not as prohibitive as it would have been south of the border.

Added to that, the process was available to the poor because they could apply to be put on the poor's roll and have their expenses paid, an eighteenth-century equivalent of legal aid. As with legal aid, those in the middle were not eligible but could not afford the process, and so they lost out. This aspect of the process once again involved the church. It was not the church's poor's roll that paid the fees, but the minister and kirk session of the litigant's home parish had to provide a certificate attesting that the litigant was poverty stricken. Few such applications were ever refused.

So if divorce was available to all social classes, was it used equally by all of them? The answer is 'no'. In the period up to 1770, 55 per cent of divorces were pursued by members of the aristocracy or gentry and the remaining 45 per cent by everybody else. This proportion changed to 28 per cent and 72 per cent between 1771 and 1830, although the reason is unknown. The reasons for the initial imbalance are probably many: cost; the greater importance of bloodlines to those with estates to pass on; greater mobility and therefore opportunity for 'discreet' liaisons and less amount of fear of the kirk session and presbytery's ability to hold them up to ridicule and opprobrium. For those at the other end of the scale, the social ills of alcoholism and prostitution seem to have been the basis of most break-ups. Later nineteenth-century attitudes, though, seem to have made divorce and remarriage less acceptable again.

Baptism

Baptism, the receiving of people into the family of the church with the symbolic use of water, was habitually conducted on babies, often within days of birth; in the Protestant Church of Scotland as it had been in the pre-Reformation church. The later limitation of the sacrament to believers came into Scotland briefly and sporadically in the mid-seventeenth century, more regularly in some dissenting churches from the late eighteenth century onward. It was recognized as one of the two 'Sacraments' by the Protestants, where the Catholic Church had previously recognized seven Sacraments.

Irregular baptism did not crop up in church records to nearly the same extent as irregular marriage, and died out very much earlier. After the Reformation, though irregular baptism was a much more serious matter. The law of the new church lay down that baptisms should not be done privately but in church preferably before or after a regular service. Private baptism was seen as a sign of Romish sympathies, or even adherence to the Roman church and therefore to be stamped out.

In some cases the father and the minister responsible for a private baptism might have to show their penitence publicly sitting side by side before the congregation as happened in Tranent in East Lothian 1581. The parish minister was the offender, but another minister was brought into his church to tell him and the congregation the error of his ways. With the ebb and flow of Epicopalianism and Presbyterianism through the seventeenth century, private baptism was sometimes legal and sometimes not. The final establishment of Presbyterianism as the form of government of the Scottish Church might have been expected to settle the matter once and for all. Certainly among the 'crimes' of ousted ministers lingering near their previous churches is found the irregular baptizing of children. Reference has been made to the baptisms recorded by John MacMillan in what became the Reformed Presbyterian Church. These technically were 'irregular' in the sense of not being done by the minister of the parish, and not being performed by someone who knew the sponsoring parent. In some cases the parents were duly summoned to their local kirk session to be dealt with their offence.

However, even in the early eighteenth century people hankered after having their children baptized at home. In eighteenth-century Edinburgh, the children of 'people of fashion' were frequently baptized at home. Robert Wodrow who complained of the practice put it down to the anglification of Edinburgh, commenting that in Glasgow the local ministers stood firm against the custom but country ministers came into the city and performed baptisms in the homes. Meanwhile, the records of Ballingry in Fife show that in the early years of the eighteenth century, fewer than half of the baptisms were celebrated before the congregation and in some years none at all.

As with marriage, 'irregular' baptism was still considered as baptism and was a once and for all sacrament if it was performed in the proper form. For this reason, those who had been baptized in other traditions, whether Episcopal, Roman Catholic or Orthodox, were never re-baptized on conversion. Where an irregular baptism had been performed by someone not ordained in any church, it might however be regarded as void.

The question of second baptism has occasionally found its way into the courts of the Church of Scotland, with a handful of ministers being censured for administering or receiving baptism for the second time. Those churches who insist on 'believers' baptism', that only those who believe can be truly baptized, may well not have recognized prior 'infant' baptism. A baptized member of a church who was then baptized again as an adult would be seen as denying the validity of their original baptism and hence be open to church discipline.

The unbaptized child was always a source of worry in the days when infant and child mortality were common. Part of the gothic horror of Burns' *Tam O' Shanter* was the mention of the witches coven in the Alloway Kirkyard where they are dancing in the ruined church and 'Tam was able To note upon the Haly Table, a murderer's banes in gibbet airns: Twa span-lang, wee, unchristened bairns; ... ' In earlier times, a father who allowed his child to die unbaptized might have to do a pubic penance before the congregation, a judgement that seems particularly cruel to modern eyes. By the eighteenth century though, it was recognized by the church formally, if not by public opinion, that a child of Christian parents was, by that fact, part of the Church and as such entitled to Christian burial.

Baptism was taken as an opportunity to examine the father (rarely both parents) on their religious knowledge, and the father might be required to show that he knew the Ten Commandments and the Lord's Prayer. Failure to show this knowledge would result in a fine and a publicly shaming delay in the baptism; a second failure might result in someone else having to be found to take responsibility for the child's spiritual upbringing. This might be grandparents or even neighbours. In the case of foundlings and some illegitimate children, the kirk session took on the role.

As a further sidelight on the church's role in the upbringing of children, at least up to the eighteenth century and possibly later, ministers were instructed not to allow names that were of pagan origin ('Diana' was given as an example) or names that were associated with God, such as 'Emmanuel'. Instead, the names of 'holy men and women in scripture' were to be used.

Despite this, only a few names were in common use and several of the common ones had no scriptural background. Of the 2600 or so women charged with witchcraft and listed in Edinburgh University's *Survey of Scottish Witchcraft* between the Reformation and 1710, the ten most popular Christian names accounted for 85 per cent of the female population: led by Janet (19 per cent), Margaret (17 per cent) and Elizabeth (11 per cent). Isobel, Agnes and Marion and Katherine represented between 6 and 8 per cent each, with Christian, Helen and Jean making up 7 per cent between them. A further thirty names covers 99 per cent of the population, with a final thirty or so names being found only in single instances.

Taking the 470 men's names from the same database (a much smaller sample obviously), 75 per cent shared one of only ten Christian names: John, with 25 per cent, William, James and Thomas with between 8 and 11 per cent each, and George, Patrick, Alexander, Robert and Andrew with between 3 and

6 per cent. A further twenty-two names took up 20 per cent of the total, with twenty names occurring as single instances.

In case it might be thought that those accused of witchcraft were not typical of the population as a whole in their names, an analysis of the Christian names of the first 124 Moderators of the General Assembly of the Church of Scotland, from 1560 to 1800, show that forty-one were called James or John and a further forty-one called Robert, William or George. There was no overlap between the two samples, but the latter sample was probably more biased to Central Scotland and urban centres, particularly Edinburgh, than the witchcraft sample. 'Noble' families probably had a wider range of names due to intermarriage with English and other foreign families.

Burial

Initially, the Reformed Church was not interested in the manner of disposal of the dead. The iconoclasm of the Reformation destroyed graves and shrines. Saying masses for the dead was looked on as mere superstition to be stamped out. The earliest instructions for protestant burial were that

> the Dead be conveyed to the place of burial, with some honest company of the Kirk, without either singing or reading; yea without all the ceremony heretofore used, other than that the dead be committed to the grave with such gravity and sobriety as those that be present may seem to fear the judgements of God and to hate sin which is the cause of death.

That said, there was wide variation in practice; a sixteenth-century burial service in Montrose for example had a special hymn, translated into Scots from German but with local additions, the whole ran to twelve verses. By the seventeenth century, it would appear that there was no burial service at all, leaving the funeral as a secular service which the minister might attend but only as an individual among the other men. From the eighteenth century, ministers began holding short services in the home of the deceased prior to the interment but still without a role at the graveside.

Nonetheless, the church did have several parts to play in the funeral some of which are reflected in the records. The bell, if there was one, was tolled. The graves were in the churchyard and the clerk was meant to record their use. The graves were to some extent private property in as much as people paid for the rights to a lair and these rights could be bought and sold, but the kirk session had to agree the transaction and often had to act as arbiter in disputes. The records of such disputes can throw light on family relationships.

The proceeds of the sale of lairs by the session normally went to poor's fund. As well as the cost of the grave, there were funeral costs too: the bellman needed to be paid; a coffin needed to be made; the grave needed to be dug; and usually a mortcloth needed to be hired.

In the case of someone with no assets, these costs accrued at the minimum level and had to be met by the kirk session via the poor's box. In the 'lean years' of the 1690s, when Scotland was struggling under famine, some of the records show the frequent discovery of the bodies of unidentified strangers in the streets of towns like Perth and Stirling. The penniless dead were as much a call on local funds as the local poor.

Although modern funerals may have other elements added to them, the more conservative churches still stick to a very spare ceremony; this description is of a Free Church funeral in Lewis: 'very simple, you have a singing, prayer, you have readings you have another prayer another singing, you have a short word from the Bible, a very short word I mean two minutes and the benediction and that's it'.

By the nineteenth century, kirkyards were running out of space for burials and commercial companies started preparing the ground for cemeteries, particularly in the cities, but by that stage, the Church was no longer responsible for the records.

Leaving aside the rites of passage, the other main kirk session record was the minute book. In some cases, this was actually described as the register of discipline, but it really was much more than that. It records such of the misdeeds of the parishioners as came before the session's gaze. At different times as with different clerks there may be more or less detail of the sins and of the witnesses' statements. The minute book may also show other areas where the church was concerned: records of who needed help from the poor's box and for how long; records of help given to students needing support on the long route to becoming ministers; records of help given to Christians in other parts of Europe; of ransoms raised to redeem slaves taken by North African pirates; or records of church funds being used to build or repair bridges locally.

Discipline

Inevitably, it is the discipline records that draw the most attention. Many, perhaps most, of these involved fornication. It seems fairly clear that these tended only to come to attention if a child was born as a result. It was described as 'antenuptual fornication' if a child was born too soon after a marriage (a slightly lesser offence). There was always a possibility of serial offenders, bearing or fathering multiple offspring. A common currency for penitence was used: three appearances before the congregation in 'the place of repentance' or 'on the pillory' for a first offence; six for a second (relapse); and twenty-six for a third (trilapse), making that on a par with adultery. Sackcloth was to be worn for the occasion, supplied by the session. It was fairly normal that the two people involved did not do their penance at the same time, even if they were sentenced together. In theory, punishment was equal for both parties but this varied at different times and in different denominations. It was always easier for a man to physically escape from the parish; therefore, women tend to figure more in the punishments.

The numbers undergoing punishment were never large even in the bigger Burghs. That might in itself imply that such offences, or being caught in those acts, were not common. A visitation of twenty-four parishes in the Diocese of Dunblane in the 1580s inquired each parish about the morals of the inhabitants and a total of thirty-one cases of adultery were reported, some had been resolved, some were under process and some unrepentant. At the start of the eighteenth century, the parish of Stirling only had two sackcloth gowns, and so the convicted sinners might have to wait months before they could do their penance and be absolved, particularly if a couple of adulterers were serving out their 26 appearances. At various times, a sliding scale of public repentance was used. There was also a more private administration of justice where the rebuke was delivered only in front of the kirk session, accompanied by public mention only. The offender might be required to stand up in their place and be rebuked, they might have to stand in front of the congregation for the rebuke or they might have to spend the entire service sitting on the 'cutty stool' (the stool of repentance) or standing on the pillar/pillory. Gradually, the public nature of such rebukes began to diminish, surviving longest in some of the smaller, more conservative churches.

Even when the influence of the Session was at its height, there were people who did not recognize or cope with its authority. Few went to the extremes of Charles Stirling of Kippendavie who, when he made his appearance in the place of public repentance in Trinity College Church (Edinburgh) in 1701, was accused of 'Laughing, having of fruit, speaking to others and making of water and other miscarriages on the pillar; to the great dishonour of God and offence of the congregation.' He also denied the charges despite many witnesses. Later arraigned for treason and Jacobitism, it may be assumed that Charles had little respect for the Established Church. But if he was a fairly spectacular example of someone who declined to acquiesce in session discipline, there were many others who quietly resisted.

There were various forms of resistance; while some simply disappeared to the bigger towns, or even England, where anonymity was easier, men, joined the army or navy or foreign trade. But it is impossible to know how many moved out of the range of their home kirk session. As Scotland's industrial population grew, the effectiveness of Church discipline became almost nil by the end of the eighteenth century. For those who stayed put and resisted, options were few. Strict denial when the child was present was not convincing in the case of the woman, but she could either refuse to name the father, name the wrong father or claim rape by an unknown man. The kind of resistance represented by the first two courses of action was more likely when she was being paid by a wealthy and possibly married lover to conceal his identity for social reasons. This could lead to the woman being accused of adultery or the more serious offence of contumacy which took the case from the kirk session to the higher court of presbytery. Up until 1712, continued contumacy could lead to the offender being put in the hands of the civil authorities and residence in the local tolbooth could follow. Meanwhile, the unknown man paid no public price, although in some cases there might be an assumption that he was financially supporting the woman and her child. For the man suspected of fornication evidence was inevitably slighter; refusal to take responsibility was easier and recourse might be made to oaths taken in church in front of the congregation. This itself had its own ritual; the oath might be read publicly before the accused and the congregation more than once and the accused cautioned of the enormity of his action in swearing untruthfully. Finally, he would be allowed to swear and thereafter could not be charged unless further evidence of his guilt appeared. Then of course, perjury added to his original offence put him in a very much worse place.

Delays were frequently caused in the process by those under investigation. The easiest delay was not to turn up when summoned to the kirk session or presbytery. By the time the person had failed to attend or 'compear' which was the word used in the records, the case might again be handed to the civil powers and the hospitality of the tolbooth might beckon. Excuses might be made: a nursing mother was given some leeway and a mother in labour was given a week or two to recover. A servant involved in the harvest might also be allowed time, especially if the land was distant from the parish as often happened with semi-migrant farm workers.

Besides the stool of repentance, fines were used for offenders. There was often a bargaining process where those with funds tried to buy their way out of trouble; by the early nineteenth century, it was colloquially known as 'buttock mail'. The poor's fund would receive the proceeds but there was certainly a feeling that the better off had more options in dealing with their guilt than the poor.

By the mid-eighteenth century discipline cases were changing: Parliament removed the facility for church courts to call on the magistrates to back up their decisions in 1712; through the century, public repentance gradually fell out of favour, particularly in the cities and larger towns; the growing number of alternatives to the Established Church meant that while those who were committed to their own church submitted to its discipline, those less committed avoided discipline by claiming allegiance to any other church that did not pursue them.

Within the upper reaches of society, there was a feeling that the church should not be too interested in the lives of individuals. Additionally, industrialization, the rise in population and the rise in the mobility of population were all making anonymity that much easier. The irony is that it is easier to trace the stories of those born out of wedlock in the early eighteenth century than it is in the early nineteenth. A difference in attitudes can also be found in two civil cases, one from the early eighteenth century and one 70 years later. In the first case, a man was convicted of slander for telling the local kirk session that the wife of a local landowner was guilty of adultery. His punishment, paying a fine of 500 merks (£332.66) and standing at the kirk door acknowledging that he was a liar, was overturned by the Court of Session on the grounds that he was doing his duty. Seventy years later, the court told the minister of Dunfermline that he had no right to accuse people from the pulpit unless the Session had already tried their case and made public repentance part of the punishment. Lord Alemore, one of the judges said:

> The time was, when the clergy directed the judges, and even the Parliament, and when they used very great liberties in the pulpit. But these times are now over. ... We all know the credit that is paid by the people to whatever is uttered from the pulpit. If ministers are permitted to behave in this manner, they will be worse than mad dogs running about the country.

The times were changing; there was a reaction against the investigations of morals; one of the more outspoken critics, a missionary in Harris in the late eighteenth century, John Lane Buchanan, wrote of kirk session discipline that:

> This inquisitorial office is generally more agreeable to the elders, than to the ministers, as they are more ignorant and insignificant and consequently require more the prop of other people's failings..... In many instances they. who are at least as shrewdly suspected of lewdness as well as intemperance themselves, are the severest and most curious and prying inquisitors into the failings of others.

It is possible that Buchanan's rant was perhaps coloured by the fact that he was deposed for having sexual relations with three women, one of them married, during his sojourn in Harris. One of the crucial points of church discipline though was the intention to move on. Once an incident was dealt with that was an end to it and it should not be cast up in future. In at least two cases, errant ministers found their congregations petitioning presbytery to restore them to their pulpits after they had done their penance for fathering children out of wedlock.

The Church was not only concerned with sex; it was not even concerned with all sex. Scottish church records reveal scanty evidence for homosexuality or paedophilia, for example, reinforcing the idea that the church was really interested in sexual morals only as they affected procreation.

Temperance

The Dunfermline case mentioned above was based on the minister attacking a prominent citizen publicly for drunkenness. Drunkenness figures periodically through the centuries, particularly if it impinged on the Sabbath. Drinking in a public house while church services were being held was a heinous offence. The offence became all the greater if violence ensued. It was not unknown for ministers to have a drink problem, then as now. The minister of Lecropt near Stirling was deposed for forgery in 1724, but his case referred to a whole string of events in public houses and change houses. Even some of the prominent figures of their day were known to struggle. Rev. George Gilfillan in Dundee, so eminent in the nineteenth century that the Gilfillan Memorial Church survives to this day, was well-known for his spells of overindulgence and was rebuked by his presbytery more than once. On the first occasion, he was arrested while sitting in Dundee docks reciting from the works of Shakespeare. By this time, 1867, the Temperance Movement was very influential in the Scottish churches and his misdeeds were seen as much more serious than they would have been a century earlier when Alexander Webster, minister of the Tolbooth Church in Edinburgh and in due course Moderator of the General Assembly, was referred to as Doctor *Magnum Bonum* for his love of claret.

The churches' institutional dislike of alcoholic drink dates from the nineteenth century and gradually built up strength through the century. Drinking had been a notorious social problem, particularly in Scotland's cities for a long time. An Edinburgh bookseller, William Creech, wrote in 1792: 'The legislature would surely act wisely by reducing the duty on malt liquor and increasing it on spirits; ardent spirits so easily obtained are hurtful to the health, industry and morals of the people.' By 1832, Glasgow supported 1360 spirit dealers, one for every fourteen families, and while drunkenness had been common for years before that, there was a feeling that drunkenness combined with industrialization led to economic and moral disaster: a drunken ploughman could leave his horse to do the work while a drunken iron founder was a danger to himself and everybody around him.

Temperance Societies started appearing in Scotland from the 1820s; not being religious in origin, they rather belonged with the political radicalism of the Chartist tradition. They were initially promoting 'Temperance'; moderation, such as drinking beer in small quantities was acceptable but drinking whisky was not. By the 1840s, total abstinence from alcohol was seen as the goal and societies sprung up all over the country to promote it. The churches were not initially involved at an institutional level, although many individual church members were active in the movement. However, it was becoming more socially acceptable as the decades went on, and the unpleasant realization was that Catholic countries in continental Europe had much less of a problem than the supposedly morally superior, Calvinist Scotland. In England, the Temperance Movement became associated with religious dissent, Methodism and the Baptist churches in particular. This did not happen in Scotland; none of the biggest churches took a particular lead. Even the Scottish Baptists rejected teetotalism as a precondition for office as late as 1897, and the Scottish Wesleyan Methodists formed a Temperance Committee only in 1875. The major denominations joined the campaign earlier; the United Secession Church (United Presbyterian after 1847) had a Temperance Society from 1845 but only an official UP Church Temperance Committee from 1866. The Free Church had its Temperance Committee from 1847; and the Church of Scotland, with unconscious humour, founded a Committee on Intemperance a year later. By the end of the century though, the Established Church in particular tended to be less committed to the cause than either of its main rivals; there were said to be three times as many Free Church Ministers total abstainers than Church of Scotland ones.

Why were the churches slow to take up the cause? Perhaps it was because the cause was associated with political radicalism and subversion. Perhaps it was because one of the most prominent activists was an Irish RC priest, Father Matthew, whose visit to Scotland in 1842 added several thousands of total abstainers to the 7,000,000 he is said to have encouraged to sign the pledge in his lifetime. Perhaps it was because by the 1860s so many ministers of engaged in campaigning were involved in the anti-slavery movement. Even then, there was a negative public image of temperance reformers which some felt would detract from their effectiveness as ministers. In the 1870s, the official refreshments rooms at the General Assemblies of both the Church of Scotland and the Free Church sold alcoholic liquor for the refreshment of commissioners.

But if the churches were slow to be involved institutionally, individuals were very active and gradually persuaded their churches to take on the crusade. Much of this came as a result of the growing campaign to return to a more widespread observance of the Sabbath. Industrialization had brought in its wake a culture of relaxation and recreation on the one day of the week that was not dominated by employment and this was seen as an attack on religion. The campaign to have public houses closed on Sundays therefore appealed to two camps, and gradually the temperance campaign came to be adopted as a policy by those intent on keeping Sundays non-commercial.

The United Presbyterians were perhaps the most temperance minded of the major churches, which is possibly why Rev. George Gilfillan's failings in Dundee were made public, but of all the Scottish churches, only the Evangelical Union voted to support total abstinence, shun those who made their living from alcohol and to use non-alcoholic wine for Communion services.

By the end of the nineteenth century, the temperance campaigns gained impetus again. An American import; the Blue Ribbon Society specifically based their campaign on biblical texts and religious revivalist methods. The result a few decades later was Prohibition in the United States, despite concerted attempts this was not the result in Britain, but it did harden attitudes within the churches, and by using public halls rather than churches, by using choirs to enhance the emotional impact it had a considerable but short-lived effect. The Band of Hope which concentrated on persuading children to sign up to total abstinence within a religious, Sunday-school-like atmosphere was much more long-lasting. Founded in Leeds in 1847, it had British membership peaking in the 1930s at around three million but it dwindled dramatically in the 1950s. Its successor organization is still involved in preventative work with young people, educating them about alcohol and drug use. Until the 1950s, though, children attended regularly and also gained from the organized 'trips' that took them to places they would never otherwise see.

The use of unfermented wine for Communion services caused ructions in individual congregations. One UP Church in Motherwell split in two, the teetotal group's church being known locally as the 'Jeely Watter Kirk', and others followed. Teetotalism for some became more important than their actual faith. Seventy Free Church congregations had turned to unfermented grape juice in 1870; by 1914, the figure was 734. As well as the total abstainers' argument, there was also the fear which is still around, that the sip of an alcoholic communion wine might be enough to re-trigger an addiction. As late as the 1970s, there was a church in Glasgow which served alcoholic communion wine in two sections of the pews and non-alcoholic wine in the other two sections; to add to the complication, in each case, there was a section that used the 'common cup' and another section that used individual glasses.

After the Great War, there was legislation which allowed for local voters to vote against licences being issued within their locality. Church members played a significant part in these veto campaigns; however, despite left-wing political support for temperance, there was a growing opinion among working people that associated 'Temperance' with a middle-class desire to control working-class behaviour. However, many of the keenest supporters of the movement were those ministers, particularly in the Free Church, who had come from lower social backgrounds and saw drunkenness as one of the major evils of the society that they had come from. The attempt to prohibit the sale of alcohol either locally or nationally may even have helped alienate ordinary working people from churches that seemed intent on trying to control them.

Sabbath observance

A more biblical issue was the observance of the Sabbath. The observance of Sunday, or lack of it, was indeed a regular feature of session minutes. Folk history looks back with various degrees of horror at a time when everyone went to church on pain of appearing in front of the session, but in reality, it does not appear to be the case. Session minutes do record efforts to patrol the streets and bring to justice those most flagrantly abusing the Sabbath, but actual cases are rare. Public drunkenness on the Sabbath appears periodically as does the occasional tradesman plying his trade: a barber in Stirling, for example, was caught shaving army trumpeters from the castle garrison. One minister in Larbert was asked in 1695 whether he always preached and replied that he normally did but sometimes the smallness of the congregation discouraged him and he did not bother. The pursuit of farm work on the Sabbath does figure periodically in the records, but people working on Sunday in large numbers was more a feature of the eighteenth century onwards when industrial processes were much more efficient if they were allowed to run seven days a week and therefore required workers to be present. The advent of railway travel added another field of conflict when the Sunday running of trains became a significant issue and the freedom of workers and their families to travel on the one day of the week that was available for their recreation was seen by some as desirable and by others as a breach of God's Law.

Even without travelling, though, Sunday recreation was resisted by many in the churches. An open-air prize-fight in Govan in 1862 was broken up by the local minister, fully robed, striding into the ring and sending the entire audience home. In 1865, a letter to the newspapers commented on the fact that a dozen policemen had to be employed in preventing people from skating on St Margaret's Loch on a Sunday. On the other hand, another suggested that street lights should be left on from Saturday through to Monday morning to save lamplighters having to light and extinguish them on Sunday. The matter of the trains came to a head in 1865, the year when a merger of the 'North British Railway Company' with the 'Glasgow and Edinburgh Railway Company' led to the likelihood of the resumption of Sunday running of trains.

Note the word 'resumption': the same battle had been fought and won by the Sabbatarians at an earlier stage, but by 1865 there was a growing number in the churches who saw a relaxation in the rules as worthwhile and a corresponding hardening of attitudes by their opponents. In due course, the Sunday running of trains became the norm, but it is a battle that has raged intermittently over the ferries to the Western Isles ever since. Taken to a modern extent, those strictest in their observance of the Sabbath will close down their websites or part of them on a Saturday evening.

As a final note to this survey of the interactions of the churches with sinners, it may be appropriate to challenge the modern view of the historic church as glorifying a 'holier than thou' attitude. On the contrary, an argument can be made for it to continually remind the people that congregations, then as now, were made up of sinners and were not just the preserve of the pious. The case of James Gourlay, minister of Tillicoultry Church, Clackmannanshire, can be taken as a case in point. In late 1772, he asked to be relieved of his charge on account of his health; he had been advised to take a long sea voyage. A month later, Dunblane Presbytery was summoned to an emergency meeting to consider his confession of fornication with his maidservant Agnes Drysdale. This in itself was not unique but Gourlay, having voluntarily confessed, was summarily deposed and ordered to be rebuked in front of the congregation by three ministers on successive Sundays. At the same meeting, there was presented a petition signed by no fewer than 130 land-owners, elders and heads of family asking that the Presbytery should execute its punishment on him as quickly as possible and then restore him as their minister. In the event, the patron declined to reappoint him, for Gourlay had already resigned, but the support of so many in the congregation suggests that a record of public penance was no barrier to being acceptable as a minister. Indeed, he later became a minister in the American colonies. His successor followed a similar trajectory, being deposed for fornication twenty years later. By then, the tariff of public penitence had dropped from three to two appearances for a first offender.

The involvement of the churches in moral matters has changed over the centuries; on the whole now they tend to speak on the principles rather than involve themselves in individual cases. Private censure for moral lapses was still found in the twentieth century but the stool of repentance was long gone, public censure for the moral lapses of church members is now the province of tabloid journalism.

6

Non-Presbyterian Dissent: Congregational, Baptist and Methodist Traditions

The chapter considers the origins of three of the largest non-Presbyterian traditions as they have developed in Scotland. All three traditions have a long and strong history in the rest of the United Kingdom; however, the Congregational and Baptist traditions have a particularly Scottish development, while the Methodists in Scotland trace a much more British path.

The Congregational tradition

Congregational churches, churches which recognized no human authority from outside the individual congregation, first appeared in Scotland soon after the Reformation with the attempt of Robert Browne to escape from English persecution and set up an independent church in Edinburgh. He was soon sent on his way by an equally unsympathetic Edinburgh. A scatter of others followed but there was no identifiable Scottish church until the invasion by Cromwell's army brought large numbers of what were known as 'Independents', the majority religious group in the army, following Cromwell's own line. Individual congregations rejected control by bishops and also by presbyteries. Cromwell's rule in Scotland favoured Independents, and the recognized place of the Church of Scotland, whether Episcopal or Presbyterian, disappeared until his hold on the country was released. Such Independent churches as there were seemed to have little attraction for the local population. At most eight ministers in Scotland were convinced of the cause and their influence disappeared with the Restoration in 1660.

Glasites

A more native form of Congregationalism arose in Scotland in the 1720s with the deposition of John Glas as minister of his church in Tealing near Dundee. Glas was disturbed by his congregation's enthusiasm for the Covenants of the previous century and felt that they should have no place in the thinking of the church. He rejected the idea that the magistrates should have any responsibility for supporting the church or that the state could insist on particular religious views. Instead he, like many after him, tried to bring his flock to a state more like that of the early church. He formed a separate congregation of about 100 people of those who shared his views within his parish. At a Communion Service he conducted with a neighbouring and more orthodox minister, he preached in such a way as to show his rejection of the authority of the Church of Scotland. At the next Presbytery meeting in 1726 he was accused by his colleague of opposing the doctrine and authority of the church. This led to his final deposition from Tealing in 1730. A later judgement in 1739 declared him still to be a minister, but not of the Church of Scotland.

The result was the denomination which became known as the 'Glasites', although their own preferred term was 'Church of Christ'. The remnants of his Tealing congregation were joined by a group in Arbroath, led by a minister of similar views. By the time of Glas's death there were fourteen churches in Scotland, with others in England and the United States. A daughter of Glas married a Perth weaver named Robert Sandeman; he became a strong promoter of the denomination, so much so that they became known as 'Sandemanians' in England and in the United States. Their Scottish strength was tiny, perhaps 1000 members at most, with the strongest centre being in Dundee. In the 1790s Dundee was said to have 1160 people attached to the congregation; this may have represented about 250 members.

They were generally regarded with suspicion; they celebrated communion weekly, and also celebrated a 'love-feast' or 'agapé' between services on a Sunday. This idea intrigued those who heard of it and added an air of mystery. When the mystery was resolved in later days proving to be no more than a communal plain meal, it gave the denomination its nickname of the 'Kail Kirk'. Other characteristics which set the Glasites apart from other churches were the practice of feet-washing and strict dietary rules banning the eating of blood and of meat which had been strangled.

It was a strict church, with a combination of Calvinism and rationalism which demanded conformity to strict standards. Despite being founded by a minister, it was non-clerical, with each church being led by a minimum of two elders who had no formal training and were drawn from the membership. This lack of formal theological training was yet another reason for their being mocked by those outside, although the elders generally were chosen from among the best educated members.

People joined by declaring their faith and convincing the rest of the membership that their faith conformed to that of the membership. In the services, the Bible was read four or five chapters at a time until every word of every chapter had been read in order, with Psalms sung, equally systematically. There was no attempt to pursue a theme in a service. Communion, the 'Lord's Supper', was celebrated at the evening service, with a real innovation, the singing of hymns. Discipline was as strict as in any Presbyterian Church, with expulsion or excommunication as the final sanction. Marriage was seen as a duty to be undertaken young, preferably around sixteen, and marriage within the community was virtually compulsory.

Like so many of the smaller denominations, the Glasites appealed to the weaving community, but it took root also in the business communities of Perth and Dundee. Several printers were also members in the late eighteenth century and perhaps because of this, the Glasites were active and influential in print.

Perhaps because of its insistence on uniformity of thought in individual churches (or perhaps just because they were Scottish in origin), the Glasites were prone to splitting and several non-communicating groups of churches existed at various times. Gradually the church declined; it died out in the United States by 1900; its last church closed in 1984. The death of the second last elder spelled the end, for without two elders they could not appoint any new ones or celebrate Communion. The last elder died in 1999, coincidentally a Sandeman and a descendant of the founder.

Aside from its influence on the ideas and theology of Congregational and Baptist churches, the Glasite church is notable for the quality of its records, many of which are preserved in Dundee University and which give a detailed picture of the community. Several of their churches are still in existence, though converted to other use.

Sporadic independent congregations began to appear from the time of Glas onwards; two Church of Scotland ministers in the borders for example started a small congregation in Maxton in 1732 as a protest against the restoration of patronage, and although they carried on as ministers in the national church, the congregation remained independent.

Old Scots Independents

A second congregationally minded group came into existence in 1760 founded by two Fife-based ministers who had been influenced by Glas. They founded a church and they became its 'elders'; they were joined by a congregation in Glasgow whose members had left the Relief Church. They had wealthy men in their number, including a prosperous candle-maker called Paterson whose funding of their church building led it to be known as the 'Candle Kirk'. The Glasgow Church was the subject of fairly robust opposition and sometimes pelted with missiles, but its eldership contained influential people like David Dale, founder of the New Lanark Mills and its community. Some of these churches were rigorous in their standards even by the standards of the day. The church in Paisley was notable for its strictness so much so that when it closed after twenty-one years of existence, from their total membership of 164, seventy-nine had withdrawn and thirty-nine had been 'cut off' for various reasons. Having said that, they were also extremely generous in time and kind, indeed the closure of the church owed more than a little to the debts the congregation had accrued as a result of its generosity. The spread of Old Scots Independents came slowly. By 1814 there were twelve congregations with a membership of about 500 people. Unlike many independent churches, they did not actively promote evangelism and this may have contributed to their gradual fading away.

The Bereans

A third group of independents thrown up by the eighteenth century were the Bereans. As churches go, they do not loom large in Scotland's consciousness. There were never more than a handful of congregations, although they had a presence in London as well, and the total numbers can never have been more than 200 or 300. However, they did survive for seventy years or so and appear in published statistics of church membership.

Once again, like the Glasites, the Berean Church was the product of one man's falling out with his local presbytery. John Barclay trained to be a minister of the Established Church. As a probationer he was placed as assistant to the minister in Errol but was dismissed for 'teaching obnoxious doctrines'. He was then appointed as assistant in Fettercairn in the north-east of Scotland and remained there for nine years, aiding the ailing and elderly Rev. Anthony Dow. He might have expected to succeed Dow, and indeed the congregation were keen that he should, for he was an effective preacher and well liked, drawing listeners from miles around. However, he was also writing and it was his writing that drew attention to unorthodox views. As a result, when Dow died, the local presbytery cancelled Barclay's appointment. Indeed they went further and forbade him from preaching within the presbytery bounds, refusing him the certificate that would let him preach elsewhere in Scotland.

Barclay appealed to the General Assembly, which upheld the presbytery's decision. Barclay found himself outside the Established Church and set up as an independent preacher, erecting a church in Sauchieburn. Many of the people of nearby Fettercairn followed him there and made up the bulk of his congregation.

The people of Edinburgh had heard Barclay defend himself at the General Assembly and many were impressed. No sooner had he set up his church in Sauchieburn, than he was persuaded to open another in Edinburgh, following that with several in London, and soon there were other congregations building up in Glasgow, Stirling, Crieff, Dundee, Arbroath, Paisley and Fettercairn.

The Berean Church's beliefs came out of the Calvinism of its time, but were quite individual. Heavily Old Testament based, they believed that the prophets and the Psalms presaged Christ's life, but should not be applied to modern lives. They kept the practice of the Sacraments, but objected strongly to the word 'Sacrament' and to the concept of 'consecrating' the elements. They were also among the early users of hymns, largely if not entirely written by Barclay himself.

Little remains of the life of the church. They had ministers; Barclay was ordained by a 'class' of five dissenting ministers in October of 1773 in Newcastle and he then ordained others. They never had a formal presbytery or 'class' which met, but there is, or was, a manuscript record of the Bereans in Edinburgh which gives some details. As was usually the case with these small offshoots, discipline was strict and they believed themselves to be the only true Christian Church. In some places they owned or leased their own property; in others such as Stirling they made use of a local school, spilling over into premises across the road if large numbers were expected, while in Paisley they apparently owned and met in a grain store which was sold to a Seceder congregation in 1785.

By the 1820s there were few Bereans left; Glasgow had ninety-six members in 1823 and Stirling about thirty-three. The Edinburgh church voted to close in 1834, and there were said to be four ministers still working in seven small congregations in 1843. That was the last reference to them in any records and they must have died out soon after, although Barclay's writings were reprinted during the 1850s. Thereafter the Congregational Church kept alive their memory for several decades with an annual service at Sauchieburn, where it started, and look on the Bereans as part of their history and heritage.

The Bereans do not offer much information for family historians and their records appear to be lost, but they do make up part of the story of the church in Scotland for a small number of localities.

The Brothers Haldane and their churches: The Congregational Union

If the Glasites, Old Scots Independents, and Bereans were all small and of importance only to their adherents, the same could not be said of those churches that arose out of the work of James and Robert Haldane. The Haldane brothers came from a wealthy family; both had brief naval careers, one in the Royal Navy and the other in the navy of the East India Company, but were able to retire at an early age. Their spiritual 'awakening' sprang from awareness of the French Revolution and what it meant for human freedom, but this was transformed into an evangelical fervour. Robert sold his estate at Airthrey (now the site of Stirling University), with the intention of going to India as a missionary but this was prevented by the East India Company. Instead the brothers put their energies into mission work at home; initial financial support gave way to actual mission work and James Haldane's tour of Scotland to spread the Gospel. The tour made a considerable impact, with many conversions, and led to the foundation of 'The Society for Propagating the Gospel at Home'. This was intended to be non-sectarian and inter-denominational, indeed the Haldanes were still members of the Established Church at this point, but Robert gave the proceeds of the sale of his estate to the Society. Church buildings soon followed; 'The Tabernacle' in Edinburgh which could hold 2500 people and others in Glasgow, Dundee, Perth, Elgin and Caithness. James Haldane was himself ordained as a minister in 1799, by which time the brothers had been joined by Greville Ewing, who looked after much of the administration as well as ministry. By then they had withdrawn from the Established Church and formed their new association of independent congregations. There was naturally opposition from existing congregations, but there was also a trickle of ministers dissatisfied with life in the Church of Scotland or the various Seceder churches. Inspired by the Haldanes, other congregations formed and loosely associated themselves. By 1800 the churches were able to open a seminary to teach new ministers and the responsibility for this fell to Greville Ewing. It was reported that the first twenty-four students all started as Presbyterians but were Congregationalists by the end of the course.

By 1807 there were eighty-five churches but as so often happened, divisions appeared. The most serious one, and the one that finally split the movement, was the question of infant baptism. Both Haldanes were converted to Baptist views by 1809 and large numbers joined the Baptists with them. The task of rebuilding was left to Ewing; but some of the buildings legally belonged to the Haldanes, and others belonged to congregations who were in debt to them. The seminary was also the property of Robert Haldane and entirely supported by him.

The remaining churches were therefore in a crisis, both financial and personal, and it was at this point that the Congregational Union was formed, not as a ruling body but as an association for helping each other out. Gradually some congregations from the other independent strands joined them, Old Scots Independents and Bereans. Occasionally individual churches fell out with each other, but this did not lead to expulsion. One particular controversy led to four Glasgow churches being out of communication with their neighbours. It was, however, over the same topic as that which led to the next strand of Congregationalism, the Evangelical Union.

Evangelical Union

At around the same period, dissent was growing in the United Secession Church. One of its ministers, James Morison, gradually came to a different view of Calvinist doctrines from what was accepted at the time. This became known as the 'Atonement Controversy'. Morison came to believe that Christ died for all believers, not just the elect; he gradually moved away from many of the tenets of the Westminster Confession and finally he was deposed as a minister. In 1841 Morison and his congregation opened an independent church; a second church followed when his father was deposed by the United Secession the following year, followed by a further two in 1843. These four, with an evangelist and eight elders formed their new denomination that year; the Evangelical Union. As with so many other organizations, it was not meant to be a new denomination, but that is what it became. It had stipend funds and building funds, a theological hall and all the other elements that a Victorian denomination felt it had to have. The original churches had grown to thirteen in 1843 as it quickly also gathered in some churches from the Congregational Union which had been facing the same questions over atonement. By 1896 there were ninety churches in the Union. The EU quickly became one of the chief promoters of the Temperance Movement in Scotland and it was also promoting missions throughout the country, although with particular strength in west-central Scotland.

Partly because of continuing coolness over the controversy that led to the founding of the EU and its inheritance of former Congregational churches, the Congregational and Evangelical Unions were not close allies in the mid-nineteenth century. However, it was recognized that their actual differences were few; the liberalism of some late Victorian theology was gaining ground and gradually a movement towards union began to form from about 1867 onwards, at much the same time as the dissenting Presbyterian churches also started considering re-union. It took nearly thirty years, but in 1894, both churches voted to unite. The union took place in 1896 under the title of the Congregational Union of Scotland. As an omen of what was about to happen in the Free and United Presbyterian Churches' union of 1900, a minority in the Congregational Union who were against union went to court, but finally, and unusually, all the dissenting congregations were gathered back into the united Union within a few years.

Some expansion followed; eight new congregations were formed by the outbreak of the Great War but twice as many had closed by 1924. From that time, the organization became much more of a denomination and less an association of separate congregations; there were campaigns put churches into particular areas with ministers appointed centrally to them, there was a movement towards controlling who could become ministers and there was a full-time and very influential Secretary of the Union. One ground-breaking development was the ordination of Vera Findlay, later Kenmure, as the denomination's first woman minister in 1929. Her appointment to her first charge in Partick was met with enthusiasm, and although her marriage soon after did not seem to cause ripples at a time when female school-teachers were expected to resign on marriage, Vera Kenmure's status as a mother was another matter and she was forced out of her first charge after the birth of her daughter. However, part of her congregation also left that church and they formed another which amalgamated with Hillhead Congregational Church under her ministry two years later.

The Second World War came at a point when the Congregational Union was already struggling. Numbers were down and the enthusiasm of those who remained was low. By 1944 there were 158 churches and about 39,000 members. The Forward Movement was begun in 1944 and some new churches did come about as a result. About half of the Congregational Union of Scotland united into the United Reformed Church in 2000. This denomination based on an amalgam of English Presbyterian and Congregational Churches was founded in 1972 and initially its only Scottish representatives came from the Church of Christ which joined the URC in 1981. The remainder of the Scottish Congregational Churches remained separate and formed the Congregational Federation.

The Baptists

One of the first intimations of the Baptist tradition being present in Scotland after the Cromwellian period came from the *Scots Magazine* in 1765. It described how an 'antipaedobaptist' had baptized two adults in the Water of Leith in Edinburgh.

The two persons being first stripped, were cloathed in black gowns, and then went into the water with their minister who, after repeating some words in their ordinary form took them by the nape of the neck plunged them down over head and ears and kept them for a little time wholly under water.

Strictly speaking, Baptists in Scotland would not see themselves as a denomination but rather as an interdependent collection of churches who share certain common characteristics. The most obvious one of these is the insistence on 'Believers' Baptism', the belief that only those who have had a conversion experience should be baptized into full membership of the church. This was completely at odds with the normal practice of infant baptism which had been part of most other churches' life from earliest times. Allied to this belief is practice of baptizing by immersion, by dipping the person under water, rather than by the sprinkling of water which is the usual method in most other major churches. However, baptism by sprinkling is perfectly acceptable for modern Baptists if, for example, there are medical reasons against immersion.

The Baptists in England take their origin from the early seventeenth century and were present in Cromwell's army when he invaded Scotland in 1651. There were Baptist services held throughout the country and even a handful of local ministers were convinced, but when the army left it took its Baptists with it. The handful of churches which they had planted disappeared within twenty years and thereafter there was no Scottish Baptist tradition for nearly a century.

When the tradition did return it came in different forms. The first of these was a single church formed in Caithness by a landowner, Sir William Sinclair, who had been converted while soldiering abroad and founded a little church at Keiss, largely for his own estate people, in 1750. This congregation still survives and is therefore the oldest Baptist Church in Scotland. The Glasites were an early influence, particularly on the second strand, a group known as the 'Scotch Baptists' which took their origins in the 1770s. A third strand was formed around the brothers Haldane in the first decade of the nineteenth century. The fourth major strand in the history of Scotland's Baptists was the influx of English Baptists who, like English Methodists, brought their own forms of worship which gradually became part of the Scottish tradition and took on their own Scottish characteristics.

The Scotch Baptists were the first of the groups to have a presence as more than a single congregation. They were founded by Robert Carmichael and Archibald McLean; the former had been an Anti-burgher Seceder minister who had become convinced of the need for believers' baptism and taken himself to London to be baptized there in 1765. Archibald McLean was a printer and became *de facto* leader of the Scotch Baptists with his occupation providing him with the means of propagating his own particular version of faith. Calling themselves 'Scotch Baptists' to make clear their difference from their more numerous English counterparts, they soon had congregations of like-minded people in England and Wales and indeed it is in Wales that they still survive as one of many independent church groups. In Scotland they spread gradually through the lowlands, although they were never numerous. They had a strict set of principles, largely laid down by McLean. Some of these they shared with the Glasites. What made the Scotch Baptists individual was their insistence that each congregation had to have more than one elder and that only those that shared the beliefs of the congregation could take communion, which had to be administered by an elder. These elders were not paid, with the sole exception of McLean, who finally accepted a salary to release him from his printing business. Like the Glasites their intention was to run a church on the same lines as the early Christians; their ethos was largely Glasite and they sang some of Glas's hymns. They differed on baptism, and like the Old Scots Independents, they were actively evangelistic. There were no full-time clergy; the elders generally came from the congregations' own resources, although some did move around. Unanimity in all matters was insisted upon and disagreement led to expulsion. As groups of people frequently took issue with one or more of the church's tenets, splits and the forming of new churches was fairly frequent. As each congregation was also legally independent this led to a position where it was very hard for the ordinary person to know whether any Baptist Church was deemed acceptable by any other Baptist Church. One bone of contention was over the numbers of elders and whether they were needed for Communion services. This was also the issue which divided them from the English Baptist tradition and the other Scottish ones. Another equally divisive issue was the question of who could be admitted to the Sacrament of Communion; some felt that it was only members of congregations known to be in close agreement; others felt that anyone who claimed a conversion experience was eligible. After a series of splits most of the Scotch Baptist congregations gradually fell into line and accepted the other traditions.

In early days there were a number of people of substance drawn to the Scotch Baptists, the occasional physician or advocate but by the 1830s, the dominant economic status of members of the Edinburgh congregation is described as 'largely poor and working class in composition' and this fits with evidence from Stirling that members lived close to the church and unlike many dissenting congregations, did not draw membership from the suburbs where the wealthier citizens lived.

One of the curious facts about the Scotch Baptists is that they usually founded churches in communities which already had Glasite churches and often where there were Old Scots Independents as well. It is fairly general that the mind-set of a small dissenting church in the eighteenth and nineteenth century led to a tendency to further dissent, and this is seen in many of Scotland's towns and villages. In the early nineteenth century it was quite normal for any or all of these groups to have tiny congregations co-existing in the same town. They were all independent and might or might not recognize each other as sister churches. Within the individual churches, their structure was largely determined by their origins.

The timetable for a Scotch Baptist on a Sunday was a morning service that lasted from 10am till shortly before 1p.m. After a gap of an hour, a service of similar length would follow which included the Sacrament of Communion, held weekly by Scotch Baptists, fortnightly by other Baptist groups on the whole. The pattern followed 'psalm or hymn, prayer, psalm or hymn, prayer, psalm or hymn, Old Testament reading, New Testament reading, prayer by the preacher, exhortation, exhortation, exhortation, psalm or hymn, prayer, sermon, hymn, benediction'. Each of the prayers and exhortations might be undertaken by a different person and the exhortations would be called for without notice. One result of this form of worship is that potential leaders and pastors were quickly recognized by congregations from within their own number.

Those from a Presbyterian background among the Baptists would have found the use of hymns quite foreign to them, but in fact the Baptist Church at Keiss has the distinction of producing the first Scottish hymnbook, in 1750, although it was never used beyond the congregation.

The third strand of the Scottish Baptist movement was that founded by the Haldane brothers. In a country known for its secessions, they were unusual in actually seceding from their own denomination which they had founded only a few years previously. Because their church was called 'The Tabernacle' this group were known at the time as 'The Tabernacle Connection'. Although largely lowland based, it had a strong missionary tradition and also located churches as far afield as Thurso and near Lochgilphead. One visiting Baptist from England commented that these churches were the only Baptist churches in Scotland where English Baptists would be admitted to communion. That fourth strand, the 'English Baptists' began to appear at much the same time as the Tabernacle Connection.

The 'Englishness' of this group is perhaps a misnomer; some chapels were described as English only because they differed in structure from the Scotch Baptists; some of them were founded as a direct result of the Scottish universities' openness to students of differing Christian beliefs drawing English students. As a result of this Baptist students were able to get the university education in Scotland which was debarred to them in England until the foundation of the University College London in 1826. The early 'English Baptist' churches tended to be short-lived and liable to schism. It was only in 1806 that the first congregation to survive to the present day was founded,

Richmond Court Church (now Charlotte Baptist Church) in Edinburgh. The 1820s brought an increase throughout the country, and enthusiasm for mission work throughout Scotland has meant that almost all Baptist churches in the Gaelic-speaking Highlands came from that tradition.

The growing strength of English Baptists was parallel to a crisis in the Scotch Baptists who were carrying on their propensity for schism; an attempt in 1834 to heal the split of 1810 led to further splits, but gradually the more liberal congregations drew nearer to the English/Haldane-type churches.

Baptist churches have always been independent of each other, maintaining links with like-minded congregations by meetings and correspondence, but several attempts were made to create a more formal structure. An attempt in the 1840s failed but a later attempt in 1869 united fifty congregations with 3700 members. This body, the Baptist Union of Scotland, enabled the majority of Baptist churches to work together and co-operate much more effectively and in due course became the means that new congregations could be helped to build churches.

The late nineteenth century brought to the Baptist churches, as to others, challenges and opportunities. In the industrial lowlands new communities arose round the rapidly expanding new industrial sites. Around the ironworks of Lanarkshire, the shipbuilding communities and the mills of Paisley, where the new communities of migrant labour lived in largely slum conditions, the existing churches made little initial impact and were often in the wrong place. The field was open for churches and people with a passion for evangelizing. Added to that the evangelizing campaigns, particularly of the Americans Dwight Moody and Ira Sankey, brought a great awakening of evangelical fervour in their train. In this the Baptists had their part; their churches grew in number so that by 1914 they had about 20,000 members.

In a migrant community a small church of kindred spirits was a useful social support group. For semi-skilled people with some education and aspirations, the ethos of these congregationally-run Baptist churches standing for self-improvement and a shared set of ethical values was more attractive than the more rigid hierarchical approach of the Presbyterian churches. Having said that, it is easy to overestimate the attractiveness of the Baptist Church; the numbers involved as members were always tiny compared to the various Presbyterian churches; perhaps one percent.

The Baptist Church was always evangelical; their prime aim was the conversion of people; such a conversion could bring people also to a better life as it would reduce the threat of social evils to converted families. That was the theory, but equally many saw the social evils as a barrier standing in the way of conversion. Chief among the evils was the demon drink, and the Baptists were prominent in the temperance movement in the late nineteenth century and beyond, although they were late in joining it. The Free Church and the Established Church both had Temperance committees in the 1840s; the Baptist waited till 1881. Once espoused, though, the cause of Temperance was promoted with vigour with Baptists joining with the other denominations in their political pressure groups. On the other hand, it can also be said that the emphasis on teetotalism did not endear the evangelical abstainers to those in lower reaches of society who saw in alcohol a way of blunting the impact of their economic conditions.

It was not just the campaign against alcohol that began to bring denominations together. The revivalism of the second half of the nineteenth century began to break down barriers too, as the evangelical movements in many of the major churches began to see that what united them was more important than what divided them. Public, often open-air, evangelical meetings brought together speakers from the Presbyterian churches, Congregationalist and Baptist churches, even Episcopalians, and this gave rise to non-denominational missions in the poorest areas. If the Baptist Church was aware of its lack of impact on the poorest layers of society, some were also aware of its lack of impact on the more educated. Others also worried that the Baptist principles were in danger of being swamped by their being involved with Christians whose views were different and so they spoke out against too close a cooperation with other denominations.

The early twentieth century saw the Scottish Baptist Union healthy, achieving steady if unspectacular growth. The high point of membership was reached in 1935 with 23,310 communicant members. Churches were being planted in areas of population growth such as Mosspark in Glasgow and Rosyth in Fife. Churches were even being replaced or upgraded. Church membership in different areas waned and grew at different times. With as many of the churches being in industrial areas, the ebb and flow of manufacturing industry had a clear effect on the congregations. Like several denominations, Baptists also emigrated in large numbers when times were bad in Scotland.

At the same time, Baptist churches were growing more outward looking, taking part in national campaigns, supported by a range of churches, to try to convert more of the unchurched and to encourage those already involved. In particular, Billy Graham's visits to Scotland in the 1950s brought Scottish Baptists particular satisfaction as he is himself a Baptist. Despite that though, numbers were dwindling fast and Scotland was beginning again to be seen as a possible field for missionary endeavour by some American Baptists. Meanwhile the Baptists themselves were struggling with their relationship to other churches, first joining and then withdrawing from the World Council of Churches when they felt that Baptist and evangelical views were not being heard. Nonetheless, at a Scottish and local level, Baptist churches are fully involved with other churches.

The congregational nature of Baptist churches remains; as a result, some individual churches have remained outside or left the Scottish Baptist Union. Equally those inside the Union, although subscribing to the same principles may take different lines on, for example, whether women can be pastors.

Methodism in Scotland

Unlike Baptists, Congregationalists and Episcopalians, the Methodist Church in Scotland had no real Scottish roots. While the former denominations can trace their antecedents back to small Scottish groups that later merged with their English and Welsh equivalents, the Methodists were entirely the result of a religious movement south of the border, although it was a movement that developed its own Scottish flavour. The core of the Methodist movement in Scotland takes its origin from the twenty-two journeys that John Wesley made between 1751 and 1790, although there were some Methodists in Scotland prior to this.

The evangelist George Whitefield had made a foray into the country in the 1730s and although the early Seceders, who might have been expected to be his closest allies, could not accept his non-exclusive views, he found the people of the country eager to hear him. He is reputed, for example, to have preached to 20,000 people at an outdoor communion service in Cambuslang. Whitefield though was basically Calvinist at heart, even though he was an Anglican priest. He disagreed fundamentally with Wesley and never formally joined the Methodist movement. Nonetheless, the reception he got from the Scottish people, if not from the Scottish clergy, showed that Scotland had ears for preachers from other traditions than Presbyterianism. At the same time the 'revivals' that began to appear throughout the country, most notably at Cambuslang and Kilsyth, showed that a different spirit was afoot in the land. The growth of the Methodist movement and the revivals within Presbyterian churches were just two aspects of a movement that was widespread throughout North America, where it is referred to as 'The Great Awakening', as well as in Britain and northern Europe. Although there are few records, evidence does remain that shows that English and Continental soldiers stationed in Scotland had become Methodists and held meetings in various places in Scotland. One preacher serving among soldiers in the Netherlands described how soldiers who had been in Scotland had lost their 'simplicity and zeal for God' and instead had acquired that very Scottish habit of arguing about doctrine.

One of the earliest references in Scotland was to be found in the *Scots Magazine* of 1839 which lambasted the Methodists for their enthusiasm, always a seen as a dangerous trait by those less enthusiastic, their rejection of set forms for religious services, and for their habit of extemporary prayer. Adding more fuel to the fire was the allegation that laymen and even, perish the thought, even women, led worship. Two years later a further article showed how far Wesley was from Calvinism in affirming that all had free will and could be saved by faith. This was a far remove from the orthodox Calvinist view that people were predestined to salvation or damnation regardless of any good works they might have done.

Most of these early Methodists came to Scotland with the army, although there were others. In the wake of the '45, Scotland also heard examples of that new-fangled and slightly suspect form of religious verse, the hymn, being sung by soldiers. After his discharge from the army, one of these soldiers, Sergeant Robert Channon, was employed to train a church choir in the Aberdeenshire village of Monymusk and then in the city of Aberdeen itself, where he taught a repertoire of psalm tunes quite different from those habitually used throughout Scotland.

If Channon was still limited to psalms in Aberdeen, an Established Church minister in Glasgow, Dr John Gillies of the College Kirk, was not afraid to try out some Methodist hymns on his congregation at a weekday evening service in 1753. Gillies became a close friend of Wesley despite serious religious differences, as did a number of other Scottish ministers mainly in the cities. For fifteen years, Methodism grew quietly, without much controversy, with small societies founded here and there whose members also attended local parish or Seceder churches without criticism. It was not at this time seen as an alternative to existing churches, but rather as an additional enrichment.

So what then were these Methodists offering to the people of Scotland? In its earliest days, Methodism was an offshoot of the Church of England; John Wesley remained an Anglican priest all his days, but what he brought to his religion was a high sense of mission, and especially a mission to take the Gospel to the least educated and poorest classes in society, a strong feeling that all who believed could be saved and that those who were to be saved showed it by good works. Many of Wesley's friends tried to persuade him that Scotland had no need for his message due to the differences between it and England. In England it developed very strongly as a ministry of non-ordained lay preachers. Wesley resisted ordaining his followers in England because he did not think of Methodism as a separate church, but simply a different way of worship and evangelism. In Scotland he had no such scruples. Because the Church of England had no presence in Scotland and had no close relationship with such Episcopalians as there were in Scotland, Wesley had no hesitation in ordaining preachers there. On the other hand, he did find that congregations had a prejudice against his preachers because they were not as well educated theologically as the Presbyterian ministers of all varieties whom they were used to. In England, the two universities were barred to all except Anglicans until the foundation of University College London in 1826. Englishmen of a dissenting background who wanted higher education could receive that education in three ways; they could attend any of the five Scottish universities, St Andrews, Glasgow, King's College Aberdeen, Edinburgh and Marischal College Aberdeen, they could cross to Trinity College Dublin, set up for the late Elizabethan puritans, or they could attend what were generically known as 'dissenting academies', private colleges set up to educate non-Anglicans, Baptists, Congregationalists and Presbyterians. On the whole Methodist preachers did none of these, doing their training on the road without any formal education.

Trouble came for the Methodists of Scotland in 1765, though, when Dr John Erskine took umbrage at some theological writing of John Wesley which seemed to him to attack some of the fundamentals of Calvinist theology. Wesley's idea that Christ had died for all, not just for the few, the 'elect' was heresy to orthodox Calvinists and suddenly the differences between Methodists and the bulk of the population became important beyond the circles of theological pamphleteers.

Other differences came to seem important. The necessity for Methodists to raise money to build chapels or pay preachers was seen as socially exclusive, they were accused of denying Calvinism but saying they were Calvinists when it suited, their weekly meetings were seen as sources of salacious gossip, their preachers were criticized as ignorant and uneducated and their style seen as commonplace. As a boy, the future novelist Sir Walter Scott heard Wesley preach and found he was far too 'colloquial for the taste of his listeners'. Worse still their preachers travelled from place to place, never settling for long and were often seen as a threat to local ministers.

The numbers of adherents declined; 735 for the whole of Scotland in 1774 had dropped to 481 ten years later. There was opposition but it was much gentler than other groups had met with through the eighteenth century, and indeed much gentler than the violent treatment other Methodists had met with throughout England and Ireland. John Wesley was accorded the freedom of both Perth and Arbroath in 1772, and commented of the people of Dumfries that 'surely the Scots are the best hearers in Europe'.

After 1765, Methodism began to settle down in Scotland, but its reliance on self-funding meant that congregations appeared and disappeared with great regularity. Preachers tended to come from England and were encouraged to be itinerant. The response to the falling numbers was that 'Conference', the governing body of Methodism, decreed that the preachers in Dundee and Arbroath should never stay more than a week in any one place. From a Scottish perspective this 'Conference' began to be seen as more and more authoritarian and remote. Worse still, to Scots who had fought for the right to call ministers, it exercised patronage by decreeing which ministers should go where. However, it did take on a characteristically Scottish nature in some ways. The style in which the Scottish Methodist churches celebrated Communion was far more like the traditional Presbyterian way than in England. Individual churches might have 'elders' a concept entirely alien to their English counterparts, and, as already mentioned preachers were more likely to have more formal education.

Methodist congregations, whether in Scotland, England or elsewhere, proved just as likely to split themselves or split away from their parent bodies as any Presbyterian congregation. This was usually over the amount of control that the central body of each group tried to assert. The 1851 Census shows England with about ten varieties of Methodism, and although Scotland only showed four at that time, others of the ten had already sprung up in Scotland and as quickly disappeared again.

One group that did survive longer in Scotland was the Primitive Methodists, sometimes shortened to the 'Prims', but probably not by themselves. Primitive Methodists were so called because they tried to look back to the primitive pre-institutionalized Methodist church as envisaged by John Wesley, not because their habits lacked modern polish. Originally they laid great store by open-air worship and in a completely 'lay' church. Preachers were not ordained as in Presbyterian or Episcopalian churches, but they could be paid for their labours and if they were not confident to lead the singing at services, a singer would be at their side to help. Singing indeed was always a characteristic of Methodist worship which drew many people in a manner not shared by Presbyterian churches till a century or more later. In Scotland the Primitive Methodists came initially as missionaries from England and targeted some of the poorest areas in the country. The mission in Edinburgh for example centred on the Grassmarket, and in February 1826 the missionaries visited '300 abjectly poor' families in that area, including hundreds of children too poor to attend school. They soon took on the lease of a former weaving mill and created a chapel with seating for 600–700 people with the help of £100 raised locally 'from respectable people' as it is recorded. However, the old bugbear of central control raised its head and the Superintendent, Nathaniel West, split from the parent body and split his congregation irrevocably. Meanwhile in the west of the country, one James Johnson, a hatter to trade, started his mission by preaching on Glasgow Green, moving successively to Gorbals, Bridgeton and Calton. The following year a satellite mission started up in Paisley. The Primitive Methodists, like some other small denominations, saw their mission as being to industrial workers, mainly in heavy industry or weaving. Virtually all their congregations were to be found in the industrial towns of the central belt where the local churches were struggling to make contact with the great influx of workers. In particular many of the churches that grew up in west central Scotland took their origins from English workers who flocked there from Staffordshire or Shropshire to the ironworks of Lanarkshire. As further ironworks were set up, further Primitive Methodist congregations would soon follow. Curiously enough, a hundred years later, workers from some of these communities re-migrated to central England taking Scottish Presbyterianism with them particularly to Corby in Northamptonshire. Of course English ironworkers were not the only immigrants to industrial Lanarkshire, and there was some opposition to the Methodists from Irish Catholics who resented their missionary endeavours. So it was that the Lanarkshire village of Carfin produced a minor riot where Methodist missionaries were drowned out by the beating of kettles and pans and driven from the village.

The language of worship was intended to be down to earth and comprehensible to ill-educated people, so high-flown language was discouraged. One meeting affectionately requests Brother Murray 'to try.... to use no words but such as are generally understood'. If preachers were not ordained or formally qualified, they were still set apart, or 'called out' to be probationers and undertook various pledges. If things did not work out, they were pledged not to sow discord in the congregations they served; they were also, rather surprisingly for the early nineteenth century warned against 'sex in church work'. This last reflects the fact that the Methodists were the earliest of the major churches to use women as preachers and missionaries, although possibly less so in Scotland than in England.

With such a concentration in the poorest areas and the poorest parts of society, Methodism suffered perennial financial problems, probably more so in Scotland than in England. If chapels were set up, financing them was always a problem, with individual members of the congregation taking on responsibility for the debt. Membership of a congregation tended to be of two sorts; communicants and class members. These latter were the full members of the congregation and were pledged to attend weekly classes regularly and pay their dues which were intended to support the work of the church. Many others attended regularly but their contributions were much smaller and could not be relied upon. If class members did not attend they would be removed from the roll. Non-payment of class fees, on the other hand, was a clear signal to the central authority that a local minister was not liked or was failing.

Perhaps because of their non-Scottish origins, Primitive Methodists could be innovators in a way that the Presbyterian Seceders could not. Although the Methodist practice of allowing Christians of other traditions to take Communion was also found in the Presbyterian Relief Church from the late eighteenth century. It was the Methodists who broke the ban on celebrating the festivals of the church by instituting a Christmas Day service in 1861 in Motherwell. Some Church of Scotland and Free Churches started holding Christmas Day services by about 1890.

The Primitive Methodists, despite their best efforts, never caught the Scottish imagination; they served faithfully in the communities they targeted, but their people were attracted by any new body just starting and aimed at the same part of society. The Salvation Army with a very outgoing, socially aware and recognizable identity took many of its first members from the ranks of Methodist churches of all kinds, as did the Brethren movement. The Primitive Methodists never had more than 2500 members in their existence and for their first fifty years never topped the thousand mark, although their influence was on a much greater number of people than actually signed up as members. By the turn of the nineteenth century, Primitive Methodists were involved in politics, some in the Independent Labour Party, some in trade unions and some in speaking out against Clyde ship-builders for penalizing their engineers in support of a dispute in Belfast. In the economic circumstances of the 1920s, the industries associated with Primitive Methodist communities were in deep trouble, and the depression hit the churches hard while at the same time increasing the need for their social services.

Meanwhile the bigger group, the Wesleyan Methodists also had their areas of strength; fishing communities were a particular source of new recruits, perhaps because the men travelled to England. Methodist congregations still worship in many of the fishing towns and villages particularly on the east coast. Many of these churches were tiny; Dunbar had a membership of twelve people in 1889 and yet by dint of the minister, John Holdsworth's work among the fisherfolk, the following year they were able to raise £544 and totally renovate the building. Interestingly stained glass and wooden furnishings were donated to that project by a Presbyterian. If Holdsworth was popular with the fisher community, the local publicans were less enthusiastic; on one occasion they burned him in effigy as a protest against his work against drink trade locally, a very Methodist concern.

With an atmosphere of reunion in the air between 1890 and 1930, Methodists saw some of the old divisions in Scottish churches healed, even if the process led to some new divisions. There were those who saw in the existence of a variety of Methodist churches an unnecessary duplication and in 1932 the three biggest groups, the Wesleyan, United and Primitive Methodists, reunited. In Scotland the Wesleyans provided about three-quarters of the membership of around 12,000, with the Primitives providing the rest. The United Methodists had never had more than a handful of members and had long since disappeared in Scotland. Membership of the new body remained stable until about 1970, when a steep decline took place.

So what characterized Methodism after it became one? The Glasgow East Mission targeted the poorest in society, the numbers attending doubled between 1935 and 1936. All strands of Methodism were tied to opposition to the demon drink, opposition to the liberalization of drink laws was consistent and teetotalism was seen as compulsory for ministers. From the outside, it was still seen as an 'English' church, though members saw it differently and during the 1950s and 1960s there were some moves towards reunion with both the Episcopal tradition and the Presbyterian one. These came to nothing, although cooperation with other churches at local levels became the norm. As of 2014, there are about forty-five Methodist congregations throughout Scotland.

7

Overview: Disruption to Diversity

The story of the nineteenth-century church in Scotland is dominated by the Disruption, but amid all the hype and oratory, the Church of Scotland survived. It had lost about a third of its ministers, most of them taking their congregations with them; it had lost large numbers of members, often the most active, and it had also lost large numbers of elders and other office bearers, but it was still the national church and it was still building new churches in the 1840s.

In a sense, the church went on with 'business as usual'; presbyteries still met, albeit with reduced numbers; kirk sessions met as well, also with reduced numbers, though some kirk sessions ceased to exist and had to be reconstituted.

The Presbytery of Dunblane, for example, met in June 1843 with those who had not left for the Free Church. They scored out part of the minutes of the last pre-Disruption meeting as not legal but left it legible. They confirmed that their commissioners who had walked out of the General Assembly had been deposed and had their names struck from the roll of Dunblane Presbytery; they accepted a letter of resignation from another minister and then they arranged for each of the ministers who had seceded to be visited to formalize their intentions. Then, they had to arrange for the various churches involved to be visited on a Sunday and 'preached vacant'; that is, the congregation was told that they had no minister. Then the long task of filling the vacancies started, with the patrons identifying their favoured candidate.

There was also recognition of a further personnel problem. Parish schoolmasters had to be members of the Established Church in good standing. The schoolmaster at Doune was known to be no longer a member, so he was dismissed; this action was repeated across Scotland. The parish school system was showing signs of descending into chaos.

At the level of kirk sessions, there were different responses. In Doune, where the minister stayed put, several elders left for the Free Church but no one would know this from the Session minutes. Their names simply ceased to appear and a few months later some new elders were ordained. It is only by looking in the Free Church Session minutes does their secession become apparent. On the other hand, Stirling lost all its four ministers; they each had their own kirk session but three of the sessions also met together as the General Session of Stirling. Here, a neighbouring minister came in as Moderator and the eight remaining elders met with him as the General Session. The names of those seceding were reported, their departure formalized and arrangements made to retrieve the key to the Burgh church from the beadle, who had also left.

The most urgent matter was what to do about the poor, specifically about the ninety-nine paupers who received regular relief. Like education, this was an immediate and crucial role of the church and it too was thrown into chaos. As well as the ministers and a majority of the elders, the majority of the people had seceded and the church door collections slumped. Prior to the Disruption, the weekly collection had averaged just under £6; a month later, they were gathering only a quarter of that. Being a Burgh, Stirling had resources which country areas did not, so the Session was able simply to pass the whole problem to the Town Council and wash their hands of it. Country parishes did not have that luxury. Stirling's loss of church door collections though was nothing compared to some others. St David's Church in Dundee found its entire church door collection on the Sunday after the Disruption amounted to sixpence; 2.5 pence in today's money.

The question of poor relief was in fact a national crisis. Members of the old Church of Scotland did not need to pay for their minister or the upkeep of their church building or the manse, but they did have to pay for poor relief in the parish. The same issue had arisen with the previous secessions, but the numbers of Seceders, though large, had grown gradually and the church never lost such a large proportion of its funding at one time. However, the system had been creaking badly for a long time and from 1817, a series of reports and studies had tried to address the problems. Legal assessments of everybody, church-going or not, had been attempted in some parishes amid much disagreement. The big urban parishes had the greatest need for poor relief but the least ability to provide it. Among them, there were few who could afford it and it was extremely difficult to collect from a largely unchurched population.

Even before the Disruption, the medical profession had been trying to force a better poor law system. Their argument was that the causes of poverty were not moral shortcomings but economic ones. At its simplest, bad harvests led to high prices which led to poverty and hence to disease and starvation. Relief was only provided as a last resort but earlier intervention might have prevented the problem in the first place. The situation was made worse by a depression in trade that struck with full force in the textile industries. Paisley in particular was effectively destitute in 1842. Industrialization was killing the handloom industry so that 14,000 people were on poor relief in February 1842, and the further collapse of a local Trust meant that local funds were lost.

The Disruption brought the situation to a crisis, but there can be little doubt that it would not have lasted much longer. Already a Royal Commission into the Poor Law was collecting evidence throughout the country. Shortly after the Commission reported, the legal responsibility for providing poor relief was removed from the parish church, where it had lain since before the Reformation. Only its timing in 1845 was the direct effect of the Disruption.

So far as the churches themselves went, there were problems and issues needing immediate attention. There were about 400 empty pulpits to fill possibly slightly fewer, because some of the departed congregations were legally entitled to keep possession of the churches that they owned and in some cases had built. Congregations like the thirty-eight former Old Light Burgher congregations who had rejoined the establishment in 1839 promptly left again in 1843, taking their churches with them and were simply removed from the list.

This was not a new problem for the church: the post-Reformation church and the post-Revolution church both suffered from a severe lack of ministers, but in 1843, the solution was different. The revival of strength in the church had brought about a glut of men wanting to be ordained and so the gaps were made up relatively quickly. There is an argument for suggesting that some of the incoming ministers were not of the desired quality, that some had been looking for a charge for a long time for very good reasons, but the same arguments also held for the young Free Church.

The progress of the Free Church will be dealt with in Chapter 8, but how did the Disruption affect the Established Church? In areas like the Highlands, the membership left in huge numbers but the churches remained in the hands of the Established Church, paid for as a legal obligation on the heritors. They may have been largely empty, attended by the minister's family and occasionally the laird, but the Established Church remained the national church with a presence and a minister in every parish. To take one of the more extreme examples, the 1851 Census shows that on a particular Sunday there were over 36,000 attendances at a Free Church in the County of Ross & Cromarty, as against 3500 attendances at the Established Church. In those eight years since the disruption, the Free Church in the county had built or acquired forty churches to match the twenty-seven of the Established Church. Furthermore, within them the Free Churches could seat more than twice as many people.

But that was the Highlands; over the whole country the picture was different, as it still is today. Nationally, the equivalent number of attendances for the Free Church was about 490,000; 360,000 for the Established Church and for the United Presbyterians 300,000. Orkney & Shetland had the greatest number attending the UP Church with the Free Church the least attended of the three. These figures do not allow for people attending more than one service in a day. So, the figures cannot be taken to be accurate but only indicative.

There were social variations too. Because the Free Church had ministers to pay and churches to build, members were expected to give and to give sacrificially and substantially, just as they had been in the Secession tradition. So for many of the poorest, the Established Church (by the time referred to as the 'Auld Kirk') remained the obvious option, for there, they would not be expected to pay more than the contributions to the poor fund. At the other end of the scale, the landowners who were paying for the parish churches tended to attend them unless they were Episcopalians. That being so, it may well be that those whose livelihood depended on the landowning cases also remained in the establishment. So in the lowlands in particular, the group that the Established Church lost tended to be of the middle and lower middle classes. On the other hand, the new industrialists and manufacturers expected to manage their own religious life as much as they managed their secular lives and so were drawn to the Free or, especially, the UP churches.

The 1840s were dominated politically throughout Europe by revolution and thoughts of revolution, culminating in 1848, the year of revolutions. In Britain, the main movement in this trend was provided by the Chartists. The Chartist Churches will be considered in Chapter 9, but generally there is a good deal of evidence that the ministers of the Established Church were more sympathetic to the Chartist cause than were those of the Free Church. Most notable of these was Patrick Brewster of Paisley who was disciplined by the church for his political activities. In fact, Brewster was far more radical a Christian than the Free Church fathers were and saw them as more inclined to protect the economic *status quo* than to preach the Gospel to the people. He particularly disliked Thomas Chalmers on political grounds as Chalmers was adamant in holding up the social order of the day and attacked those who sought to change it.

It has to be said though that Brewster was a maverick and far from typical of the average Auld Kirk minister. Nonetheless, his remaining does show the width of opinion that still remained in those who stayed. There was still an evangelical party; there were still those fighting against Patronage; and there were still those arguing for the right of the Church to govern itself without interference from Parliament.

One thing that those remaining in the Establishment did not have was the marketing expertise that the Free Church was building up. Within a decade of the Disruption, its history was being written. Not unnaturally, these histories were as polarized in their views as the churches themselves. The early death of Chalmers gave the Free Church a head start in producing books which emphasized the role of the Free Church as God's chosen instrument in Scotland. The Free Church fully recognized the hunger for the printed word in mid-nineteenth century and tried to feed it. All sorts of magazines appeared both officially and unofficially. Local newspapers found themselves with local rivals if they backed the wrong ecclesiastical view. An event such as the Religious Census of 1851 brought distrust as to its bias and intentions, so on Census day, alternative censuses were organized by some newspapers to check the official figures. Incidentally, they did not show significant variations. The Free Church press busied itself too with a stream of biographies and autobiographies of those who had led the Disruption and with printing official accounts of its debates. This passion for biography and publishing did not extend to the Auld Kirk, giving the effect to anyone reading nineteenth-century material that the Free Church had a dominance which it did not have. The Free Church expected the Established Church to wither away and leave them as the new 'Free' national church: it did not happen. The Auld Kirk largely just got on with the job of providing a church nationally, whether or not the local people attended it. Crucially, the rump of evangelicals who had not left the church, the 'Middle Party' as they came to be known, the 'Forty Thieves' as the Free Church called them, came to prominence later and led a resurgence in the church which they stood by.

Meanwhile, beyond the turmoil in the national church, things were happening in the other churches too. Most of these will be dealt with in the chapters on the individual denominations, but the 1840s was the decade that the Mormons made their biggest impact on Scotland; the Episcopalians had their own disruption which led to several churches rejecting the local hierarchy and putting themselves under bishops in England; while the United Secession Church lost several ministers over what became known as the 'Atonement Controversy'. That group became the 'Evangelical Union' and formally broke with the United Secession just days before the Disruption but in 1847 the United Secession Church and the Relief Church united becoming the United Presbyterian Church. This time, unusually, the union did not spawn two further minority churches; those who did not join the UPs, as they quickly became known, either joined an existing denomination or became independent churches.

So the 1840s were a time of turmoil; denominations split and united, denominations arose and disappeared. It was a time of economic turmoil in Scotland as in the rest of Europe. It was a time of political upheaval in Scotland as in the rest of Europe. At the end of the decade, the potato famine brought in large numbers of largely indigent Irish but also accelerated the movement of people from the Highlands to the industrial lowlands. Both of these migrations changed the religious landscape of the country.

Amid all this, in England and Wales, the government had introduced compulsory civil registration of births, deaths and marriages in 1837; there was an impetus for Scotland to follow England's example but the first attempt at a Scottish Registration Bill failed to become law. Meanwhile, at the beginning of the next decade, Parliament introduced a religious element in the National Census for all of Britain.

Why civil registration was implemented only much later in Scotland is due, in no small part, to the religious situation. The arrangements to introduce civil registration assumed that in most cases, the new local registrar would be the session clerk of the local Established Church. The Free Church, and even more so the UP Church, complained bitterly at this favouring of one particular denomination. For many years, of course, the same session clerks would have had theoretical responsibility for recording such events as they were made aware of, but dissenters had the choice of having burials, baptisms, etc. recorded (at a cost), or not. The Civil Registration Act of 1854 finally made it compulsory.

Meanwhile, the Established Church was not happy about civil registration either. Their complaint was that the records which individual churches had kept with various degrees of care and competence were to become the property of the state. All registers had to be handed over; the older ones to Edinburgh and the more recent ones to local registrars. This was bad enough, but in many cases they were kept in the same volumes as other session records, whether at the other end of the book or mixed in. In the former case, the new arrangements required the books to be split and the appropriate bits sent to Edinburgh. In the latter case, Edinburgh asked for transcripts of the relevant material. This in itself created problems though as many churches felt their session minutes were too sensitive to be put in the hands of others. There were attempts to claim that the Act covered births, marriages and deaths, and therefore, records of baptisms, proclamations of banns and burials were not covered. Of course, these were the records that churches had and the government was adamant that those were required. It took many years for everything to be gathered in but gathered in it was. The resulting piles of records were often in such a condition as to make them unusable until they had been substantially repaired but that too happened in due course. With hindsight, it is clear that it was the compulsory ingathering that allowed the surviving records to be properly repaired, conserved and made available.

Perhaps just to be contrary or perhaps to make a point of claiming equality, some of the better organized dissenting churches offered their records too but the Act was clear in only asking for the Established Church records and the others were declined. This is why any search of the records accessed through the ScotlandsPeople website brings up 'Old Parish Registers' which exclude hundreds of churches throughout the nation.

An equivalent controversy had arisen around the Religious Census of 1851. The gathering of information was not like the questions about religious affiliation in the most recent censuses. In 1851, the questions were about churches: number of seats available, number of people attending in the morning, afternoon and evening (with no means of knowing how many individuals were counted more than once) (see Figure 2, Census 1851, see p 214). There was also a series of questions about church-sponsored schools. Needless to say, not everyone was happy. Coming just eight years after the Disruption, the Established Church saw it as a threat, as giving governmental credence to the Free Church's claims about overtaking it in influence. Meanwhile, the Free Kirk saw it as a threat because it expected the census to show that their belief that the Established Church would disappear without them was not true; they also expected the figures to be manipulated. The UPs just did not trust the figures on principle. Some in the smaller churches did not want to be bracketed, so they just described themselves as Christians; some had religious scruples about taking part in a census at all. In some places, rival censuses were held to check the 'official' figures; in Stirling, for example, the Free Church supporting newspaper *The Stirling Observer* held its own headcount on census Sunday. The Established Church in Stirling, as already noted, had lost all its ministers to the Free Church, so in 1851, all their ministers were relatively new and the Free Church resented those in their congregations who had not followed their ministers out. It comes as no great surprise then that the *Observer* accused those churches of massaging the figures by bringing in large numbers of soldiers from Stirling Castle and children from children's residential homes to show a greater strength.

Nationally, the result is very incomplete. Those collating the data noted how many churches failed to provide responses and in some cases tried to estimate the data. The data is still a tremendous source of information about the churches in mid-nineteenth-century Scotland, but like all data though, it needs to be treated with caution. What is clear though is that the idea that 'everybody went to church' in the nineteenth century was never true; at most probably one-third attended.

In 1801, Scottish Presbyterianism had one dominant national church and about five smaller Presbyterian denominations. There were two Episcopal church regimes, Scottish and English, and a growing Roman Catholic community. There were also a number of tiny churches either new or new to Scotland. Fifty years later, the picture was very different. The national church had split and three of the smaller churches had come together, so there were now three denominations sharing the allegiance of the vast majority of the inhabitants of the country. The Highlands were dominated by the Free Church, the south west remained with the Establishment while the UPs were strongest in Glasgow, Lanarkshire, Orkney and parts of the borders. Edinburgh was largely Free Church, but most of the countryside around it tended to remain with the Establishment (see Figures 7–10, United Presbyterian, Free and Established Churches in 1851 and the Majority Churches in each county in 1891, see pp 214–222).

In short Scotland, although still predominantly Presbyterian, did not have a single denomination which could speak for the country and all three were quick to disparage any claim that the other two might make to do so. The real bitterness lay between the Established and Free Churches, where any opportunity to display a holier-than-thou attitude was quickly attacked.

Gradually, however, Scotland settled into a state of acceptance of the situation and church life began to develop in the wake of the Disruption. One historian has described the development of the Victorian church on Scotland as a series of simultaneous revolutions, Biblical, Confessional, liturgical, social and life style. With hindsight, all of this was happening to the accompaniment of discussion of developments in science.

The Biblical revolution was a change in attitude to the Bible led largely, and to modern eyes surprisingly, by the theologians of the Free Church. Some of them were strongly influenced by trends in Germany as a result of studying there and the trend was to look at the Bible critically, almost treating it as evidence to be tested. Part of this was reconciling the Bible with the science of the day and part of it was fitting the Bible into what was known of the history of the period from other sources. In many ways this was not new but simply an extension of the enquiring mind of the Scottish Enlightenment. A Scottish Roman Catholic priest was removed because he had suggested earlier in the century the Creation story was not literally true, and eighteenth-century figures such as the judge James Burnett, Lord Monboddo, used his study of languages to argue for a much longer and more gradual development of the human race than is implied by the Creation story. To some extent, he can be credited with developing a theory of evolution and natural selection long before Darwin. It was also true that he was deeply religious and had no difficulty reconciling his scientific beliefs with his religious ones. Others, however, found that the easiest way to resist the challenge of these new approaches was to stress the idea that the Bible should not be examined critically at all.

The Biblical revolution led to several high profile cases in the Church Courts and perhaps it was those cases that gave publicity to the ideas rather than the original teaching. Foremost of these was the 'Robertson Smith Case'. William Robertson Smith had been a brilliant student in Edinburgh who was appointed to be Professor of Hebrew and Old Testament at the Free Church College in Aberdeen at the age of twenty-three. Deeply influenced by the work being carried out in Germany, he had been teaching his students for several years until his articles for the new edition of *Encyclopaedia Britannica* brought his ideas to a wider public. In particular, his article on *The Bible* in volume 3, published in 1875, treated it as a document to be examined critically, not merely accepted word for word. Opposition grew and a series of cases went through the church courts for several years. Robertson Smith's defence scraped through by the slimmest of margins and he was merely admonished and cautioned to be more careful. A further article in the *Encyclopaedia* reopened the whole affair and its publication gave the impression that Smith was contemptuous of the entire proceedings against him. This time, the case led to his deposition as Professor. Finally, in 1881, he moved to London and became joint editor of the *Encyclopaedia*, still regretting the loss of his opportunity to teach a new generation of students. Despite his condemnation by more conservative opponents, Robertson Smith was deeply committed to his faith and essentially orthodox in it.

Some historians have drawn a contrast between the opposition to Robertson Smith's approach to the Bible and all the major churches' quiet acceptance of Darwin's theories. Part of this may have been because ministers were expected to have a scientific education as part of their training for the ministry and therefore were open to ideas. Be that as it may, by the end of the century theories of evolution, though challenged and rejected in points of detail, were generally accepted as not being a challenge to faith itself. Of course, what is believed by professors is not necessarily believed by the man or woman in the street, or indeed in the pew. There were those who saw the idea of evolution as pernicious and damaging, but people like Henry Drummond, a professor at the Free Church College in Glasgow in the 1890s, were also teaching their ideas in series of lectures aimed at ordinary working people. Drummond was perhaps the most extreme promoter of evolutionary theories, although he disagreed with Darwin on many points, and he was attacked from a number of angles, theological and scientific. Nonetheless, in his time he brought a reassurance to many people that in an evolving world, God was still in charge of the process.

The Free Church dismissed Robertson Smith but never defined his 'heresies' and so a succession of scholars were able to build on his work despite opposition from a substantial part of the church and despite periodic trials. It may seem surprising to those who recognize the present Free Church as conservative to realize that in the late nineteenth century parts of it were at the leading edge of radical theological thought.

If traditional views of the Bible were being challenged, so too was the Presbyterian idea of a faith based on the *Westminster Confession* of 1647. This still remains as something that all Church of Scotland ministers and elders have to subscribe to. Nowadays, a conscience clause allows people to disagree with parts which are not central to their faith but some of the more conservative churches still hold on to it in its entirety. The early challenges to it tended to lead people out of the Presbyterian churches; John McLeod Campbell's condemnation and deposition from the ministry in 1831 for preaching that Christ had died for all, not just for the elect, was only the first. A decade later, James Morison left the United Secession Church over a similar issue, ending up as founder of the Evangelical Union; further cases were quietly dropped. A few years later it began to be realized, particularly in the UP Church, that the doctrine of 'the elect' was no longer very important; although it was never formally dropped, it ceased to be an issue. Part of the impetus for this came from mission workers who realized that they could not take the Gospel to Africa and India and tell people there that they should believe and follow the Bible but that their future salvation had nothing to do with their actions and that whether they went to heaven or hell was already decided. Heresy trials continued through the late nineteenth century but gradually took on less importance in the life of the church and still less in the lives of ordinary members.

A number of changes made the three mainstream Presbyterian churches quite different at the end of the nineteenth century from how they had been fifty years earlier. The openness to new thought about religion was at the heart of it, but there was little difficulty about accepting the scientific advances of the age and the science teaching which all Scottish ministers had as part of their training reflected that. The revivalism that came to Scotland from America in the 1870s also brought with it a view of conversion that put emphasis on the convert's decision and again went against traditional Calvinist views of conversion.

With all this happening, the *Westminster Confession of Faith* came under attack as being outdated and not reflecting the Churches' views, but it survived as the 'subordinate standard' of the churches' views, with the conscience clause introduced in all three major denominations.

At the same time as all these challenges were taking place in the realm of religious belief, others were affecting how the church worshipped.

Since the Reformation, the Presbyterian churches had sung only Psalms. These were not the Psalms of the Authorized Version left as prose and chanted as in Episcopalian practice but adaptations written for singing which rhymed and scanned so that they could be sung to a range of tunes. From there being a 'proper' tune for each of the 150 Psalms in 1564, the number of tunes in use dwindled to twelve during the seventeenth century. Other songs were written and used for private worship, but in church the Psalms were sung exclusively. Meanwhile in England, Methodism in particular was encouraging a much greater range of both hymns and tunes.

Gradually, this changed in Scotland too; the Glasites published their own hymnbook in 1749; the first Baptist chapel in Scotland had its own hymnbook in 1750; the Episcopal Church of Scotland produced a hymnbook in 1781 and the same year saw the Church of Scotland take their first step by authorizing a book of 'Paraphrases of parts of Scripture' which were written in a form for singing and included five hymns. The Relief Church was the first to bring out its own collection of hymns and other churches joined in too. The Church of Scotland brought out its first hymnbook in 1862; the UP Church and the Free Church followed. A short while later, controversy about the use of musical instruments to accompany worship followed. Episcopalians had no scruples about using them, but for Presbyterians, the use of an organ to accompany public worship was tantamount to sacrilege. Again the Relief Church came to the fore with one of their Edinburgh churches voting to install one in 1829. A broadside preserved in the National Library of Scotland called 'Organic Affections or an Account of a meeting held in the Relief Church St., James Place' satirizes the arguments for and against the installation of an organ, with one speaker attacking the idea on the grounds that 'He held that the organ was shadowed forth by the beast with the seven heads and ten horns in the Revelations.' Much of this broadside was really concerned with poking fun at the Relief Church because the people in positions of authority were tradesmen and includes the question: 'Is it not absurd for such illiterate and vulgar speaking men to be rulers of a church?' On the other side of the country though, a Glasgow minister entered the argument, writing An Apology for the Organ as an Assistance of Congregational Psalmody in 1829.

Since part of the argument against the organ was that there was no warrant in the Bible for using such things, another minister published a satire in which he claimed to show there was no warrant in the Bible for using spectacles to aid reading in church and therefore they too should be banned. A salient argument indeed. In the Church of Scotland, the first organ to be successfully installed crept in behind a curtain in Greyfriars Church in Edinburgh in 1863. Even the choir did not know of its impending use until its sound burst forth at an evening service.

The argument went on for several decades but the visit of the evangelist Dwight Moody and the evangelical singer Ira Sankey in the 1870s made the harmonium or 'American Organ' familiar in a religious context, and soon many churches had first a harmonium and later a full pipe organ installed.

Other practices also changed: printed service books appeared, baptismal fonts replaced the bowls by the pulpit and church services gradually slipped into a form that they largely retained until the 1980s.

That said, some of the smaller and more conservative Presbyterian churches retained the ban on singing anything other than unaccompanied psalms and do so to this day. The part of the Free Church which stayed outside the Union of 1900 voted to cease using their hymnbook shortly after the Union and a hundred years later, its decision to permit hymns and musical instruments caused some members to leave.

Underlying all these changes though was a much bigger one: the growth of choice in what church to attend or indeed not to attend at all meant that faith was seen as more personal and less a matter of the automatic glue that held a society together. In the past, if the church had held society together, it had done so by reinforcing the social and political *status quo* and not by challenging the existing order except where it impinged on the churches' interests. Even social reformers such as Thomas Chalmers operated on the assumption that they had to defend the existing order by preaching submission to superiors, suitable gratitude for charity and patient endurance in this world. The well-off on the other hand were guided to act in the best interests of all the people. As the well-known hymn put it:

> The rich man in his castle,
> The poor man at his gate,
> God made them high and lowly,
> And ordered their estate.

Despite the adulation for Chalmers in some quarters, his lack of support for the Reform Bill of 1832 led to his windows being broken by the Edinburgh mob. His religious faith led to missions to the poor and not to a church among the poor and for the poor.

This was a point of view shared by all the major churches; even the very occasional political radicalism of some of the eighteenth-century Seceders had disappeared. The Seceders' support for the parliamentary reforms of 1832 was based on their belief that it would strengthen the existing social order by giving them their place in it. Although it is clear that the Highland communities' rejection of the Auld Kirk at the Disruption was a rejection of the church's close ties to landed interests, there is little evidence to suggest that their new Free Church ministers were politically involved on their behalf; they simply did not see it as their role. The Free Church's support in the famine which struck the Highlands in the late 1840s was purely meant as a short term relief under exceptional circumstances and not aimed at trying to find a long term cure.

There is an argument for saying that in the middle of the nineteenth century, the major churches in Scotland had lost their way. Their energies were being spent on heresy hunts; squabbles over doctrines which barely mattered to the man in the pew and mattered not at all to the man not in the pew; disagreements about worship or church union and generally on topics which distracted from the recognition that the churches' influence was sliding downwards and that swathes of the population were largely unchurched.

Finally, it began to be noticed. One preacher referred to the attitudes of mind that led to this drift; the hostility of some types of socialism, infidelity, the stolid indifference of practical agnosticism and the hopelessness of the poor. Finally and gradually, the churches began trying to understand the point of view of those that they were failing to reach. This recognition brought tremendous efforts to reach the industrial poor and all the churches had their own campaigns. Other mission bodies also started to do the same, sometimes more effectively, and the process brought both rivalry as missions competed for the same souls and cooperation as missions recognized that to be effective they had to work together.

Environmental and social conditions then came to be seen as an appropriate area for the churches to campaign about, although not by all churches, even now. There was still a reluctance for the main churches to become involved in the politics of labour relations but by the beginning of the twentieth century, even that was changing and major reports to both the United Free Church in 1911 and the Church of Scotland in 1918 spelled out that the churches' spiritual teaching could only be honest and effective if the churches were in the vanguard pressing for social reform and a good environment for the people they were trying to reach.

By the last twenty years of the century, however, the church as a whole had lost its overall responsibility for poor relief (in 1845) and for education (in 1872) and some realized that it was being marginalized and had lost a huge part of the influence it had had a hundred years previously. Many regretted the loss of influence on the young caused by placing the control of parish schools under political control. Some realized that it was a problem of the churches' own making; one anonymous pamphleteer of 1874 asked the question

Are the churches in Scotland mere conservative institutions existing for themselves and for the salvation of individual souls, or do they exist for the salvation of society and for the sweetening and sanctifying of all relations; between man and man as well as between man and God?

Some foresaw in the dwindling of the churches' influence the potential for a proletarian revolution.

Finally, the churches as a whole began to take notice; in an 1888 report to the Church of Scotland came the hard-hitting statement

[the Church] has to reach that it has more to do for these so-called 'lapsed masses' than to assault them with armies of district visitors and to shower upon them tracts and good advices, while we are leaving them to swelter in dens and under conditions where Christian life is difficult if not impossible to realise.

Meanwhile, some of the Free Church ministers in Edinburgh began to realize that it was much harder to be a Christian in slum conditions. One of them,

William Mackenzie of North Leith Free Church, became involved in a scheme to build 'improved dwellings for artisans', building sixty-two houses in all but providing a model for other schemes in Edinburgh. Others ministers became involved in improving standards of lodging houses and in providing green spaces for recreation and drying clothes. In rural areas, they were campaigning against the feeing fairs which led to many agricultural workers having to move position and home every six months.

This changed view also took as its basis a new interpretation of the Bible and saw within it how often care and justice for the poor are a feature of Biblical teaching in both Old and New Testaments.

Amid all this change, one Act of Parliament was passed which might have changed the course of nineteenth century Scottish history had it just happened thirty years sooner. Patronage, that practice which caused the first major Secession in 1734, which caused the foundation of the Relief Church in 1761, which was the prime cause of the Disruption in 1843, that great bugbear of the history of Scottish Presbyterianism, Patronage was abolished finally and irrevocably in 1874.

In fact, the Established Church had gradually been moving away from being subject to Patronage. There were many churches where the congregations had the same right to call their own choice of minister as the Free Church and there were many churches where the choice was nominally under the control of a patron but where the patron had effectively handed over the decision to the congregation. There were few disputed presentations after the Disruption, perhaps because in almost every parish there was an alternative church to attend. Nonetheless, in the 1860s, the Established Church started to agitate for the repeal of the Patronage Acts. This was not necessarily to be seen as an attempt to work towards a healing of the Disruption but as an act that was good in itself, although there were some in the Church of Scotland who saw the current divisions as damaging to Christianity as a whole. By the end of the decade, the Church was petitioning Parliament for the end of Patronage in return for financial compensation and substituting for it the election of ministers by heritors, elders and male communicants. The Bill finally passed in 1874.

To modern eyes, it might seem that the removal of this huge bone of contention would have brought the churches which had seceded as a result of it back together. But this did not happen for a long time. The hurts on both sides, the pamphlet wars, the newspaper campaigns and the sheer dislike of each other between the Established Church and the Free Church made any union impossible while any of the protagonists from 1843 were still alive and active. Meanwhile, union between the Established Church and the United Presbyterians was equally impossible while the Established Church was seen to retain its role as 'established by law' because the UPs were by this time firmly against the idea of any church having strong ties to the state and the government.

However, there was some movement. The Free Church and the UPs, together with the much smaller Reformed Presbyterian Church started to explore a three-fold Union. It did not happen then, although the Free Church and the greater part of the RP Church did unite in 1876, but the scene was set for much better relations among the churches; for the recognition of each other's ministers; and for a good deal of local cooperation both in Scotland and in their respective missions.

Among the signs of change in the churches as a whole, there were changes in entrenched attitudes and there was a growth in organizations attached to churches.

Perhaps the clearest sign of the former was in the growing awareness of the festival of Christmas. The Reformed Church had a rigid rejection of all pre-Reformation festivals, Christmas included. The church used to refer to it as 'yule' and thought of it as pagan or papist or both. By the late nineteenth century, following on its growing popularity in England, it began to make inroads in Scotland. Institutions, orphanages, asylums, and the like regularly began to have Christmas treats. The Episcopal and Roman Catholic churches began advertising Christmas services and then gradually some Edinburgh Presbyterian churches started having concerts of Christmas music, such as a performance of Handel's 'Messiah' on Christmas Day (if not a Sunday). Finally, the unthinkable happened and a Christmas Day service was held. Country areas took longer to change and it was a very slow process, but even country churches were being decorated for Christmas by the early years of the twentieth century.

The growth of church-based organizations was also a feature of the later nineteenth century. The Temperance ones have already been mentioned, but bodies like the Women's Guild were founded and they channelled a large area of previously underutilized potential into the churches as well as into their social programmes, giving women their own voice and providing a major source of strength for the churches in general at a time when women were still debarred from the courts and hierarchies of the major churches.

Sunday Schools had long been a feature of churches both as a means of Christian education and of general education for those unable to access other education, but the late nineteenth century also brought the advent of the Boys' Brigade which was aimed at attracting boys to an organization that acted as an agent of Mission, of discipline and of social improvement. With its military framework, it echoed the Salvation Army but also tapped the enthusiasm for home military service which was prevalent at the time. Soon there were few areas of the country that did not have their BB battalions drilling boys from the age of six upwards, and service in the BB began to be seen as a desirable attribute by employers appointing young workers.

By the end of the nineteenth century, the churches as a whole had changed substantially from the days of the century before and were facing up to the challenges of an age which was radically different from all those which had gone before. With the start of the twentieth century, they were going to have to face problems of a new and ever more challenging nature.

8

The Disruption Tradition

This chapter discusses the denominations which arose out of the Disruption of 1843: the Free Church, the United Free (UF) Church and the Free Presbyterian Church. The first and the last of these have both split in the last twenty-five years. The Free Church split into 'Free Church' and 'Free Church (Continuing)' while the Free Presbyterians split into 'Free Presbyterian Church' and 'Associated Presbyterian Churches'. Both these schisms fall beyond the scope of this book.

The Free Church of Scotland

With the formal act of signing the Deed of Demission on 24 May 1843, the Free Church of Scotland came into existence. It had no official name, it had about one-third of the ministers of the pre-Disruption church, it had some thousands of elders, it had an unknown but small number of church buildings, it had some money, but it had big plans to be the new national Church of Scotland. These plans included a strategy that involved mirroring as far as possible the establishment of the Established Church. There was to be a church in every parish and, since the church had responsibility for education throughout the land, a school in every parish. The intention was clearly stated: the Free Church was to take the place of the new National Church when the old one withered away as they expected it must. It was to be a new National Church unrestricted by the rights of heritors and patrons and by the interference of an unsympathetic Parliament. Given the initial numbers and the local enthusiasm in many areas, in those first few months it must have seemed a real possibility.

There was a list of priorities both in decision-making and action. The ministers who left the General Assembly and walked down to the Tanfield Hall in May 1843 remained in Edinburgh for a few days to settle some of the immediate issues regarding their new church as a whole, but they had to go back home to very uncertain futures. Most of them had congregations to go back to, there were few ministers who were not followed by substantial numbers of their parishioners, but they had to leave their manses and find new accommodation; they had to find somewhere to use as a church and they had to adapt to life on a much smaller and less certain income.

However, despite the pressures on them to find somewhere to live and somewhere to preach, most of the ministers did find time for one action that must have surprised many at the time; they had their photographs taken. The day after the historic walk-out, an advertisement appeared in *The Witness* for an engraving of the historic event to be produced 'in two or three years' by the artist David Octavius Hill. His method of producing this was to invite all those who were present at the great event, and indeed many who only wished they had been present, to attend him in his garden studio where they were photographed by the new 'calotype' process. Many of the photographs were taken in these first few days, but the process of gathering them all carried on for about three years. The painting itself, a gigantic multiple portrait of hundreds of men at the signing of the 'Deed of Demission' with a small number of women watching, was not unveiled until 1866 with the published copies following shortly after. By the time it actually appeared other painters had used photography as the basis of paintings, notably William Powell Frith, but at the time of conception it was a revolutionary idea.

The question of church buildings gave huge problems; a few buildings came with their congregations. Chapels of ease which had been built with locally raised funds and former Old Light Burgher churches which had come back into the establishment in 1839 belonged to the congregations so they were a start. The former were usefully in areas of expanding population. The latter were more randomly placed and it may have been that the ambience of them was not felt welcoming by who had not come from the Secession tradition. Certainly even in a village the size of Doune, where the minister remained in the Parish Church the people who left it formed their own Free Church and ignored the existing former Old Light Burgher Church which had also joined the Free Church. The two congregations did not unite until many years later (see Figure 9, see p 221).

In some places sites for new Free Churches were not a problem. Because the Disruption was planned and orchestrated, some plans for alternative accommodation were already well in hand. In Tain in Easter Ross virtually the whole congregation followed their minister out. Prior to that, by April 1843, £500 had already been raised to build a temporary wooden church on the links for the minister to preach during the summer while the new church was being built. Tain's premises did not pose a problem because the Burgh council was also in favour of the Disruption and paraded in all their finery to the new church when it opened in June 1843. The permanent church was opened a mere four months later on 17 October 1843.

Many communities pooled resources to provide wood and quickly built temporary structures; more temporary still were the tents. One enterprising tent-manufacturer from London had spotted the opportunity for sales even as the first Assembly was meeting and brought north a supply, but even at a local level the minister of Blairgowrie returned home from the Disruption Assembly to find that a tent was already in place. His new church was able to seat 1000 people under recycled sailcloth provided by a Dundee ship-owner and stitched together. It was seen as providential that the first few weeks after the Disruption were marked by good weather. Some land-owners were perfectly happy to sell or even give land. In some areas, particularly in towns and cities, the landowners were themselves joining the Free Church. These can generally be identified where the Free Church was put up directly across the road from its rival, just to rub home the point. In more rural areas negotiations were protracted and it was many years before every parish had its own church building.

The minister stayed put in Portree on Skye and the half of his congregation that left his church had to make new arrangements using an old schoolhouse which was later extended. The local laird refused land for a replacement for many years. Nor was a minister immediately forthcoming; the minister of the neighbouring church at Snizort looked after the parish for six years, forming its new Kirk Session and preaching there on Sunday evenings after looking after his own flock in the morning.

In the meantime, other congregations worshipped in barns, in the fields or in public halls. They used anywhere that would accommodate the numbers who attended. Perhaps the most imaginative solution was a ship specially built to act as a floating church in Loch Sunart in the north-west of Scotland. Finally, though permanent churches were built for Free Kirk congregations throughout the land. Most initially conformed to a very austere economical design and were built equally economically because a depression in the building industry had made both labour and materials cheap.

One early series of decisions involved stipends; money had been gathered in expectation of the schism over the previous few years and this became the Sustention Fund, to be used to lay down the new stipends for the ministers who came out as well as for those they hoped to recruit. Most, possibly all, ministers, though, suffered a severe cut to their income by leaving the Establishment. By 1891, nearly fifty years later, the average Established Church minister was receiving £289 in stipend per year against £243 for a minister in the Free Church and £247 in the UP Church.

At the level of the new presbyteries and synods, these courts also had to decide how these ministers might be best used. Ministerial support for the

Disruption had geographical variation; strong support in the Synods of Ross, Caithness and Sutherland contrasted with the heartlands of the Covenanters in the southwest which showed little enthusiasm, probably because they already had an alternative in the Reformed Presbyterian Church. Towns were more enthusiastic for the cause than the countryside; Stirling for example had had four Church of Scotland ministers who all joined the Free Church. One had been a minister in the Old Light Burgher Church which had reunited with the Establishment in 1839 and promptly joined the Disruption in 1843. The decision was early taken that Stirling's Free Kirk congregations only needed two ministers. Despite the fact that ex-Secession church was the property of the congregation, their minister was one of the two declared to be transportable and he ended up rather unwillingly in Huntly. The other one was called to the new Free Church in Doune, some eight miles away. After his death, the local headmaster summed up the latter in these words, '*he was a terrible father, and in his covenanting Calvinistic rigidity, a perfectly awful man'*. What an epitaph! Perhaps his congregation in Stirling was glad to foist him off on Doune. Similarly, in Aberdeen, all fifteen ministers left the establishment and six congregations simply ceased to exist. With those fifteen also went the most active elders and members, leaving as the remnants of their congregations the poorest members of society.

Readjustment using those who were available was only possible in a handful of cases though, it could not disguise that the new denomination had only about 40 per cent of the ministers it needed to settle a minister in every parish. The denomination which the 40 per cent had left had a similar problem for the Established Church had several hundred vacant pulpits and an even greater number of congregations which had suffered severe splits. The Census of 1841 had identified about 2950 ministers, clergy and divinity students in Scotland of all denominations; ten years later that figure was about 3800. Much of that increase must have been due to the duplication of ministers in so many communities. Fortunately for both churches the religious turmoil of the previous ten years had encouraged many to seek to enter the ministry and there were many qualified, at least on paper, to take up the challenge. It has been said, however, that the standard of new ministers ordained in the aftermath of the Disruption was lower than it had been and that men were accepted for the ministry who might not have found a church in previous generations; certainly some in the Free Church made those charges against the new ministers who replaced them in their previous churches. The Free Churches' own figures show that after a sharp rise in the numbers of their ministers in the first ten years of the new denomination it took about twenty years for full coverage of Scotland to be achieved, with numbers steadily rising to a plateau by about 1880.

To cope with this, facilities for education for the ministry had to be organized quickly. New colleges were set up in three of the four university cities of Scotland, Christ's College in Aberdeen, New College in Edinburgh and Trinity College in Glasgow. These were all incorporated back into the universities they came out of after the Union of 1929 and form the current Church of Scotland's presence within them, although only Edinburgh's buildings are still in use.

Not only ministers suffered financial loss if they joined the Free Church; parish schoolmasters were appointed by their local kirk sessions and had to be members of the Established Church. Large numbers of schoolmasters therefore had to give up their schools and sometimes homes when they joined the new denomination. At the very least, the Free Church wanted to provide a means of support for those who had sacrificed their careers; some thought that was enough, that there was not money to support a national education system such as the Established Church did. A brief battle was fought in the Free Church, but by the Assembly of 1844 it had received promises of £50,000 to establish 500 schools. Unfortunately promises did not always develop into real money, and the cost of training new teachers also took much of the available funding. Ironically the problem was resolved by the government deciding that the grants it gave to Church of Scotland schools should also be available to schools run by other denominations. Accepting the money did raise qualms among some of the brethren who wanted their church to have no links with the government, but pragmatism won through at the cost of creating a split between the two parties. By 1851, though, the Free Church ran more schools than the Established Church, no mean achievement in eight years.

At congregational level, changes were necessary too: the concept of elders survived and they were crucial to the continued existence of the new congregations, but the congregations were responsible for far more than they ever had before. They had churches and manses to fund and maintain, they had ministers and schoolmasters to support financially and they had foreign and home missions to support as well. Much of this was new to them, for they had been the responsibility the heritors in the Established Church.

As a result, a new layer of church court was introduced, the 'Deacons' Court' took responsibility for some of the temporal matters just as the Managers had for the earlier Seceding churches. It all meant that a bigger proportion of the congregation, or at least of the male part of the congregation, had to have a greater commitment to maintaining the church as a whole.

Not surprisingly, much the Free Church's energy in the 1840s was spent simply in surviving, in continuing to raise money for their future survival. The whole church was made aware of the financial implications of the Disruption both for the ministers and schoolmasters who lost homes and livelihoods and for the ordinary member or adherent who had to give sacrificially at a level far higher than they had been accustomed to giving under the old heritor-funded regime.

Despite this, when the potato famine hit Scotland, it was the Free Church which responded most resolutely. The famine hit Scotland in 1846, a year later than in Ireland; in many areas, particularly in the islands, the whole crop was destroyed. Even more critically this was in areas where potatoes formed anything from half to 88 per cent of the diet of the people. Starvation was a very real possibility. Adding to the complications the government had taken over responsibility for Poor Law in the previous year. The Church of Scotland's response was at best half-hearted. It called for a national day of fasting and recommended individual congregations to contribute special collections. The Free Church, with such a strong following in the worst affected areas worked far better and by February 1847 had raised £15,000. They were also able to call into service a boat to take people on fact-finding visits to see where the need was greatest and made the decision to concentrate the aid on the poorest classes in society. Aid was also distributed on the basis of need without any consideration of the church allegiance. In early 1847 the decision was taken that the various agencies involved should combine their efforts. It is interesting to note that the combined committee included the current Moderators of the Church of Scotland, the Free Church, the Relief Church, a Roman Catholic bishop, not to mention the provosts of all the major cities and various senior law officers, possibly the first time that the Protestant churches had had formal links with the Roman Catholic Church in Scotland. This body continued the relief along the lines set up by the Free Church, including the strict principle that relief had to be worked for. The number of 'Destitution Roads' created in the process bears witness to the extent of the relief.

The Free Church's response to the Famine cemented the highlanders' general adherence to it. It may also have smoothed relations with the landowners who were also involved.

One major difference between the Established Church and the Free Church was in its use of the printed word. The Free Church was far superior as a propaganda machine. For one thing, the debates at the General Assembly were carefully revised and published, in contrast to the Established Church which only published its Acts and Reports, not the debates. The struggles and privations of the Free Church ministers were, right from the start, to be written up and published to drive home the need for financial support for the denomination and also to make it seem the heir of the Covenanters. Newspapers and magazines were firmly entrenched on one side or the other and some were specifically founded to put the Free Church point of view. Minister after Free Kirk minister was commemorated by a biography, while almost none of the Auld Kirk was so honoured. Thomas Chalmers, who had died in 1847, was seen as the great hero and martyr of the cause. There is a mass of history of the time, but all of it was written from a partisan point of view and in the war of words the Free Church always held the upper hand. The greatest exponent of this war of words was Hugh Miller, a stonemason from Cromarty who became editor of *The Witness*, a journal published by the evangelical party in the church in expectation of the coming Disruption and afterwards funded by the Free Church. Miller was an accomplished amateur geologist and his writing on that perhaps eased the way for the Free Church to have a relaxed view of scientific advances of the day even if many of his conclusions now seem entirely wrong. In *The Witness*, he also wrote tellingly of the events in his church; estimates vary as to how much of the witness he physically wrote but it was an immense amount. *The Witness* ran to 56,000 words each issue and for much of the time appeared twice a week with the help of a minute staff. Its circulation and hence its influence was immense in Scotland. Tragically Miller ended his own life, probably as a result of the pain brought on by physical illness and overwork. There is no evidence for the statement that occasionally appears that he was traumatized by the conflict between his faith and his knowledge of science.

As well as a propaganda campaign of words, the churches also indulged in a propaganda war of statistics. This was one of the reasons that the 1851 religious census was so contentious, but throughout the nineteenth century church statistics appeared in print more and more. Many of these were gathered together in a book called *The Churches and the Churchless in Scotland; Facts and Figures* compiled by Robert Howie and published in 1893. The statistics he gathered give information down to parish level and including such other non-Presbyterian denominations as made information available. From this can be seen the levels of congregational giving and hence the degree of financial commitment expected of the various churches; it is a valuable resource for information about local churches, but it is partisan and the figures and conclusions need to be treated with caution.

If the Free Church had won the war of words, it fairly quickly became clear that its early belief that it would replace the Established Church was not going to be fulfilled and it had to adjust to being simply one of three major branches of Presbyterianism that dominated Scottish church life throughout the century.

One fairly early action was to try to consolidate Presbyterian dissent. Most of the Old Light Burghers had already joined them via four years in the Established Church; a slightly lower proportion of the Old Light Anti-burghers, by this stage called the 'Synod of United Original Seceders', joined the Free Church in 1852. Even before the Disruption they were providing support to the evangelical party in the Church of Scotland and sent a delegation of deputies to the first Free Church General Assembly in 1843. These deputies addressed the Assembly at some considerable length and were cordially answered at similar length. The Free Church reciprocated by attending the Seceders' next Synod meeting and negotiations for union were soon under way hindered only by the fact that the Seceders looked on the Free Church as somewhat lukewarm in their view of the Covenants. This problem in fact led to a Disruption among the Seceders and thirteen of their thirty-six ministers declined to join the Free Church, remaining as a separate denomination until the tiny remnant was absorbed into the re-united Church of Scotland in 1955.

However if the smallest churches were being drawn to union with the Free Church, united in their opposition to Patronage, the bigger ones were not, for the United Secession Church and the Relief Church had meanwhile united as the United Presbyterian Church (UPs) and were pursuing voluntarism. This was completely against what the Free Church and Established Church stood for. This is largely dealt with in the chapter on the Secession Churches, but it posed a major stumbling block for any negotiations with the Free Church. The idea that, effectively, what church you went to was your own business and the state had no place in governing, funding or preferring any one denomination over another was already well entrenched in the United Secession Church before the Disruption and was a major reason that the evangelical party in the Church of Scotland wanted to form their own national church rather than joining the existing alternative one. When it became evident that the Free Church was not going to take over as the national church moves began to unite the Free Church with the UP Church and with a section of the Reformed Presbyterians. The negotiations between the Free Church and the UPs foundered. It was one of the rare occasions where the majority in the UP Church, which was in favour of union, recognized the deep antipathy of the minority to the idea and decided that the unity of the existing denomination was more important than their dream of future wider unity. In 1876, though, most of the Reformed Presbyterians joined the Free Church keeping their identity as a separate presbytery of the Church for some time.

Coincidentally, or perhaps not, this union came just two years after the original trigger of the Disruption ceased to have relevance, for Patronage was abolished, and this time it was final. No longer did anyone other than the members of congregations themselves have any right to choose a parish minister. Certainly, the underlying causes had not changed in the sense that it was still Parliament that claimed the right to decide the policy, so the Free Church still felt entitled to maintain its distance. A handful of congregations did rejoin the Church of Scotland as a result, but only a handful. Gradually though, the Voluntary principle began to gain in its attraction and there was a feeling abroad that union between the Free Church and the United Presbyterian was inevitable but not to be rushed.

Amid all this concern for union or not, theology had not been forgotten; and the Free Church was in the fore of the debate over the age and historicity of the Bible. The controversy over Professor Robertson Smith and others who followed his lead was widely reported and followed avidly in the Press. Perhaps its biggest effect was to highlight the difference between the Highland Free Church and the lowland Free Church. In the Highlands and Islands, the Free Church was the church of the people. In some areas, the poorest part of society had almost total loyalty to it, although there were exceptions. In the lowlands, particularly in the cities, the Free Church had a much wider economic basis; wealthy businessmen were likely to be supporters, while the poorest members of society were likely to remain in the Auld Kirk if they had any church connection at all.

Meanwhile a resurgent Church of Scotland began to reassert its position as the national church with historically based social responsibilities that the other denominations did not possess. It even tried to reclaim the Free Church hero Thomas Chalmers as a model of Christian social idealism and recognized the idealism and sincerity of the original Free Church supporters. This let it attack the 'new' policies of the Free Church which were taking it away from the historic basis of the Disruption as an alternative untrammelled national church and into the ideas of voluntarism and disestablishment that sought to break down completely any links between church and nation. The main charge was that the leadership of the Free Church was out of touch with the membership. This had been the main sticking point in the abortive attempt at union with the UPs in the 1870s, but the Free Church was seen as moving closer to the UP position and accepting that churches should not be part of the national establishment. Meanwhile in parliamentary politics, the whole concept of disestablishing the Church of Scotland was looking increasingly possible and was widely supported by those who had the ear of the Free Church Assembly. Gladstone's defeat in the election of 1895 however removed the disestablishment question from parliamentary politics.

1893 saw the fiftieth anniversary of the Disruption; the Free Church celebrated, yet it was severely divided. A large part of it now saw a union with the UP Church as essential, but to unite with it, the Free Church had to recognize that it had changed its views over the previous half-century. The first attempt to prepare, the passing of the 'Declaratory Acts' led to the secession of those who became Free Presbyterians. They could not accept these acts which a majority of the church voted through. That particular rift was so serious that when the Union of the Free Church with the United Presbyterians did go through in 1900, the Free Church minority who could not accept that union were still shunned by those had who left to form the Free Presbyterian Church seven years previously; a rift which persists to this day.

United Free Church: 1900–1929

The UF Church came into existence in 1900 as a result of the union of the United Presbyterian Church with the majority of Free Church. As such, it represented a very large proportion of the church-goers of early twentieth-century Scotland. Its early years were dominated by the controversy as to the whether they or those who had remained as the Free Church (Continuing) had the right to the property of the pre-1900 Free Church, but aside from that the new denomination had an energy gained from uniting two of the three biggest denominations in the country. Right from the beginning they had an eye towards future union with the Church of Scotland. At a local level cooperation was well established. The problems lay at national level and were in some ways the same as had led to the loss of the continuing Free Church, the concept of an 'Established Church'. One thing that the old UP Church had taken into the union was the idea that no church had any civil rights greater than another, that no church should be specifically favoured by the state, that no one church should accept money from the state while as a corollary and that no church should accept direction or control from the state.

The Church of Scotland had moved some way to fulfilling the voluntarists' conditions. The big problem, Patronage, had disappeared in law in 1874 having disappeared largely in practice some years previously. National education had gone from being the responsibility of the church in the same decade and poor law, thirty-nine years before that. So what was left? What was left was the responsibility of the heritors to pay stipends and to repair churches. The UF Church would not re-join the Church of Scotland until its members paid their own way, but even from their very first General Assembly in 1900, members were speaking of the possibility of the UF Church being part of a wider union that would re-unite Presbyterianism nationally, apart from all the surviving splinter groups which had resisted previous reunions, Free, Free Presbyterian, Original Secession and Reformed Presbyterian.

Leaving aside this crucial stumbling block, there was really very little difference in beliefs or practice between these two denominations. Each accommodated a range of theology from the conservative to the liberal, with the UF Church slightly more to the latter tendency, and with the UF Church also formally embracing a more relaxed attitude to the *Westminster Confession*. Each had policies for attacking unemployment, poverty, alcoholism and other social evils. In both churches there were real efforts to bridge the divide that had grown up between the Labour Movement and the churches despite the significant Christian origins of the Independent Labour Party. There were of course many in the churches who were far from convinced that this was the right course to follow. In its attitudes to some of the contemporary challenges to faith, the UF Church was more open-minded and began to realize that non-Christian faiths had much to teach the Christian churches too.

Preliminary work was taking place towards a potential union by 1911, but it was put on hold by the Great War. At the same time, working together became much more the norm and the two denominations broke down many of the barriers between themselves at a personal level. At an institutional level, towards the end of the war the two churches began working together on a scheme for social reconstruction, supporting the coalition government of the day in its plans. The vision was for a land where those who had borne the burden of war could find their reward in a 'worthier social environment'. As well as healing these social divisions, the church leaders saw that the divisions in the churches were as damaging and so in the final months of the war, the two churches again began formal talks to unite the two churches with the ideal of 'of a united National Church leading a covenanted Christian commonwealth in pursuit of social justice and harmony'.

To prepare for this, various steps had to be taken. Some of the issues perhaps seem pretty trivial nowadays such as how appropriate it is in the united Church for the monarch to appoint a 'Lord High Commissioner' to attend the General Assembly as observer. There were other issues that were much more important. Perhaps the most crucial of these were questions about the right of Parliament to make laws about the Church and the financial arrangements that the Church of Scotland operated under. Once these were sorted out, however, there was still a proportion of the UF Church which did not want to be part of a national Church of Scotland.

Finally, the changes that the UF Church wanted in the Church of Scotland were made; the teinds that heritors paid to support ministers' stipends and repair churches were converted to a single cash balance; a 'Declaratory Act' clearly stated the limits of state authority over the Church and when passed through Parliament, clearly showed the Church's autonomy. When these were passed through Parliament, the way was clear for a reunion although about 100 ministers out of over 1000 remained out of the union with a rather larger number of congregations.

This group who resisted the union were laid by the Rev. James Barr. As a UF minister, he was allowed to stand for Parliament; an action that was forbidden to the ministers of the Church of Scotland. His entry into Parliament as a Labour MP for Motherwell did lead some of the Church of Scotland to think that he had an unfair advantage in speaking on the church affairs that were going through the Parliament.

This time however, the churches had learned from the legal problems arising from previous unions and the process was completed without recourse to the courts. In return for an agreement that taking cases to court was not an option, arrangements were made to recognize the strength of votes in congregations and allocate resources fairly. Even the dispersal of records was allowed for. Existing records for United Free Congregations and Presbyteries were allocated to the Church of Scotland or the UF Church according to the proportion of the congregation or presbytery adhering to the Union or opting for the UF Church (Continuing). The minority staying separate were allowed to keep the name 'United Free Church of Scotland', but for the first five years they agreed to be known as 'United Free Church of Scotland (Continuing)' before reverting back to the old name. A proportion of the assets of the old UF Church was allocated to those going their own way; it has to be said that this was not overgenerous. In cases where congregations were split, it was found that the wording of title deeds of individual churches from years before tended to favour remaining in the union over seceding.

After the union, the strength of the UF Church (Continuing) stood at about 14,000. Four years later, it stood at 20,000 and new churches had been built or bought for the new congregations throughout lowland Scotland, mainly for congregations made up of a grouping of minorities from several churches in a locality. It was and is a largely lowland church, those highland Free Churches which had gone into the UF Church in 1900 mostly rejoined the national church rather than joining the continuing UF Church. They were perhaps always less convinced by the anti-establishment arguments than the lowland churches of the UP tradition.

The UF Church as it continued through the 1930s remained evangelistic, with a strong interest in social questions; it also moved forward in other ways; recognizing that the strength of any church lay in tapping into the gifts of every member, it was the first Presbyterian denomination in Britain to ordain women as elders and as ministers equal in every way to men. This had been part of the agenda of the UF Church before the union of 1929 and indeed women had been eligible to become deacons in 1918 but a decision was deferred at that time; however, within eighteen months of the formation of the UF Church (Continuing), women began to be ordained as elders. The distinction of being the first woman ordained to a charge in the UF Church belonged to the Rev. Elizabeth Barr, daughter of Rev. James Barr, its first Moderator, who was ordained to the UF Church in Auchterarder in Perthshire.

Since then, the UF Church continued to grow until the 1950s. This was as a result of both growth within the denomination as well as occasionally receiving congregations of the old UF Church which had initially gone into the union and then changed their minds.

Free Church from 1900 onwards

There was a Free Church minority therefore that refused to join the UF Church and clung to the Free Church name; they also tried to keep possession of the Free Church property, churches, manses, Assembly Hall and colleges. It seems to have been the United Free supporters who gave them the name 'Wee Frees', a name that is resented by the present Free Church members and gives considerable offence.

The argument was that in uniting with the United Presbyterians to form the UF Church, the Free Church had abandoned its Disruption principles. That being the case, the remaining dissenting Free Church ministers and congregations laid claim to the whole property of the old Free Church. A series of court cases ensued. The core legal point was whether the UF Church could consider itself to be the 'true' heirs of the Disruption when it had deserted from the 'establishment' principle on joining with the UP Church. Ironically for a Church which resented Parliament's attempted control of the Church in the 1830s and 1840s, the minority took the matter to the House of Lords to judge whether they or the majority were more true to Disruption principles. The House of Lords found in favour of the minority leaving the new UF Church with only its former UP property, and the remnant Free Church with a vast number of churches and manses for which it had no possible use. Finally, largely as a result of the UF Church's tactics in building public support, a more demographically equitable settlement was reached based on the proportions of congregations adhering to each side in the dispute. The continuing Free Church did fairly well from this settlement, but the case left a very substantial legacy of bitterness on both sides of the divide.

The Free Church which was left had then to decide its future course. By 1904 the legal cases had drained their financial resources significantly while they only actually had forty ministers and so had no realistic hope of establishing themselves nationally in the foreseeable future. Attempts to reconcile with the Free Presbyterian Church, of similar size, failed although a handful of ministers did come over from the FP Church over the years. But as great a legacy of hurt remained from the 'Second Disruption' of 1893 as from the House of Lords case of 1904, and the Free Presbyterians disapproved of the Free Church practice of holding such non-religious events as bazaars and soirees.

That group of forty ministers included twenty-six from the original split, but the remainder came in from other Presbyterian churches particularly in England and Ireland who did not necessarily follow the same ethos. The Church appointed a full-time General Secretary, J. H. Thorburn, to look after administration but it soon became evident that he was out of kilter with the views of those who had declined to join the UF Church. Thorburn wanted a national church and consequently wanted to downplay doctrinal issues and concentrate on building numbers. He encouraged an open door policy for communicants and ministers which did not sit well with the church as a whole. Finally, his contract was terminated and he left the Free Church, writing a very hostile pamphlet accusing it of being a 'Celtic Free Church' rather than what had been envisaged in 1843. In the wake of this controversy, about thirty of the younger ministers left the denomination in the following decade.

Early decisions about worship saw the post-1900 Free Church drop its use of hymns and revert to the old practice of standing to pray and sitting to sing psalms.

Nothing could now disguise the fact that it was a small minority church with a geographical basis almost entirely restricted to the Highlands and Western Isles, together with some of highland extraction in the cities of the central belt, and in fact the 'establishment principle', while never actually abandoned, has no relevance for the denomination today.

Beyond the Highlands though, the Free Church is active in foreign missions. All the pre-1900 missions remained with the UF Church, but new ones were established in South Africa, India and Peru. Modern Free Church historians tend to concentrate on the nineteenth century and on the controversies of the early years, and there is a need for a history of the church in the twentieth century.

Free Presbyterian Church of Scotland

Moving back to the position before the Union of 1900, shortly before the Union of 1900, the Free Church suffered its own 'Disruption' with the foundation of the Free Presbyterian Church.

The immediate cause was the passing of an act by the General Assembly of the Free Church, the 'Declaratory Act'. By this act, the Free Church was saying that the principles that it had stood for at its founding in 1843, and particularly the principles of the *Westminster Confession of Faith* (1647), could be changed. This led to the opposition and finally secession by some of the members. However, the controversy did not come out of the blue and although the passing of the act was the trigger, the actual division was much deeper and longer lasting. Within ten years of the founding of the Free Presbyterian Church, it had seventy-five congregations. Seventy of those were north of the Highland line, the remaining five, in Glasgow (2), Edinburgh, Greenock and Dumbarton served congregations founded as Highland or Gaelic speaking. There is a strong argument for saying that Free Presbyterian

Church was a reaction to the Gaelic highlanders' feelings of alienation and separation from the lowlands and from lowland values, the same feeling that had led to the highlanders' almost total rejection of the Established Church in 1843.

One of the problems faced in the abortive attempt at three-way union in the 1870s was that the highland portion of the Free Church had little in common with the lowland UPs in particular. Union with the Reformed Presbyterians, which came about in 1876, was not an issue as their theology was acceptable to the most conservative of Free Church members and their numbers were small. By the 1890s though union was back on the agenda; the lowland-dominated Free Church was once more intent on union with the United Presbyterian Church. Many of the major figures who had opposed the attempt at union in the 1870s were by this stage dead and, led by Robert Rainy, Principal of the Free College in Edinburgh, negotiations were proceeding with a denomination which seemed to stand against most of what was most important to the highland Christians and was entirely foreign to the Highlands and Islands.

The Declaratory Act seemed to many of the members a legitimizing and validation of a process which they had been fighting for many years. It was also the method by which UP and Free Church beliefs were to be reconciled.

Aside from making possible the shelving of some of the basic tenets of Calvinism, the modernizers were reacting to modern developments in science and in other forms of scholarship in ways which challenged a literal interpretation of the Bible. Among some, there was a real distrust of scientific advances and to the movement that applied the techniques of literary criticism to the Bible. They did not like the idea that the Bible was written, copied and recopied by real people who were prone, like everybody else, to make mistakes. This issue came to a head with the Robertson Smith case and those that followed it.

The third major cause of concern was simply the feeling that the Highlands and Highland Christianity were seen as a backwater with nothing to give to the national church as a whole. Meanwhile, the Highland church saw itself as the home of spiritual truth with a spirituality and purity at odds with modernizing lowland influences. Scripture in Gaelic and preaching in Gaelic were seen by some as the essence of Christianity. This was a view not shared by many of their lowland counterparts.

The fourth major concern with both the Declaratory Act and the proposed union with the UPs was that it seemed to many that the Free Church was become a 'Voluntary' church and giving up the position that the national church should have a mutual legal and moral dependence on the state. The Free Church never achieved its aim of being recognized as the state church, but many in it thought that that was the goal they should still be aiming at.

So how big was the Disruption that gave birth to the Free Presbyterian Church? Initially it was tiny. Despite the opposition to the Declaratory Act, when the act was passed most ministers sat tight. The ministers who opposed the declaratory act most loudly (known as the 'Constitutional Party') nonetheless accepted it. Only one, Donald MacFarlane of Raasay, walked out together with a group of divinity students. Fortunately for the fledgling denomination, a second minister joined the secession in a very short time, enabling them to form a presbytery. The real strength of feeling was among the laity. It was the elders who really drove the new denomination, conducting much of the worship and keeping the congregations together. Reading the obituaries of some of the founding elders, it is clear that the spirit of 'The Men' from the early nineteenth century was still represented in these people. Like virtually every other seceding group in Scottish church history, they saw themselves as a suffering persecuted remnant, and certainly the Free Church was in no mood to make any concessions to the fledgling denomination.

The Free Presbyterians were never numerous. It is hard to get accurate figures for congregations especially as numbers attending were always far in excess of the paper membership. The highland churches had, and still have, a long tradition of only a small minority of their congregations being communicant members. By 1895, the Free Presbyterians claimed to have seven ministers, eighteen students and 20,000 people in connection with the church. But in the highland population, as a whole this was a tiny percentage. In addition, adherence to the Free Presbyterians was uneven in the region. On the Isle of Lewis, for example, the Free Church suffered little loss, whereas in Skye and the far north of mainland Scotland, the Free Presbyterians were much stronger.

When, in 1900, the Free Church did finally unite with the UP Church as the UF Church, there might have been an expectation that those of the Free Church who did not favour the prospect would join with the Free Presbyterians but that did not happen. The wounds caused by the Declaratory Acts still festered and those who refused to join the union did not show any great enthusiasm for joining with those who had seceded a scant seven years previously. There were talks and indeed the 'new' Free Church (Continuing) even repealed the Declaratory Act in 1905 but not in terms that satisfied the Free Presbyterians, and the wounds proved too deep. A few Free Presbyterians switched back to the Free Church after 1905, but in general the two denominations go their separate ways.

Over the 120 or so years of its existence, the Free Presbyterian Church has been characterized by an unassailable piety, commitment and Biblical knowledge. In the course of that time though, it has also lost the services of many able men through its inability to accept divergence from the uniformity of belief that is its strength. It was recorded in an obituary of an elder in

1939 that 'he had the melancholy experience of seeing three ministers in succession in the Inverness congregation, separate from the church'.

So, what do the Free Presbyterians believe that makes them apart from other conservative offshoots of Presbyterianism? This can be summarized as a belief that the Bible is the Word of God, inspired and infallible, from beginning to end, best represented in English by the Authorized Version of 1611 and a full acceptance of the terms of the *Westminster Confession* as drawn up in 1647. This in turn has led to distinctive features in worship such as the exclusive use of Psalms for congregational singing on the grounds that only the psalms are divinely inspired and sanctioned by scripture; standing for prayers at public worship; and the rule that women should keep their heads covered during worship. The feasts of the church such as Christmas and Easter are not celebrated on the grounds that they are unscriptural and an invention of the Roman Catholic tradition. Despite this, many of their views on abortion, homosexuality and on other ethical issues would not be so very different from those endorsed by the Vatican. A strict observance of Sunday as the Christian Sabbath is perhaps the most visible symbol of Free Presbyterian practice, shared with the other conservative traditions of Presbyterianism. A fuller explanation of these practices can be found at the Church's own website.

9

Non-Presbyterian Dissent; Other Small Churches

There are many small denominations which have filled the niches that the larger ones did not reach. Many were specifically missionary enterprises; some were home-grown, some others imported from elsewhere in the United Kingdom while yet others were imported from beyond Britain.

Largest of these is the Brethren tradition, followed by the Church of Christ and those churches which owe some of their thinking to the 'Holiness' movement which itself grew from an American development of Methodist ideas. Other than those, there is a variety of churches which do not fit comfortably with other traditions: Gibbites, Buchanites and Moravians, Catholic Apostolic Church and Chartists.

Brethren

The Brethren are one of the most widespread of the smaller Scottish churches and yet one of the hardest to identify. Their buildings never identify themselves as 'Brethren' but are more likely to be called 'Gospel Hall', 'Hebron Hall', 'Olivet Chapel' or any of a number of other names. Why should this be so? This was simply because there never was a 'Brethren Denomination' as such; each hall or chapel was a separate entity entirely self-regulating and independent but part of a Brethren 'movement'. It was part of the ethos that the Brethren were not members of a denomination or an institution but were Christians worshipping in the way the early Christians worshipped.

There were elements common to all chapels. They held to 'believers' baptism' and a weekly communion service open to all Christians and they did not hold with an ordained ministry. The 'Open to all Christians' did depend on who they considered to be Christians and could be quite restrictive.

The movement itself started in Dublin in the 1820s among radical evangelicals dissatisfied with institutional Christianity. From there it spread to the south-west of England where it became known as the 'Plymouth Brethren', a name which survived until well through the twentieth century but is now largely disused.

A bitter split in 1848 over the expected second coming of Christ led to one group of congregations disowning the other and developing in its own direction. This latter group became known as the 'Closed' or 'Exclusive' Brethren, the remainder being called the 'Open' Brethren.

By the late 1830s, the movement had spread to Edinburgh but it was slow to spread in Scotland. By 1860, there seem to have been about six assemblies of each group. The 1851 Census is not helpful in making a closer estimate as the lack of an accepted name makes identifying Brethren congregations largely impossible. In addition, the Closed Brethren took a biblical text to be an injunction against taking part in censuses at all. Early Brethren groups allowed women to preach in some circumstances, mainly to other women, but later the preaching role became restricted to men. At the same time it was made clear that, although there was no ordained ministry and the dispensing of communion could be performed by any member, it was inappropriate for a woman to do so.

The substantial growth in Brethren communities came after the beginnings of the revival movement throughout Britain in the later nineteenth century and it is to this period that the particular association of Brethren Halls with the east coast fishing community belongs, due largely to the work of the North East Coast Mission. By the mid-1880s there were 115 Exclusive Brethren assemblies and 185 Open Brethren assemblies. The latter figure had grown to 373 by the 1930s when there were believed to be about 30,000 adhering to the movement. The Exclusive Brethren probably never had more than about 6000 members in Scotland. Both groups were conservative, Bible-based missions which rejected the more emotional appeal of the 'holiness' churches in favour of a closely argued intellectual religion. The Exclusive Brethren generally call their buildings 'Gospel Hall' while the more biblical names such as 'Bethany', 'Bethel', 'Olivet' and others tend to be associated with the Open Brethren.

Despite the popular association of the Brethren with the North east fishing communities, these were largely small groups and did not form a large part of the membership. Much of the numerical strength of the movement came from its activities in newly industrial areas in the lowlands with many of the most flourishing churches being in areas reliant on mining or iron industries. The crucial point for the growth of Brethren congregations was that they grew best in communities subject to considerable social change.

Like so many other Scottish churches, the movement had a tendency to fragment; the Open Brethren lost a group of Assemblies who became known as the 'Churches of God' in the 1890s. This group took on a more institutionalized and organized structure, taking perhaps 10 per cent of the members with them. Despite splitting again in 1905, the Churches of God still have a small presence of about a dozen congregations.

The Exclusive Brethren split even more often and their lack of records makes any research very difficult. There are currently about five main groupings of Exclusive Brethren in Scotland, but all very small, largely as a result of scandals which hit the movement in the 1970s. Perhaps the strictest of all groups, some Exclusive Brethren refuse to eat with those who are not members; members are not allowed to go to university or join professions, watch television or keep pets.

Considerable research has been carried out on the Open Brethren; a history 'The Brethren in Scotland 1838–2000' by Neil Dickson has an immense amount of detail. The best archive resource is to be found in Manchester at the John Rylands Library.

Churches of Christ

A look at the 1851 Religious Census for Scotland will show up various small churches described as 'Campbellites', 'Christians', 'Isolated churches'. Some of these groups later amalgamated into the 'Church of Christ', a small denomination which remained independent until 1981 when about forty churches in Britain voted to join the United Reformed Church and about twenty-four formed a new organization; the Fellowship of Churches of Christ. The Churches of Christ are generally looked on as a North American import, but in fact had their beginnings before their North American cousins became organized. In North America, they represent a grouping of six strands of churches in the 1830s. The biggest strand was founded by father and son Thomas and Alexander Campbell. Thomas Campbell was from the north of Ireland but trained as an anti-burgher minister in Scotland before being ordained to a charge back in Ireland. Like many others he moved to the United States and was soon at odds with the Presbyterians there. Two central reasons were his beliefs that all Christians should be able to share the Sacrament of Communion and that people should be baptized as adults not as children. The former was a view he shared with the Relief Church, the latter put him in the Baptist grouping, but he had a much less strict view of what a believer needed to do or show than conventional Baptists, and that was a difference that lasted throughout the history of the denomination.

No- one in the church thought of themselves as a denomination as they believed only in what was in the Bible with none of the statements of belief or institutions that so many other churches had gathered. Small churches had developed in Scotland, as in the rest of the United Kingdom, on very much the same principles. In 1807 the first congregation came into being in Auchtermuchty largely in the wake of the Haldane brothers, but led by two brothers John and George Dron.

By the 1820s, Campbell's writings were available in Scotland and found approval in these churches. Other churches soon formed. The influences behind them tended to be Presbyterian but rejecting certain crucial elements, such as the system of courts and control. As a result many came from dissenting churches which themselves were splitting over doctrine, such as the Glasites and the Old Scotch Baptists. Both the latter groups had a policy of requiring unanimity in decisions; in practice this meant that anyone not agreeing with a decision had to leave. The openness of the Churches of Christ to a variety of opinion therefore was attractive to many. It was a movement coming from the same roots as Methodism or the Brethren, but was different in its prime aim of uniting Christians and openness to independent thought. In 1834, John Dron visited the United States and met Alexander Campbell and closer links followed.

By 1840 there were churches in Glasgow, Dundee, Perth, Banff, Turiff, Edinburgh, Cupar, Dunfermline, Montrose, and Dumfries, the majority coming from the Scotch Baptist tradition. The leader of the Dundee church, George C. Reid, was an independent evangelical minister who was converted to the Campbellite view and convinced 110 members of his congregation to follow him.

In 1840 the British and North American groups joined although they had fairly significant differences in their attitudes. The British side though was always a very small church, numbered in hundreds by 1840 it never rose above 20,000 and by the time of the union in 1981 it had fewer than 3600 members. Even by 1840 the American Church numbered 40,000 and it went on to grow into the millions. The North American Churches were more evangelical, more clergy-minded than the British ones. A joint meeting in 1843 showed that Scotland had twenty-one churches with 608 members while England had nineteen churches with 530 members. Edinburgh, Cupar and Dundee were among the largest congregations in Britain, all having between seventy and hundred members.

A visit by Campbell to Scotland in 1847 led to a bitter attack on him by the anti-slavery movement which culminated in a short stay in prison in Glasgow, so this cast a shadow on the Churches. Nonetheless, trans-Atlantic relations remained good, with strong mutual support. Individual churches were run by elders who retained their normal secular work to support them. Each church might have one or more elders and if they had no-one theologically trained enough to act as an elder, the congregation might have one or more presidents to run its affairs.

Unfortunately from the point of view of the British Churches of Christ, an evangelist Dr John Thomas, from the American Churches proved to have views which diverged sharply from either body's norm. The Churches of Christ did not have a history of 'heresy-hunting', so Thomas had developed his views without hindrance but adopted a position where he insisted on re-baptizing those who had been convinced by his arguments. Not unnaturally, this upset those unconvinced by him. He later became the founder of the Christadelphians (dealt with in the next chapter).

As a result of Thomas's activities, seven Scottish congregations left the Churches of Christ during the 1850s and many others were weakened. The Edinburgh church however survived a substantial loss of members and soon numbered several hundred in a newly bought building. Also in the 1850s, Charles Abercrombie became a teacher in Slamannan in Stirlingshire. He soon began to preach in the open air to the miners leading to the baptism of eighty in the open air. Through Abercrombie, churches were founded in Bo'ness, Bathgate, Crofthead, Whitburn and Hamilton.

Each congregation was independent and decisions of the Association had no force. If a congregation was believed to have adopted wrong beliefs, they were not expelled as they might have been in other denominations but it was left to each individual congregation to decide its own relationship. That said however, the Churches of Christ did gradually formulate stricter views: for example, they condemned the practice of allowing non-Christians to take communion as had grown up in some North American Congregations.

Like several other churches, individual congregations might become the uniting factor for emigration. In 1857, the Church at Cupar, which had already lost members through Dr Thomas's activities, suffered heavy losses when twenty-five members of one family emigrated to New Zealand, later forming a church in Dunedin. A similar grouping from Ayrshire had already left for Australia.

Like so many other small churches, the Churches of Christ was almost entirely lowland in nature. It appealed to the newly displaced workers in heavy industry but also to coastal communities. In this aspect, it shared similarities with both Brethren assemblies and primitive Methodists. Another split in the 1940s led to a small remnant group of churches, but the majority joined the United Reformed Church in 1981.

The 'Holiness' churches

The Churches of Christ were not the only ones to have a fairly small presence in Scotland but a substantial following abroad and sometimes an influence out of proportion to their size. One particular group arose out of what is now known as the 'Holiness Movement'. Initially, this emerged from developments in Methodist churches, particularly in the United States and especially from revivals around the year 1800. These were religious events, often unplanned, where mass religious conversions took place in a spirit of high emotion. They have occurred at many times in the history of Church but those in the United States were particularly influential. It was a religious movement that concentrated on the work of the Holy Spirit on the believer and demanded almost an instant coming to faith rather than the slow dawning of faith that many Christians experienced. People in large numbers felt themselves to have been 'sanctified' or 'baptized in the Holy Spirit'. Many of the early followers also expected an imminent day of judgement and the Second Coming of Christ; however this 'Millennialist' view also coloured the beliefs of other religious groups becoming active in the early nineteenth century, Mormons, Catholic Apostolic Church, and others. The earliest Scottish manifestation of this viewpoint was the growth of the Primitive Methodists.

Although the Brethren had some links with the movement, they were never a Holiness church as such, largely because they rejected the emotionalism and dependence on the experience of the Holy Spirit which the Holiness churches made central. Fifty years after the establishment of the Brethren, several other 'Holiness' churches also appeared in the United Kingdom and in Scotland. Partly, this was a result of a wave of revivals and mission work embarked upon as an effort to reach the unchurched, although several of missions were far more effective at attracting members from existing churches than from those that the churches were not reaching. In particular, the efforts of the North American evangelists Dwight Moody and Ira Sankey, the former preaching and the latter singing, made a significant impact on the people of Scotland with their campaigns in the 1870s. Moody's practice of asking for a commitment to Christ immediately after preaching struck an emotional chord with many people and the results were impressive. In their wake, other missionary endeavours were started. Some were within the existing churches and indeed united 'rival' congregations locally in joint missionary enterprises and in building mission halls. Others were beyond the institutional churches and targeted particular groups of people, fishermen, railwaymen and industrial workers.

These last missions could often be seen as a threat by the older denominations, especially as they realized their own difficulties in reaching migratory workers. A Church of Scotland commission reporting in 1894 claimed that in mining villages of East Lothian:

A difference was drawn between the native mining population and immigrants, the former being fairly regular in church attendance but the latter it seemed utterly impossible to get hold of. Among both the fishing and mining population in the Presbytery, Plymouthism, Salvationism and Christadelphianism seemed to have taken a deeper root than generally in the other districts visited; and Mormonism was reported to the Commission for the first time as a source of evil.

Meanwhile, in Biggar(Lanarkshire), one of the campaigns of the Faith Mission was accused of alienating people from the worship of the Church. One recurrent theme was the worry that people were discouraged from going to the churches by a lack of fine clothes and that the mission halls were less particular about and more accepting of people attending in whatever they wore on a daily basis. Perhaps, the most serious charge though was that made against the East Coast Mission was that it encouraged its target audience 'to regard themselves as a class separated from other working classes and to remain unattached as communicants to any regular denomination'. Other differences too were obvious in the mission's approach; emotions were allowed to run high while ministers tried to suppress emotionalism. One description of a revival meeting in Port Gordon in north-east Scotland described how

> the school got heated almost to suffocation by the people's breath, and in this state of atmosphere the meeting was kept up for nine and a half hours, many of the people remaining there the whole time without meat or drink. Hymns and spiritual songs were repeated numerous times until the audience was quite in an excited state, boys and girls holding one another by the hands and rocking and rolling with their bodies, and even beating with their feet on the floor to the time of the music.... However the greatest commotion did not occur until around midnight when during a period of prayer a number of women shrieked loudly and then fell into an unconscious state. Finally the meeting began to draw to a close around 1.30 am, only because the lights were nearly all burnt out and the meeting place was beginning to get dark.

Clearly this was religious experience quite outside the teaching and preaching models followed by more traditional churches. Despite this though, there is a fair amount of evidence to suggest that those involved in such missions were as likely to come from churched backgrounds as unchurched.

The missions gradually came to have their own organization even if they stemmed out of work from existing churches. One such was the Faith Mission. This was founded by a Glasgow business man, John George Govan in 1884. Initially concentrating on the west of Scotland, it soon spread its efforts throughout Scotland and Ireland and still exists with, among other activities, a college for training evangelists in Edinburgh.

The pattern of its early activities was for the workers, 'Pilgrims', as they were known, to concentrate on a community for a few weeks at a time with daily meetings in whatever accommodation they could book before moving on to another town or village. Govan himself described their early efforts in Fife in 1887:

All the pilgrims then in the Mission, eight in number, congregated in the County, and with open-air marches, shouting, choruses, solos, testimonies and Gospel appeals, pushed the battle to the gates in towns and villages, sometimes amid much open opposition, and achieved some splendid conquests for Christ.

A permanent hall in Fife was one of their earliest buildings.

The Faith Mission was relatively unusual in having Gaelic speakers available and indeed was invited by at least one Church of Scotland minister to provide a Gaelic-speaking assistant for his parish. One of their basic tenets was to be non-sectarian and they maintained relations with many of the more mainstream churches. The Faith Mission became the model for several other mission based groups, particularly as individuals of strong convictions argued about various aspects of their faith. Unlike many of the new mission groupings, it concentrated on country areas rather than urban ones; in 1924, they held missions in 326 different places throughout Britain and Ireland. This was the high point of the organization, with over 3000 conversions recorded, a figure that reduced to 650 by 1954. The problem of gaining access to halls for meetings they solved by commissioning 'portable halls' that they could take round, erecting them easily wherever they wished to hold meetings, while the Pilgrims latterly were equipped with caravans to stay in for the duration of their missions.

One of those to leave the Faith Mission at an early stage to pursue their own style of mission was William Irvine who became the founder of the 'Go-Preachers', or '2 by 2s'.

Irvine devoted his life to mission work largely in Ireland, but the groups that he founded, known as Go-preachers, tramp-preachers, and many other epithets spread throughout Ireland and into Scotland, England, especially the north, and beyond to the rest of the English-speaking world where they are now generally referred to as '2-x-2s'. Gradually, the movement became very anti-clerical, claiming that no ministers would ever be saved, and exclusive, allowing no questioning of doctrine. Irvine himself was excommunicated and written out of their history to a great extent, dying in Jerusalem in 1947.

The ethos of the sect was the mission statement in Matthew's Gospel to go out into the world in twos with no possessions, hence their nickname; those going out are called 'workers', those supporting them are called 'friends'.

They practise baptism of believers by total immersion, preferably in the sea or rivers, and there are accounts of these baptisms in many local papers in their early years. They left behind many of the beliefs of the churches they came out of, including the belief in the divinity of Christ. They have their own hymn book, published by a Scottish publisher with both their own hymns and others borrowed from other traditions and altered to suit. Scottish members tend to belong to the fishing communities of the north-east. There was an annual convention in Scotland, meeting in Findochty (Moray) from about 1930 until 1985, at least with around 240 attending from all over the country and from further afield. The convention was held in the Fishermen's Hall with a dining tent erected nearby. All visitors were able to stay with local 'friends'. The 'workers' would sit on the stage with the 'friends' sitting in the hall with men on one side and women on the other. The addresses and testimonies were interspersed with hymns. There are still conventions in Scotland but it has a philosophy of secrecy and it is impossible to know how many adherents the movement has.

Pentecostalism

A further group arising from the holiness movement was the Pentecostalists. 'Speaking in tongues', 'glossolalia' is a phenomenon first recorded in the New Testament in the Book of Acts, when the disciples of Jesus spoke fifty days after his resurrection and each was heard by the listeners in their own native languages. Throughout history, examples were recorded but after the first event, it was never deemed to be quite respectable by the Church, being seen more as a form of hysteria.

In Scotland, there were well-recorded instances in the 1820s in Ayrshire. There the phenomenon was associated with Edward Irving. 'Speaking in tongues' was initially associated with people involved in the 'Holiness' movement, itself evolving out of Methodism. There were links both with the annual Keswick Convention in the Lake Districtt and with the great Welsh Revival movement of 1904, but what really crystallized was the activities of a vicar of the Church of England in Sunderland, Rev. Alexander Boddy, who was himself influenced by groups who practised speaking with tongues in Kansas and Los Angeles. Boddy never left the Church of England but gathered round him a number of people who had experienced speaking in tongues. They met not in his church itself but in its premises. The group included several Scottish residents, two Norwegians, Eilif and Christina Beruldsen, who lived in Edinburgh and started a group at home before opening a church in Leith; another was a Presbyterian elder in Kilsyth called Andrew Murray.

Taking the history of the movement in Kilsyth as an example, Murdoch was involved in a joint mission of the three major Presbyterian churches there in the 1890s aimed at evangelizing those brought to the area by employment in heavy industry. This was the same mission that provided a base for the early mission work of William Irvine before he moved to the Faith Mission and then the Go-Preachers. Murdoch's Mission hall ultimately became a Pentecostal Chapel but was also the centre from which a periodical called *'Confidence'* was published from 1908 until 1926. This gives information for a substantial number of chapels throughout central Scotland with 600 baptisms. Following only the Bible and no other written theology or formal training, those identifying with these groups were reliant on direct experience of the grace of God and were baptized as adults once they had shown themselves to be truly converted. 'Speaking in tongues' was seen as a sign of 'coming through' into faith; it was not necessarily a regular feature of believers' lives though. Healing through faith was also a significant part of belief and was particularly associated with baptism.

The groups were similar to Primitive Methodists, Brethren and the Church of the Nazarene in being aimed specifically at groups that the major churches were not reaching; the dispossessed, particularly those following the growth of heavy industry in the central belt. Sometimes this could lead to friction; it was recorded in 1907 that an open air meeting in Perth was interrupted by members of the Pentecostal League; 'a heated altercation ensued, the different sections excitedly proclaiming their religious beliefs and introducing personal references into their remarks'.

Pentecostalism was perhaps one of the least gender conscious of churches. Women were at the centre from the beginning. The church in Leith, now associated with the Assemblies of God, was founded and led by Christina Beruldsen; her husband was also involved but she was very much in charge as were other women elsewhere. Mission work overseas was a priority; three Beruldsen children went to China as missionaries.

A significant group from Pentecostal believers became conscientious objectors during the Great War. The awkwardness of explaining their beliefs without an externally recognized 'label' gave many of them difficulties, particularly when not all Pentecostals agreed with them. One result though was a gradual gathering up of the congregations into three different groupings; by 1924 there seem to have been about eighty-four such congregations split among twenty-three Elim Pentecostal, a church organized from the north of Ireland, forty-five Assemblies of God, which includes Beruldsen's Leith Church, and sixteen Apostolic Faith Churches. Historically, the first two operated in the industrial central belt while the Apostolic Faith Church tried to maintain a presence in the Highlands as well.

Numbers of Pentecostalists in Scotland were never large, although it was recorded that 3000 were converted in Dundee in 1933; but numbers of churches in all three denominations still exist. Outwith Scotland however, Pentecostalism is one of the largest and fastest growing forms of Christianity worldwide. It has also become more accepted among the charismatic movements that started in the traditional churches from the 1960s onwards.

Church of the Nazarene

Not all the churches that arose from the Holiness Movement came down through the migratory missionary ideal presented by the Faith Mission and similar organizations. In September 1906, Rev. George Sharp, minister of Parkhead Congregational Church in the east end of Glasgow was ousted from his pulpit and manse by a congregational meeting barely more than a year after he was called there. About eighty of his congregation followed him and he started a congregation known locally as 'Sharp's Kirk', worshipping where they could. Within a few weeks they had a congregational structure, a Sunday School and land for a church.

Sharp was influenced by the 'Holiness Movement'. Brought up in Motherwell, near Glasgow, he was converted at the age of seventeen and briefly considered ministry in the Church of Scotland but instead emigrated to the United States and became a Methodist minister there. Fifteen years later, while at home on holiday with his family, he preached in a Congregational Church in Ardrossan which was without a minister and was promptly offered the position. Four years later, he moved to Glasgow.

His theology did not sit comfortably with the Congregational Church but his new church thrived. A new building was opened as Parkhead Pentecostal Church in 1907 and was the first building in the area to be lit by electricity. The Church grew and became a small denomination, with churches in Paisley and Uddingston; however, despite its name, the Pentecostal Church of Scotland quickly decided that that the practice of 'speaking in tongues' which became characteristic of many Pentecostal churches had no place in their worship.

In 1909, Parkhead Pentecostal Church received a new member, an American called Olive Winchester. With an American degree in Hebrew and Arabic, she became the first woman to graduate in Divinity at Glasgow University, or indeed at any British university. In 1912, she became the first ordained woman minister in Britain. She returned to the United States in 1914, and the remainder of her career was spent there. Meanwhile, the

Church had spread to Edinburgh, Leith and Perth and even had a small Bible College to train new ministers. In 1915, the church united with the Church of the Nazarene which had grown out of a similar movement in America and which had drawn members in England and Wales. The new church became the British Isles District of the Pentecostal Church of the Nazarene. One early crisis came when rules of the church banning membership in 'oath-bound orders' meant that it was not possible for members to be members of the Orange Order, celebrating Northern Irish Protestantism. Some left the church while some left the order.

Other written rules encapsulated a way of life expected of evangelical Christians, including a ban on alcohol, attending the theatre, entering pubs, etc. It was, like many small evangelical churches, strict and backsliders soon left so that early membership figures tended to dwindle after a few years. The practice of ordaining women continued and the church also was able to send members as missionaries, George Sharp himself going to Swaziland in 1925 on a visit as superintendent of missions.

As congregations grew, new churches were built. It was never wealthy and many of these new churches were built of corrugated iron, just as some of the early Free Churches were. It was also never a large church, but it was continuing to expand in numbers and planting new churches into the 1950s and beyond in new towns and housing estates and has currently seventeen churches in Scotland affiliated to an American based mother-church with over two million members worldwide.

Salvation Army

Perhaps the best known of the Holiness churches is the Salvation Army. Founded in 1865 by William Booth to evangelize the London slums, the Salvation Army made its first appearance in Scotland in the Anderston district of Glasgow in 1879. By 1882, it had a presence in Glasgow, Aberdeen Coatbridge and Kilsyth, and its statistics boasted forty-seven officers, 880 volunteer speakers, 1953 privates, 547 drunkards converted and an average Sunday night attendance of 15,500 per week with a further 7500 attending a mid-week meeting. The Salvation Army met with more resistance, perhaps, than any other Christian organization in modern times; its quasi-military organization, its practice of parading through the streets in uniform, its vocabulary of warfare, its focus on going into the roughest of areas made it an easy target for hooliganism and disruption. The newspapers of the 1880s are full of references to Salvation Army-centred disturbances and riots. In Scotland, these incidents ranged from Arbroath where 'nightly this week processions of about five hundred boys have marched through the streets shouting Salvation

Army hymns to the beating of drums, tin kettles etc., the whole being in ridicule of the Salvationists'. to the janitor of a theatre in Glasgow switching off the lighting on a crowded stairway of the Colosseum Music Hall. In other incidents, Salvationists were imprisoned for breaking bans on marches. By 1882, however, they were acquiring premises of their own rather than renting halls and theatres; one of the first was a disused church in Leith which is still part of the Leith Citadel.

Local authorities did not like the Army because of the disturbances; one complaint was that 100 special constables had to be sworn in to protect a parade and this prevented them going to church themselves.

The early Salvation Army must have seemed very unconventional to nineteenth-century eyes; for one thing the Salvation Army did not recognize the Sacraments of Communion or Baptism as necessary or desirable, worship might be accompanied by guitar or brass band. In 1892 one highland writer to *The Scotsman* referred to

> the irreverence approaching blasphemy that characterises the worship of Army .... Crowds may parade our streets attired like maniacs and marching to the sound of the trump and the drum, and they may conduct their religious meetings with a din and a daring more like demoniacs than sane men.

The Scotsman itself was initially pretty dismissive and patronizing

> Their *(i.e. the 'lowest classes')* conduct in face of the Salvation Army seems to indicate a perception that the real spring of the movement is the unhealthy vanity of a number of weak-minded men and women, which nurses itself in the excitement of a so-called religious movement.

From the beginning, the Salvation Army practised equality of the sexes and women regularly followed the example of the founder's wife Catherine Booth who preached more, and more effectively, than her husband.

From the earliest times though, a grudging respect was growing; the local churchmen began to realize that the Salvation Army was reaching people whom the church had consistently failed. 'With all their apparent folly', one anonymous minister wrote, 'the Salvation Army people are doing more of the real work for which Christ is generally supposed to have set up his church than any other body of Christians in Great Britain'.

What gave the Salvation Army credibility was their absolute commitment to work among the poorest and most vulnerable citizens and soon a large number of schemes to help the homeless, poverty-stricken children and unmarried mothers took their place as part of the fabric of Scottish society, giving the Army a role and a respect which has not diminished over time.

By 1902, the Salvation Army was established enough for it to be awarded an invitation (for a representative) to attend King Edward's coronation. The Salvation Army had, in other words, arrived.

The Salvation Army still retains its use of military ranks for full-time workers, its military terminology and its simple forms of worship without sacraments, but its evangelistic strategy is rather less aggressive than it used to be and it is perhaps now better known for the help it gives to the most vulnerable sections of society than for its actual mission work.

This growth of evangelizing mission groups was a worry to the larger churches. They had tried the kind of mission work that had seemed necessary, but where it worked it well in reaching the people, it seemed to grow away from the churches that commissioned it and lead to small independent congregations which went their own way and sometimes a rather unorthodox way at that. The real reason seems to have been that evangelists need to arise from the same kind of people that they work among and the fact that 'ministers' were seen as mid-class and 'apart' from the people militated against them even when they themselves had risen from the same working class. Some of the more pessimistic churchmen saw the potential for these groups yielding 'very serious and very evil fruit indeed, especially in leading people away from under the influence of the Church of Christ'. This kind of attitude may seem ludicrous a century later, but the writer's comments referred to the rivalry between the various groups being a barrier and that was also a factor in the way that many of these small groups interacted; John Long, an evangelist whose diary sheds so much light on the way these groups operated, had this to say about the various groups he came in contact with:

> Although not under the auspices of the Elim Mission, I have very largely contended for the same truths. Although they do not preach Believers Immersion, yet they baptize large numbers, as many as sixty together: does not this prove to the Faith Mission that God does and will bless a people who neglect not the ordinances of Christ? ... I regret to say from personal observation that the attitude of the Faith Mission towards them is not at all as-as theirs is to the Faith Mission. The Go-Preachers of late years are very exclusive, but wise, and more careful in what they say; but not at all as evangelical as what characterized their testimony from 1897 to 1907, ... The Brethren of late years, by means of tent missions and street preaching have made an honest effort to get people saved, by preaching the Gospel under three principals namely, sin, atonement, and salvation; without influencing converts to leave there respective places of worship: this I say to their credit. I cannot say much for the Salvation Army, overdoing collecting money is not to their credit; yet God uses them in slum districts to rescue some from depths of sin.

Small as they are in Scotland, these mission churches nevertheless were often more successful abroad and members of their overseas equivalents number in many millions. Their appeal lay in the social position of the evangelist, who was considered trustworthy because he was part of the same community and could fit his message to that community. This trust made for a different relationship than the minister/parishioner one.

Some less related churches and movements

Gibbites

The Gibbites, who were also called the 'Sweet Singers', a name shared with a separate seventeenth-century movement in England, were one of the odder offshoots of the covenanting times in Scotland. They take their name from John Gibb, a merchant sea captain from Bo'ness on the Forth. During the reign of Charles II, he acted as go-between between the Covenanters in Scotland and their exiled co-religionists in the Low Countries. However, by 1680, his beliefs had moved wildly away from orthodox, or even unorthodox, Presbyterianism and he became the object of the Privy Council's interest for his 'seditious books'. Pre-warned of the investigation, he abandoned his ship and the sea and took on the life of an itinerant preacher around Bo'ness, and it was there that the Gibbites gathered to his charismatic leadership twenty-six women and three men.

Whether he can strictly be described as a Covenanter is a moot question. He quickly fell out with Donald Cargill, who went as far as to describe him as the devil incarnate. Gibb led his followers into a complete rejection of possessions, work and secular authority, lapsing into a millenniarist view of the impending end of the world. In May 1681, the whole group was captured without bloodshed; many of the women were returned to their husbands and the men imprisoned in the Tolbooth in Edinburgh. It seems likely that James, future King James VII and II, was amused by Gibb and believed him to be mad rather than a threat to the government, with the result that he was released in August 1681. With the faithful Gibbites reduced to five people, Gibb began to attack the Metrical Psalms and the Bible itself as corrupt human distortions and dangerous extensions of royal authority, committing his own and his followers' Bibles to a bonfire near Airth in Stirlingshire. He even seems to have gone as far as renouncing his belief in God. Finally, he was arrested again and sent back to the tolbooth where his behaviour was reported as becoming more and more insane. In 1684, he was sentenced to be transported to America, where he is believed to have survived until about 1720. Several of his followers also went to America and prospered.

Buchanites

A hundred years later, a rather similar 'microchurch' suddenly appeared. The 'Buchanites', as they became known, are one of very few churches to take their name from a woman: Elspeth Buchan, who lived in eighteenth century Ayrshire. She became convinced that she was an embodiment of the Holy Spirit and managed to convince a small group of others, including the Relief Church minister in Irvine in Ayrshire, that she was 'the woman clothed in the sun' mentioned in the book of Revelation. The minister, Hugh White, was not surprisingly deposed by his church for heresy. Mother Buchan, as she became known, persuaded her band of followers to fast for forty days to ensure a bodily transportation to heaven. Although the local magistrates intervened to protect children in the group and some others fell away during the fast, those who completed the forty days found themselves still firmly, if hungrily, attached to this earth. The sect was driven out of Kilmarnock by a mob and moved to Glasgow and later to Muthil. They, including many who had joined her at Muthil, then went back to Irvine before being expelled again. This time they moved to Crocketford in Galloway where they settled. Mrs Buchan believed she was immortal and that if she did die, her embalmed body would be brought back to earth after nine days, or nine months or possibly fifty years afterwards. In the event, she died in 1791. After her death some of the community dispersed to the United States but others remained in Galloway. The death of her last believer in 1846 brought to light the fact that her body was preserved in his house still unresurrected. Just because of their downright oddness, the Buchanites has a fame far beyond their numbers and appeared in various writings both at the time and afterwards. Of these, perhaps the most famous account was the one written by Robert Burns in his letters.

Moravians

The Reformation that came to Scotland in 1560 was relatively late; other reformed Churches in Germany or Italy, for example, have much longer histories. One such is the Moravian Church, founded by Protestants in Bohemia in Central Europe. It was never large and was in decline but experienced a renewal in the eighteenth century that led to its sending out missionaries to other countries including the British Isles. As a result, missionaries came to Scotland by way of Ireland and founded two congregations in Ayr in 1765 and Irvine in 1771, although the latter was short lived. An attempt to add a congregation in Glasgow followed in the mid-nineteenth century but failed. It seems unlikely that either congregation ever exceeded 100 but the Ayr church survived until about 1916. The Moravians also ran a girls day school in Ayr for some years. They were known for their friendliness to other denominations and their minister was acceptable as a preacher in most of the other churches in the town.

The Catholic Apostolic Church

The Catholic Apostolic Church was one of the products of the 1830s. It proclaimed the unity of Christians of different denominations and only really came into existence as a separate denomination to accommodate those whose allegiance to its ideas was not accepted by existing churches. As a result, references to people who accepted the ideas of the church while still retaining membership of traditional churches are not uncommon.

Although founded in London, the initial impetus for the founding was a Scottish minister, Edward Irving. He had been an assistant to Thomas Chalmers, one of the most notable ministers of the first half of the nineteenth century and had proved particularly effective at pastoral work in the slums of Glasgow's east end, but it was one of the Church of Scotland churches in London which called him to be their minister in 1822. Once there, he became renowned as a preacher who reflected contemporary popular philosophy and literature in his preaching as well as new ideas in theology. This led to his church became a very fashionable place to worship. Irving's own beliefs developed through the decade and as a result he was condemned for heresy in 1830 and deposed from the ministry of the Church of Scotland in 1833.

Irving and his supporters had founded a new church in London in 1833 before he died the following year at the age of forty-two. The church he founded became the central church of the new denomination which took shape in 1835. Unlike many of the new denominations and congregations which appeared or grew in the 1830s and 1840s, the Catholic Apostolic Church was not designed to attract the poor and dispossessed or return to what was seen as the model of the early church. It was millennialist in its nature, expecting the second coming of Christ and the imminent end of the world and day of judgement. That was not so unusual, around that time, it was a common reaction to the excesses of the French Revolution and the political turmoils it left in its wake, but it added to that a hierarchy headed by '12 apostles' each with the responsibility for various areas of the world; below them were 'angels/bishops' each responsible for a specific church and below them priests/elders, deacons, prophets and evangelists. As time went on, they became more and more taken up with designing vestments and rewriting liturgies into ever more elaborate orders of service.

Perhaps most significantly, it was a church that appealed to an upper- or upper middle-class membership. Irving's knack of attracting the fashionable in the 1820s changed into an attraction for the professions. Of the original twelve 'apostles', three were already clergy, three gentry (including two MPs), three barristers, one merchant, one artist and one Keeper of the Tower of London. They were men of influence and their influence was matched by the fact that members were expected to give a tenth of their income and since they were well off, the church itself became very wealthy.

Thus the movement took off; there were three churches in Scotland by 1851; according to one source, they reached a high point at twenty-eight Scottish churches while there is certainly evidence for six by the end of the century. The Scottish apostle was Henry Drummond, an MP and landowner who was also a major figure in London banking. Earlier, he had come under the influence of Robert Haldane but broke with him over Drummond's acceptance of Irving's new ideas and was one of the founding members of the new church. His responsibility also included Switzerland with both nations exhibiting 'Dignified patriotism shown by nations inhabiting poor countries'. The connection between the Church with the law continued in a Scottish context, with one of its members, Sir John MacDonald, becoming one of Scotland's senior lawyers as Lord Advocate and later Lord Justice Clerk.

The Church had sown the seeds of its own destruction though for they took the decision that there should be no more 'apostles' appointed after 1855. This meant that after the last of them died in 1901, there could be no more priests ordained and the church gradually petered out. The last Scottish church closed for worship after the death of its last priest in 1958.

This last Scottish church was the Mansfield Place Church in Edinburgh, one of the most ornate of Scottish church buildings. Built at a cost of £17,000, it was consecrated in 1875 and had seating capacity of 700. Later, it was richly decorated with murals by Phoebe Anne Traquair and because of this, a successful campaign was mounted to save the church and its murals and make them available to the public view.

There are three major collections of records in existence: those of St Andrews University, Lambeth Palace Library and the Catholic Apostolic Church Trust which also retains ownership of two of the English churches and other property. The Church still has a considerable income which is used for religious purposes, including £30,000 that is being allocated annually to the Church of Scotland.

Chartist Churches

At the opposite end of almost any spectrum, theological, social or political, from the Catholic Apostolic Church, was another product of the 1830s, the Chartist Churches. With the 1830s began the long process of political democratization with the passing of the First Reform Act; that did not satisfy everybody and there was growing demand for universal adult suffrage. This was led by a group who became known as the Chartists and the advancement of their cause is parallel to other movements throughout Europe which made their opponents fear revolution throughout society. In Britain, they are seen as one of the major ancestors of the Labour Party. Some Chartists were anti-clerical and some supported 'free-thinking' or atheism, but many were Christians with a strong social and political philosophy. They found that the 'institutional' churches, United Secession and the Relief Church that many of them came from rejected their ideas: so, some of them grouped together and formed a small denomination called Chartist Churches. The first was in Hamilton, followed by another in Paisley and in time followed by a further twenty-seven. They were never large and seem to have left few records. A few ministers of existing churches extended their support; Patrick Brewster of the Established Church was disciplined for taking part in Chartist Services. The Chartist Churches never established themselves and began to decline after a couple of years. They seemed to have disappeared completely by about 1850. Most of their pastors came from a teaching background and several also ran schools.

10

Non-Trinitarian Churches

All the mainstream churches in Scotland are 'Trinitarian' in that they believe in the 'Trinity' of God the Father, God the Son (Jesus Christ) and God the Spirit acting as three aspects of a single God. However, there are a number of churches which do not accept the doctrine of the Trinity but have their origins within mainstream churches and have been influenced by them. This chapter considers the history of the Quakers from the seventeenth century; the Swedenborgians and Unitarians dating from the eighteenth century; and the Mormons, Christadelphians and Spiritualists from the nineteenth century.

Quakers

The Quakers, or The Society of Friends, to give them their proper title, are the only group in Scotland who can show an unbroken link to the many religious bodies which came into Scotland with Cromwell's Army. This may seem paradoxical when the Quakers are best known for their commitment to peace and pacifism.

Founded as a form of Puritanism in England, the Quakers initially were trying to return to a biblical form of Christianity free from later influences. As such they rejected the concept of full time ministers. They consistently referred to all clergy as 'priests' which did not go down well with Presbyterians. Among other characteristics were a rejection of 'symbolic' forms of Christianity such as the sacraments of baptism or communion, simplicity of dress and an egalitarianism which led them to continue wearing hats when convention decreed they should be removed. What made matters worse was their refusal to swear oaths at a time when oaths of allegiance were a major tool in finding who was loyal to which cause. As can be imagined, they were subject to considerable harassment in early years and many were imprisoned for their beliefs; one unexpected result is that they have kept good records of court cases they were involved with. Another characteristic that did not win them many friends in more conventional churches was that women had exactly the same status as men from the earliest times. In the early years they were distrusted and harried by Presbyterians and Episcopalians and regarded with the same sort of hatred as the Roman Catholics.

Most of the original Scottish Quakers were rural and associated either with the north-east or with the Borders and the surnames Barclay, Burnet, Haig, Scott and Swinton persist through the centuries. Many were involved in milling of flour or gardening. Quakers moved to trade and manufacturing in Scotland as in England with members involved in baking, brewing, and manufacturing. More recently Quakers have had their main strength in Glasgow and Edinburgh, although they have a presence throughout Scotland.

For a small denomination, it was relatively unusual that it made little impact in industrial areas; perhaps by the time the Brethren, the Methodists, the Nazarenes were carving out their niches, the Quakers had settled into recognition of their middle-class status. Aside from those running businesses, Quaker membership contained (and still contains) a disproportionately large number of teachers, especially university teachers. One survey has showed that 31 per cent of Scottish Quakers are involved in education and 12 per cent in medical work, with a further 14 per cent in 'other professions'.

After William's accession in 1688, in theory, persecution ceased. In practice, life was still made awkward for them. Marriage was difficult: on the one hand, they did not recognize clergy, on the other hand, they wanted to be married. In 1737, the ministers in Aberdeen were taken to court for refusing to proclaim the banns of a gardener called James Gray, a Quaker, and Barbara Bannerman, because she was 'a Protestant', and after the court had ruled in Gray's favour, they refused to carry out the marriage. In the event, the Sherriff of the court declared them legally wed. From a Quaker point of view though, Gray was doubly culpable in seeking 'disorderly marriage by a priest' and by marrying outside the Society.

Their numbers were never large, perhaps a thousand for the whole of Scotland at the beginning of the eighteenth century, declining to around a hundred by the end of the century, mainly in Aberdeenshire. The latter numbers may be undercounted as they habitually kept a low profile and the numbers of dissenters noted in the Statistical Accounts are known to be quite unreliable. Efforts by English and Irish Quakers to keep the Scottish Society alive led to visits from several prominent members. Records of the Edinburgh meeting show that thirty-five of forty-six new members who were registered in Edinburgh in the late eighteenth century came from England and eleven of the remainder were from one family of English origin moving from Aberdeen. Analysis of the nineteenth-century figures for Edinburgh shows that most who migrated went either to the North of England or London and fewer (2.5 per cent) moved to the United States, one to Australia and none to Canada. Incidentally, in the same period, 3 per cent of new members in Edinburgh came from the United States or Australia.

Later in the eighteenth century and well into the nineteenth century though, Quakers became involved in social issues. Early opponents of slavery, some were also involved in the political reform movements of the early nineteenth century, while pacifism, relief work after war and famine became characteristic issues. In the Great War, Quaker commitment to pacifism led to the imprisonment of several leaders but also to the gaining of new members. In the Second World War, exemption from military service was granted with many joining 'The Friends' Ambulance Unit' and other relief organizations.

Temperance was not a serious issue for the Quakers: some of them were successful brewers and their attitude was rather the shunning of *excess in eating and drinking*. In more modern times, the Quakers' commitment to humanitarian work in time of war has developed into a wide concern for the plight of homeless people, people with addiction problems and for refugees and immigrants. Their pacifism has led to concerted political opposition to nuclear weapons.

Numbers were fewer than 200 by 1851, with membership largely defined by family ties and exclusion from the Society of those who 'married out'. This rule was changed in 1860, and numbers started to rise with less strict regulations. They also began a process of upward social mobility which led to their being one of the most middle-class of Scottish denominations. By 1965, they had risen to a strength of 459 largely by 'convincement' (their word for conversion) rather than family allegiance and growth. With some twenty-five 'Meetings' in Scotland, most are very small but their membership numbers tend to reflect active members. Many of the 'Meetings' do not have a long history, most are of recent origin and few of them possess their own Meeting House.

Like many other religious groups, the Quakers suffered splits from the nineteenth century onwards; the splits were similar to the ones suffered by many churches between conservative and evangelical and liberal. Most of the Scottish Quaker meetings remained in the 'Liberal' category. Despite some early reservations about Darwin's findings, Quakers tend to be accepting of modern scientific views.

In recent years, their lack of any fixed creed has led to a wide variation of belief in members but despite rejecting the concept of the Trinity of Father, Son and Holy Ghost, which is a basic tenet of every mainstream Christian denomination, they have been widely accepted as Christians by most in a way which Mormons and Jehovah's Witnesses have not.

Swedenborgian Church; Otherwise known as the New Church or the Church of the New Jerusalem

The Church of the New Jerusalem was founded in England in the late eighteenth century in response to the Swedish writer Emmanuel Swedenborg (1688–1772), who had claimed a new revelation from Jesus in dreams. His beliefs put the New Church in the same category as that of the Unitarians. Initially, there was a split between those who wanted to be a separate church and those who held Swedenborgian beliefs within the Church of England. A further split occurred between those who wanted a hierarchy, complete with bishops, and those who wanted a 'congregational' approach. The latter view won out.

Early meetings saw plans to organize Scotland into four provinces but this never was necessary. The church was never large in Scotland and was largely limited to sizable towns, but as early as the first decade of the nineteenth century, it was recorded that there was a group of Swedenborgian miners (probably copper miners) in Perthshire.

Led by a former Methodist, the Glasgow congregation was founded around 1813 and numbered about 25 by 1830. It could achieve congregations of 500 in the Andersonian Hall where it was sometimes given space. The members were described as being 'of the middle rank'. There were also attempts to forge links with some of the small dissenting churches in Scotland, with the Unitarians and also some of the Original Seceders. They presented copies of Swedenborg's writings to the library of the Original Secession Divinity Hall. Later in the century, a church was established and built in Cathedral Street in Glasgow. The congregation was prosperous enough to commission a new building in the west end of the city at the beginning of the twentieth century where it survived till the 1970s when it was bought by the Methodist Church.

Other churches also appeared: Edinburgh from 1807, again with numbers in the low twenties, in Dunfermline, founded by a former Quaker. A group in Alloa was founded and largely funded by a blacksmith called Allan Drysdale, although the early impetus seems to have come from two Londoners who were associated with the copper mines at Airthrey near Stirling and operated a smelting furnace at Alloa.

The Glasgow minister of the time, David Goyder, had a parallel career as a phrenologist in the winter months but used the summer months to work as a missionary throughout Scotland.

The numbers though were never large: the Church of the New Jerusalem reached its peak around 1900. The minister in Glasgow at the time, John Faulkner Potts, edited a huge concordance of Swedenborg's works. He was reputed to be one of the first people in Scotland to own a typewriter, imported from the United States.

Swedenborgian Churches tended to be quite small; other than the Glasgow church, seating capacities in the range of sixty to eighty were commonplace. The Swedenborgian Church had a much more liberal view of baptism than most churches during the nineteenth century, baptizing children of parents with no church allegiance. One unforeseen result was that large numbers of people contacted the Church looking for baptismal certificates as proof of age when Old Age Pensions came on the scene.

Like so many other churches, the Church of the New Jerusalem suffered splits. The disagreement over 'episcopal' hierarchy led, a century later, to a 'General Church of the New Jerusalem' founded in Pennsylvania in 1897. Twelve or so Scots followed this split, giving rise to what must have been one of the smallest denominations in the country. It shared a minister with England, Wales, Belgium and the Netherlands and had services twice a year. Sixty years later, the congregation still existed and numbered five, including one of the original dissidents.

With the selling of the Glasgow Church, the mainstream Church of the New Jerusalem is now reduced to one congregation worshipping in Paisley.

Unitarians

The Unitarians are a small denomination that has had a continuous history in Scotland since the late eighteenth century and still maintains churches in the four major cities of Edinburgh, Glasgow, Dundee and Aberdeen. They are defined by their belief not in the 'Trinity' but in a single divinity, with Jesus being viewed as entirely human. Over the years, it has developed into perhaps the most 'liberal' form of Christianity with no specified creed.

The concept of Unitarianism and its allied doctrine of universal atonement which states that basically everybody will go to heaven in due course, dates back to Reformation times on the Continent, but in Britain it dates to the eighteenth century with many groups coming out of Presbyterianism in the less rigid structures of the northern areas of Ireland and England. One of the most prominent of these was James Purves who belonged to a group which had seceded from the Reformed Presbyterians in 1753. Purves was sent to train in theology in Glasgow and in 1776, he and some associates from the borders founded a Unitarian Church in Edinburgh which still exists, although without a minister between Purves' death in 1795 and 1812. Until 1813, they suffered under the same kind of penal laws as Roman Catholics; King William's Act of Tolerance of 1689 specifically excluded those who denied the doctrine of the Trinity. This meant that they were barred from pleading in Law Courts, receiving legacies and barred from pursuing cases subject to criminal proceedings.

Despite this, the movement grew; Burns refers to an English Unitarian spreading his message in Scotland and in 1792, a congregation was started in Montrose. A year later, a former Church of England curate called Thomas Palmer joined them and went on to found congregations in Dundee, Forfar and Arbroath. Palmer however was closely allied with political radicalism of the time and ended up being transported to Australia for sedition. Purves and Palmer had rather different theologies. Other congregations also appeared and joined in a Scottish Unitarian Association in 1813. This included Glasgow, Greenock, Paisley and Edinburgh groups and, like so many of the early nineteenth-century dissenting bodies, had strong support from the weaving community. Political radicalism persisted in the Unitarian Church, with their minister in Dundee who was quite outspoken in support for the mill-workers during the industrial troubles of the 1880s.

A scatter of ministers came in from other denominations, Church of Scotland, Methodist and Relief Churches all provided men who became prominent. Like many other small churches, public meetings attracted many more than ever actually joined the denomination; and attendances of 700, even 1200 were reported. The resultant condemnation from mainstream ministers advertised the movement and drew others curious to know what it was about. A refusal by Tain Public Library to accept a gift of Unitarian books in 1894 led to lectures on the subject being given in Tain, Invergordon and Dingwall.

Despite some success, Unitarianism never thrived in Scotland. It appeared early in a time of religious turmoil but never seized the popular imagination. At its peak there were perhaps twenty-two churches, and in Glasgow the congregation was large and prosperous enough to commission a new classically styled church to seat 550 people in the mid-1850s, but many congregations were dependent on a very small number of leaders and sometimes the loss of one leader was enough to signal the end of the congregation. It also was heavily reliant on preachers coming from England. Other than those coming in from other denominations, very few ministers were Scottish and the training ground for the ministers was in Manchester. The Church's aversion to creeds and dogmatic statements of belief made it attractive at one point in history, but isolated it from the mainstream churches, and while there are some 200 Unitarian churches in England, only four were surviving in Scotland by the outbreak of the Second World War although all four have continued to the present day.

There is an active Unitarian History Society and further information can be found on its website: http://www.unitarianhistory.org.uk/hsresearch4.html.

Christadelphians

The Christadelphians (Greek for 'Brothers in Christ') were an offshoot of the Church of Christ which came to Britain in the 1850s. Rev. John Thomas arrived in Leith from the United States and had made several converts among the membership of the Church of Christ before they realized that he had been disowned by the parent body. Thereupon, he founded a congregation or 'Ecclesia' in March 1853 with twenty-four members ranging from eighteen to thirty-five years of age. This number had risen to 69 by 1860. It was originally called the 'Edinburgh Church of Baptised Believers of the Gospel of the Kingdom of God'. The name 'Christadelphian' came a decade later when adherence to a pacifist policy in the American Civil War led them to decide on a name that members could be identified with in order for their beliefs to be accepted.

Soon other ecclesiae were established elsewhere in Scotland, including Glasgow, Dundee, Inverkeithing, Kilmarnock and Aberdeen. Like so many Scottish churches, it had its first split within a very few years. The minority group remained independent and survived in Dundee, the two strands being reunited in the mid-twentieth century. There was a general 'aggregate meeting' held every year which gathered members from all the Scottish congregations. A further split occurred in 1885 giving rise to the 'Conditional Immortality Mission' which reunited with the parent body in 1956.

Like many of the other small churches, the Christadelphians publicized their views by open air meetings, for example by holding rallies in the The Meadows in Edinburgh in the 1890s, and by series of public lectures. This practice continues.

The Christadelphians do not form part of the Trinitarian mainstream of Christianity which includes Protestantism, Catholicism and Eastern Orthodoxy, but share many practices including 'breaking of bread, preaching and hymn singing'. Like the older churches, they had debated about the use of instrumental music, introducing an American organ for the Bible Class in the 1880s but not using it for worship until 1904. Their beliefs are based entirely on the Bible and originally on John Thomas's interpretation of it, but there is no central authoritative organization and as a result various splinter groups also still exist.

Their conscientious objections to warfare remain a consistent feature of their belief system and although some were exempted from military service in the two world wars, others were imprisoned for their beliefs. This view also extends to refusal to join the police or to vote in political elections.

The Church of Christ of the Latter-day Saints (Mormons)

Mormonism, or 'The Church of Jesus Christ of the Latter-day Saints', was founded in the United States in 1830 and quickly spread to Canada where two expatriate Scots were converted. In 1839, the church decided that the time had come to spread its message to Europe and those two, Alexander Wright and Samuel Mulliner, came back to their native land as missionaries. In some ways Mormonism was typical of a whole group of churches founded at around that time. It was millenniarist; looking forward to an imminent Second Coming of Christ, it claimed to be taking the church back to its primitive church origins; it believed in believers' baptism and in a lay eldership with no formal theological training. All these factors made it a prime candidate for success in a Scotland that was in both a political and a religious ferment and echoed the early days of the Brethren, Baptist and Primitive Methodist movements. Where it departed from the more mainstream varieties of Christianity was in its belief in the newly discovered Book of Mormon as Scripture, its practice of polygamy (until 1890) and in its practice of retrospectively baptizing and marrying people long dead. A further major factor which made it different from other churches in Britain, if not in the rest of Europe, was in its invitation to believers to migrate to the United States where ultimately the vast majority settled in what became the State of Utah. The Church's reverence for the Book of Mormon as Scripture is the fundamental reason that few Christian churches would consider it to be anything other than a cult. This was as true in the nineteenth century as it is today.

The missionaries who came to Scotland found many converts and from the mid-1840s onwards, there was a steady flow of emigrants. About 10,000 were converted in the course of the nineteenth century and about half of them left for the United States. At the same time churches were founded in Scotland. From twenty-one members and no organized branches in 1840, the numbers rose to 3291 members in 57 branches in 1851 and about 70 by 1880. This was an entirely lowland movement, with a particular strength in weaving and mining communities. The first branch was founded in Paisley, and most of the branches were throughout the counties of Lanark, Renfrew and Ayr and many more in the vicinity of Stirling Fife and Clackmannan. This was very much the area covered by Scotland's coalfields. Mormon historians themselves acknowledge that reaction to economic pressures made the promise of land across the Atlantic a very attractive proposition.

While it is true that the strength of the Mormon Church was in the industrialized lowlands, that is not to deny their efforts made to convert those in the Highlands. Peter McIntyre spent much of 1845 in Argyll and the Inner Isles preaching to large groups in Gaelic but none were baptized.

The year of 1850 was the high point of Mormonism in Scotland with 800 baptisms of new believers; by the end of the decade though, the number was little over 100. In the same period, membership more than halved. This was due to two factors; one was emigration. A church that was losing half its members to emigration faced a severe challenge in remaining vibrant and viable. To add to that though, the Mormons went through a phase of excommunicating everybody who showed any sign of stepping outside the official line. Leaving aside those who left the country, in the years between 1853 and 1856, more members were excommunicated than joined. One entire branch was put out because one of the leading elders was too infected with Chartist views; 'fire-and-faggot principles'. Partly this reflects a very high standard of conduct expected of the members but there was also a feeling that it represented a convenient way of seeing off challenges to leadership.

So who were these early Mormons? As noted, they were lowlanders and predominantly of the working class so far as the Scots were concerned. Of those who emigrated, over 40 per cent came from mining communities, 11 per cent from the textile industry and 7 per cent from the metal-working industries. Reports of Mormon meetings in the press also concentrate on the low social origins of the people involved.

One factor which sets them apart from some of the other groups, targeting the industrial areas though, is that they were achieving their earliest converts not from the unchurched among the industrial masses but from those who had been brought up in one of the Presbyterian churches and were searching, perhaps in a new community, for a church which suited them. There is some evidence among contemporary anti-Mormon writers that the more unconventional aspects of their belief were played down in favour of a straightforward Bible-based evangelicalism. It was referred to by one writer as 'the sincere milk of the Word' which would only be followed by the 'Strong meat' of the Book of Mormon when the convert was ready.

As with many of the new churches, there was considerable bias against the Mormons, exacerbated by their less than orthodox practices. There are reports of stone-throwing, burnings of effigies and the break-up of meetings in various places. Press reports are largely antagonistic, and there were attempts to prevent people being influenced.

The movement waned from about 1870 onwards; possibly this was influenced by the growth of a new spirit of evangelicalism in the mainstream churches. Baptisms dropped to a sixth of their previous number. Emigration took more than were baptized in the 1870s but by the 1890s, only about a third of the converts were leaving for the New World. By 1890, most of the churches had gone and there were only about 200 members left in Scotland. Later efforts in missionary work brought the numbers back up to around the 3000 mark by the 1960s.

Mormonism is particularly rich in records for the family historian; its partnership with the Scottish Record Office in microfilming and indexing church records has probably brought it to the attention of more people than its theology ever did. Its foundation and stocking of family history centres makes it an extremely valuable resource. Their own records are also voluminous, and there is a strong tradition of historical research.

Spiritualist churches

Spiritualist churches appeared in Scotland from the late nineteenth century. Spiritualism as a belief system largely takes its origins from mid-nineteenth-century Unites States, but looks back to sources prior to that, such as Emmanuel Swedenborg in Sweden and the major impetus for the Catholic Apostolic Church. The Spiritualists' National Union (SNU) is the central body for many churches that follow a spiritualist doctrine, although many are independent.

Spiritualism appeared in Scotland by the 1860s, with a 'Glasgow Association' having a variety of names, finally becoming the 'The Glasgow Association of Spiritualists' in 1871. However, the time when it started describing itself as a 'church' is unclear; other spiritualist bodies did not choose to do so.

They had a hymnbook, *The Spiritual Lyre*', and also practised healing. It appears to have been restricted to men until 1872. By the 1880s, there were approximately 100 members. It met in various premises until it bought the St Vincent Street Church designed by Alexander 'Greek' Thomson, one of the architectural gems of Glasgow. This passed from their hands in 1970.

The Glasgow Association was just one of several Scottish Churches. The movement had a period of considerable growth during the 1920s, largely as a reaction to the loss of so many lives in the Great War and the wish of so many people to make contact with the dead. This growth however was much more marked in England than in Scotland where there were only five associations compared with nearly 400 south of the border.

11

Towards a Geography of the Scottish Churches

The chapter looks at a number of issues, including the different ways in which the churches developed in the Highlands compared to the rest of the country, the geographical distribution of the different denominations and the different styles of church building that have evolved.

Despite being a small country with a very strong national identity, Scotland has its own sub-nationalities. The history of the Highlands and Western Isles has often followed its own path within the history of Scotland as a whole, while natives of Orkney and Shetland may well look on Scotland as a separate country to which they have some vague, undefined relation. Needless to say, other areas of Scotland have always maintained their own cultural independence; in the south, border communities have fierce local identities with their own border history too, but the northern parts of Scotland have identities that permeate their culture. As a result, the religion of their people has its own history separate though frequently parallel to that of the rest of Scotland (see Figures 7–11).

In 1521, a historian called John Major described the Gaelic-speaking inhabitants of Scotland as the 'Wild Scots', a barbarous people needing to be subdued. Aberdeen University was itself set up in 1494 to be make education more accessible to people of the north and shortly before the Reformation, the Bishop of Caithness described his Palace in Dornoch as being situated 'among the wild and uncivilized Scots and in a wintry region'. The Highlands, in short, was an area to be subdued and controlled and this was an attitude shared by pre-Reformation Catholics and post-Reformation Protestants alike. Were the Highlands in fact Christian at all before the Reformation? It is fair to say that Christianity permeated the lives of the highlanders as much, or as little, as anywhere else and as in other areas, pre-Christian traditions and rituals were absorbed into the Christian story. There is some Gaelic Christian writing surviving, though far more survives in Latin. Many monuments, largely chapels and standing stones, still bear witness to the strength of Christianity in Scotland prior to the twelfth century. Columba, whose sixth-century mission Christianized far more of Scotland than his predecessor Ninian's had two hundred years earlier, came to the western islands of Scotland and his followers, including the monks known as Culdees, spread out from there. Place names show the extent of their reach and the Culdees are commemorated in the town of Kirkcaldy, literally the 'Church of the Culdees'. As it was originally a form of Christianity owing little to the influence of Rome, one result of this flourishing of early Celtic Christianity was the tendency for Protestant historians to hold it up as a proof that Roman Catholicism was essentially alien to Scotland and that Celtic Christianity legitimized Scottish Protestantism. By the Middle Ages, however, any independence Celtic Christianity may have had vanished, partly as a result of Queen Margaret's efforts to make her husband's kingdom part of the 'civilized' world in the eleventh century.

Today the line differentiating the Highlands from the rest of Scotland starts southwest of Glasgow with Kintyre and Arran belonging in the Highlands. On the other hand, much of the northeast is lowland and shares little in common culturally with the Highlands. Roughly speaking though, the Highlands cover about half of mainland Scotland. The Gaelic language may have dominated the mediaeval Highlands and Islands but since the Middle Ages the language has gradually receded to its present restricted area and has long since ceased to be anyone's only language. Nonetheless, Gaelic (and lowland attitudes to Gaelic) have been crucial to the way church life has developed since the Reformation.

From the start, the early spread of the Reformation in the north was hindered by a lack of Gaelic-speaking reformers and a disinclination on the part of non-Gaelic speakers to go there. Aside from the language problem, the presence of the pre-Reformation Catholic Church was very dilute, parishes could be huge with no easy or safe means of communication from one end to another and the people were poor and largely uneducated by lowland standards or illiterate. On the other hand there was a strong oral tradition of learning.

The fledgling Protestant church was chronically short of ministers even in the areas where it had support; putting such a rare commodity into the Highlands was well down the priorities in the first instance. Big as the pre-Reformation highland and island parishes were, they were to get bigger. The Isle of Lewis with an area of 683 square miles was reduced from four parishes to one at the Reformation. Further down the island chain, Protestant ministers did not appear on South Uist until 1633.

The lack of literacy amongst the people of the Highlands and Islands can very easily be put down to one simple fact; there was next to nothing to read. Gaelic was an essentially oral language at that point. The invention of printing in the 1450s only spread to Scots Gaelic after the Reformation, when John Carswell's translation of *The Book of Common Order*, Knox's work on liturgy, was published in 1567. Roman Catholic priests, of course, had no need for Gaelic liturgy, worshipping as they did in Latin, but with the Protestants pledged to preach and teach in the vernacular, the failure to do so led to a significant failure to win the hearts and minds of the people. Bits and pieces of religious writing gradually appeared in Gaelic over the next few decades. Calvin's writing began to be printed in Gaelic in 1631, the first fifty Psalms appeared in 1659, the first part of Scripture to be translated. In Ireland, the situation was a little better; an Irish New Testament was started in 1574 and printed in 1602, followed in 1620 by the Old Testament. A Scottish edition of these appeared in 1690, but the language used was classical Irish and remote from the language of the Scottish people. In fact there had been two traditions of writing Gaelic developed during the middle ages; a 'high' classical form and a more down-to-earth style. The classical style had status; it linked back to ancient bardic poetry, it appealed to such educated men as there were in the Highlands and to the chiefs who had employed the bards, but it was remote from the ordinary people. Nevertheless it became the language of the Gaelic-speaking church.

Much of the lowland Reformation had been spurred in the early 1500s by the publication of religious material from the reformers, from sermons and high piety to scurrilous broadsides lambasting the shortcomings of the Catholic Church. Material like the latter had fired the crowds in the lowlands and created a group identity, much like modern football songs; in the Highlands it did not exist and there was no group impetus to attack the existing set-up or to look for an alternative. The Gaelic-speaking highlanders actually would have looked on any such material coming from the lowlands as alien and suspect. On top of this, the main thrust of the Scottish Reformation was to take all matters religious from the Bible alone and not from the traditions built up over the previous 1500 years; so, if there was no Gaelic Bible and if the people could not read the Bible in English, they could not be enthusiastic about the new regime. As a result, with most of the priests driven out and only a few missionaries trying to regain the West Highlands for the papacy, the area was largely unchurched, and for many historians, basically pagan. This situation lasted through the seventeenth century. Gradually, though slowly, pulpits were filled, but the lack of Gaelic-speaking ministers remained a serious problem for centuries.

There were two possible, mutually rather contradictory, solutions: one was to train and encourage Gaelic-speaking ministers and the other was to drive out Gaelic and make everyone speak English. Both these solutions were tried from the beginning of the eighteenth century. Knox's ideal put a school in every parish. While this suited small lowland parishes in Central Scotland, it did not fit well with a parish spread over 683 square miles with the centre of population in one corner. In a parish of that size, a single parochial school was clearly inadequate. There is no doubt that schools in the Highlands were few in number before 1700; the situation in the eighteenth century, though, was less clear.

In 1696, an act of the General Assembly stated that the heritors in each parish were responsible for a house, a school and the salary for a schoolmaster. The heritors and the minister were jointly responsible for appointing the master, while the presbytery joined with the minister in supervising him. Many schoolmasters would be probationer ministers waiting to be called to their first charge. The salary was laid down as being between 100 and 200 merks (£66–£132 Scots =£5.50–£11 sterling).

Thirteen years later, the Act was backed up by the granting a charter to 'The Society in Scotland for Propagating Christian Knowledge' (SSPCK) with the aim of establishing schools, largely in the Highlands, to promote Protestantism and counter the efforts of Catholic missionaries. The Society's policy has been described as 'civilisation through anglicisation', for at first, the Gaelic language was banned in the schools. All teaching had to be in English, and many of the teachers had limited knowledge of Gaelic. That said, many later Gaelic scholars had been SSPCK teachers in their youth. The teachers were selected and trained in Edinburgh and had to be able to teach reading, writing, arithmetic and scripture; they were also expected to conduct worship in distant parts of their parish. As these schools were meant to supplement the parish schools, not replace them, an SSPCK school could not be erected if there was no parochial school elsewhere in the parish. This was an attempt to prevent the heritors from neglecting their duty in the expectation that the SSPCK would fill the gap.

The intention to erode the position of Gaelic can be seen in the letters of the Society to their employees, taking them to task for teaching in Gaelic. Even a letter from the minister of Balquhidder in Perthshire explaining that the parishioners were keen to be taught to read the Psalms in Gaelic was rebuffed. Gradually, the SSPCK's attitude changed, although it was over a century before it accepted Gaelic education. In 1825, it agreed that Gaelic could be the first medium for teaching and reading and that English reading and writing would follow competence in Gaelic. In the meantime, it also supported vocational schooling from the 1730s, including the teaching of spinning and helped to erect a Gaelic chapel in Edinburgh in 1769.

Gradually, through the eighteenth century, the provision of schools in the Highlands became more widespread and literacy increased. Missionaries and catechists helped to fill the gaps in the provision of parish churches. Catechists were employed to give basic religious knowledge, largely teaching set answers to the set questions in the Larger and Shorter Catechisms. This religious 'knowledge' was used as a test by ministers to establish whether people were worthy of receiving Communion. How much actual knowledge of the fundamentals of Christianity it gave is open to debate. Missionaries and catechists were also funded by the crown; the Royal Bounty Fund was set up from 1725 onwards and was used to pay itinerant preachers and catechists. They had a particular duty to parishes where the area was too great for the parish minister to function effectively or where there was a significant nucleus of Roman Catholics. This was seen as a useful training ground for divinity students during their breaks in training, but the catechists might also be local men selected by local kirk sessions.

Hand in hand with these efforts to 'civilize' the Highlands in the eighteenth century came an increase in attention to Christianity and an evangelical revival. Perhaps it was more a spiritual wakening than a re-awakening, although the covenanting movement had brought an evangelical flavour to the eastern Highlands. There was a tradition of laymen-led worship in public 'fellowship meetings' held in Easter Ross from mid-century despite various attempts to ban them by synod and presbytery. Perhaps the local presbytery was right to be concerned since one such meeting was apparently seriously contemplating the possibility of human sacrifice in 1740! Despite this, the meetings became much more prevalent, taking on particular importance as part of the 'Communion Season', when they became part of the series of services leading up to the celebration of the Sacrament on Sunday. As it developed, the Fellowship Meeting took on a regular pattern involving prayer, praise and the reading of the Bible. This would be followed by a question and answer session where the leading men would discuss a given text, sometimes with the minister, sometimes without him. The leadership that this pattern developed in the church gave rise to a particular group known as 'the Men' who have an almost legendary status in Highland Christianity.

It is tempting to relate 'the Men' back to some wandering bardic predecessors honoured in the Highland psyche. This is unlikely, but during these meetings they developed the skills to expound on Scripture and to pray publicly; those attending understood the depth of their knowledge and piety. Part of their individuality was a particular style of declaiming, full of mysticism and allegory backed up by a prodigious memory and knowledge of the Bible. Their style of prayers varied, being either long or short. One such prayer meeting held in Inverness in 1797 was described by a visitor: it 'began at nine at night and William Fraser prayed for more than hour. But such a prayer! Another hour of it would have been no burden to either a Christian or a poet'. But equally, in Skye the prayers of 'the Men' were said to be 'short, earnest and void of repetitions. If anyone transgressed the rules, he was rebuked'.

The 'Men' saw themselves as being set apart, a brotherhood with a role different from their ministers. They lived austerely, keeping their occupation, be it crofter or weaver or whatever. They dressed in an old-fashioned way, distinguished by a long blue cloak and a spotted handkerchief about their heads, with hair longer than the norm. This striking and individual look was also sometimes accompanied by a belief in prophetic powers which added to their mystique.

On the whole, they were within the Established Church, but they did see their role as pointing out and trying to remedy the inadequacies of 'moderate' ministers or indeed any minister who did not meet their standards. Occasionally, they did lead congregations into secession and some small independent churches were set up, but they were more likely to ignore a local minister of whom they disapproved and tramp many miles to find a minister more to their taste. These independent churches left few if any records; so, little is known of how they functioned. 'The Men' were seen as stern and forbidding and their shadow stills falls on Highland Christianity, not least because it was under their influence that huge numbers of ordinary Christians felt unable to take Communion from feelings of unworthiness.

Following the Disruption, the huge majority of people moved to the Free Church, but this in turn was felt to be slipping in its standards; therefore, first the Free Presbyterian Church and then that part of the Free Church which did not follow the majority into union in 1900 developed a largely Highland identity. Other churches also tried to take their own brand of mission to the Highlands and Islands. These largely failed, although there is a Highland Baptist community and there are various mission halls sprinkled through the land. There was also a continuing Episcopal tradition which persisted locally. One particular area of strength was among the slate workers of Ballachulish: when they migrated to Aberfoyle in the mid-nineteenth century, a church had to be built for them there.

Orkney and Shetland have a completely different heritage from their southern neighbours, a Norse heritage rather than a Gaelic one, although Norse culture was widespread through all of Scotland and much of England for centuries and is also strong in traditionally Gaelic areas of Caithness and Sutherland.

At the time of the Reformation, the Church in Shetland was under the control of Adam Bothwell, who had become Bishop of Orkney the year before and was a supporter of the new regime. Several of the existing priests, perhaps proportionally more than in mainland Scotland, were considered suitable to serve the new Church either as ministers or readers, and he brought in others. Where the previous priest was not converted to Protestantism, he was allowed to hold on to two-thirds of his income for his life time and the new minister or reader had to make do with the other third. By 1567, Shetland was supplied with two ministers and nine readers for its eleven parishes, with a further two ministers being in place by 1574. Generally speaking, the concept of having a minister for every parish in Scotland was not a reality before 1600; owing to a serious lack of resources to pay them, particularly when the old vicars were still drawing their share of the benefices. Stipends, and ministers still draw stipends not salaries to this day, were fixed in produce in the early days, grain, wool, fish, butter were all part of what the minister might be due, although sometimes agents converted this into hard cash for him. The Shetland ministers had an income they could live on, but being paid less than half of a ministerial stipend, readers would have had to eke out their living with other sources of income.

However, not all ministers who were appointed fulfilled their duties regularly. There is some evidence of absentee ministers living more comfortably in the south while enjoying their stipends, and there is also evidence that inappropriate people were presented to livings, for, the ideal of congregations calling their minister was far from universal in the early days and livings could still be used as rewards for other services.

So if readers were not given enough to live on, what did they do? Several opened schools. The ideal of having a school in every parish, under the control of the kirk session was a dream rather than a reality in Shetland as elsewhere. Indeed, the first 'official' parochial school did not appear until 1765. In 1700, the state of the people of Shetland was poor; 'In the matter of God and Religion the body of the people are said to be very ignorant' wrote one visitor commenting also on the lack of schools, but the general problem was simply the poverty of the islands, with no resources either to keep up buildings or to pay teachers or ministers. By 1830, at least every parish had a school, but it had taken a long, long time. This meant that the lay-leadership within the local church was largely unread and uneducated and the church stagnated. The isolation of Shetland too was a factor. It is said that some ministers who were commissioned to attend the General Assembly effectively took up to nine months over it, going south in August or September and not returning till the following June. While this was so, the diary of John Mill, minister of Dunrossness from 1742 until 1805 tells of some of his journeys south to the Assembly taking rather less time. Perhaps six days in each direction was about the minimum required, but in 1762 he combined his visit south with preaching for ten successive Sundays in the northeast of Scotland before heading for Edinburgh, where he also took the opportunity to do more preaching and meet the renowned English missionary George Whitefield. Any business in Edinburgh requiring personal attention had to be done on these infrequent trips.

So, if the ministers felt isolated how did this impact on their parishioners? Shetland ministers have been accused of being uninterested in their parishioners, but Mill shows that this was not the case. He criticized their ignorance, their immorality and their lack of interest in matters spiritual, but then which minister did not? In his diary, he recorded with joy the occasional breakthroughs with individuals and he showed considerable loyalty to his parishioners despite their perceived faults. On the other hand, he was in constant conflict with his heritors, who seem to have been most interested in taking over parts of his glebe, and with his neighbouring ministers whom he clearly did not like very much. Mill was already very elderly when the most significant event of his long ministry occurred: the arrival on Shetland of James Haldane and William Innes, self-appointed evangelists who left the Established Church and the life of a landed laird for a life of itinerant preaching and mission work throughout Scotland. The Haldanes, for his older brother Robert who was doing similar work elsewhere in Scotland, were both a cause and a sign of a revival in evangelism that was happening independently of the Established Church or its Presbyterian offshoots, the Secession and Relief Churches. What the Haldanes and their associates stood for was a return to personal religion untrammelled by structures and institutions. In due course, this led to independent 'Congregational' churches and, after a few years, evolved further to the Baptist movement. In Shetland, despite their growing independence from the Established Church, Mill met them with enthusiasm and gave them every opportunity to preach to his parishioners. In this, though, he was very much in the minority of Presbyterian ministers, most of whom mainly viewed it as a dangerous invasion of their territory.

Haldane and Innes travelled widely in Shetland and Orkney, often at risk to their lives, in small boats, and their message was well received. The stagnation which had characterized religious life in eighteenth-century Shetland was ripe to be brought to an end by a different approach and this is what Haldane and Innes triggered. The next twenty-five years brought a flourish of Independent, Baptist and Methodist Chapels throughout the islands. Further impetus came from the presence of Independents in the local garrison, in a curious echo of what had happened when Cromwell's troops occupied the islands, and from a local disagreement within the parish church in Lerwick. The initial driving force of the Baptist community, Sinclair Thomson had been precentor in the Parish Church before moving to Independency and hence to Baptist beliefs. The arrival of Methodism also had a military connection in Shetland, with the founding figure of John Nicolson, a native Shetlander, becoming a Methodist during and as a result of service in the Royal Artillery. He started a mission in the islands before persuading the national conference of the denomination to send two young ministers to develop the work.

In this first quarter of the nineteenth century, the whole religious face of the islands changed. The Established Church, whether in direct response to the 'threat' of the new churches or a new realization of the shortcomings of their own provision, was building new churches and repairing old ones, adding to the number of ministers in the process.

A few years later, the dissenting Presbyterian churches, in the shape of the United Secession, made their first belated appearance shortly before the Disruption added the Free Church to the mix. It has to be said however that the Disruption did not have the impact in Shetland that it had further south, only in Unst was there a majority who left, and while other Free Churches were formed, they were always minority groups.

The migrant workers who flooded Shetland in the summer, following the fishing, led to a new need for Roman Catholic services, provided from 1860 onwards, and periodic attention from Dutch Calvinists and Lutherans from the Scandinavian countries to look after their countrymen. Meanwhile, local fishermen mixing with those of the northeast of Scotland brought a wish for Brethren meeting houses which also sprang up in many places on the islands.

By 1881, there were eighteen Church of Scotland congregations on the islands with slightly over 7000 members, while the Free Church had ten congregations with about 2300 members and the United Presbyterians had four congregations with a total of 330 members. Of the smaller groups, the Baptists had three small congregations, the Congregationalists five, Episcopalians two, Roman Catholics one and the Methodists had disappeared entirely. It is noteworthy that the congregational giving among the United Presbyterians in Lerwick was among the highest in Scotland.

Meanwhile, further south in Orkney, much the same pressures were in evidence. Churches were allowed to fall into ruin as late as the late eighteenth century and some were unusable. One periodical of 1797 claimed that 'many of our poorer Orcadians hear about as little of our Christ in his Heaven as the inhabitants of Japan'. From that time onwards, Secession church missions began to make considerable headway on the islands with congregations founded from the 1790s and with a steady growth through the islands in the next fifty years. As a result, the Free Church never made much headway; the Secession churches had already formed a strong alternative to the Established Church, so much so that the United Presbyterian Church became the biggest of the churches in the mid-nineteenth century.

Like Shetland, Orkney was greatly influenced by a visit from James Haldane. He toured the islands holding meetings wherever he could and crowds followed him and were converted. As a result, there were several Independent chapels set up in Orkney but not as widely as in Shetland.

While these specific developments in the more remote parts of Scotland had a specific flavour, the geography of Scotland shows many variations in the penetration of the various forms of Christianity.

Patterns do arise (see Figure 11, Smaller churches in 1891, see p 223). The targeting of newly industrial areas by firstly Secession Churches and then by missions of Independent churches, Brethren, Church of the Nazarene and so on gave a situation where some towns had a multiplicity of churches, which then re-multiplied as some of them split. Coastal communities were substantially influenced by individuals hearing a preacher somewhere else along the coast and promoting his cause at home, leading again to a multiplying of small groups. From the earliest days, weaving communities were known for religious radicalism and many a new church received its first strength from the weavers whether in Paisley, Dundee or in any of the smaller textile centres. Again after industrialization of the industry there was a movement of weavers to mill communities and a resulting congregation might be formed which had little linkage to the existing community. Just as the Highland Free Church grew differently from the lowland Free Church though, the urban United Presbyterian Church was different from its rural counterpart. Always dependent on significant lay support, the supporters in the country might well have a different philosophy from the wealthy manufacturers who were the mainstay in the cities. There has been considerable research on urban congregations in general looking at the way different types of people were involved with the church, but there is much less available on rural churches.

The differences between churches were not just social or theological, but architectural.

Apart from the parts of mediaeval churches that continued into Protestant use, stripped of all decoration and often reduced in size, new churches had to be built. Likewise as new denominations arose, they needed new church buildings.

Initially these were very plain and austere. The earliest post-Reformation church, in Burntisland, Fife has the pulpit central and visible to all. Many others followed the pattern of having the pulpit in the middle of the long wall of a rectangle but while new churches were gradually added in the seventeenth century, they remained very plain with clear windows and little or no decoration. By the end of the century many were seriously dilapidated as the religious strife of the times had made it difficult to tie heritors into repairing churches they did not necessarily support.

There was a huge number of churches erected from 1800 on; sometimes because suddenly the old churches were seen as unfit for purpose, sometimes because town councils saw burgh churches as a statement of their town's status; sometimes because these were new churches in new communities or sometimes because the Established Church could not be seen to be inferior to a newly erected Secession or Relief church. The various Secession churches continued to build their plain barns, and accounts exist of how the people worked together to erect their own church building using their own resources and skills.

During the nineteenth century though, Scottish churches began to change; a new generation of buildings began to appear. Some of these were built to a standard design by the engineer Thomas Telford who was commissioned in 1823 to erect a series of about forty 'parliamentary' churches, built with government money in the Highlands and Islands to serve areas too remote from their parish church. Many of these are still in use and have a very characteristic look. Elsewhere in Scotland builders began to erect the kind of pseudo-gothic designs that English architects were producing, with increasing conformity to mediaeval design. Architects like James Gillespie Graham designed many of churches of varying degrees of size and elaboration for Church of Scotland, Episcopalians and Roman Catholics. The young Free Church, once it was able to afford permanent buildings, had a series of standard designs which were very widely used. Neo-gothic Scottish Presbyterian churches went in for galleries and lofts which would have had no place in a gothic-revival church in England and perhaps some Scottish Churches owe more to theatres than to previous churches in their design. But if neo-gothic became the standard design for both Church of Scotland and Free Church, the United Presbyterian Church sometimes took a different line and followed the classical revival with pillars and porticos at the entrance as if to stress their independence of thought, their openness to the enlightenment and their wealth. This was to culminate in the handful of churches designed by Alexander 'Greek' Thomson, one of Scotland's greatest architects. Later development in the Church of Scotland and in some other churches also showed influence from the Arts and Crafts movement and Art Nouveau, with a handful of churches and church furnishings designed by Charles Rennie McIntosh. By the end of the nineteenth century the designs were also changing to accommodate new ideas in how church services should be developed and asymmetric churches with a single side aisle and stumpy towers began to be found. At the other end of the architectural spectrum, poor congregations of many denominations have found themselves worshipping in corrugated iron churches and halls built for next-to-nothing and yet surviving for several generations and still surviving; the floating church built by the Free Church for Loch Sunart, essentially a corrugated iron barn on a barge, does however occupy a unique place for its originality. Sadly it did not survive.

Finally, Scottish churches have had an influence far beyond their numeric strength throughout the world. England's flirtation with Presbyterianism in the early seventeenth century was brief, but English Presbyterian churches survived and many formed Presbyteries of one or other of the Scottish churches until the creation of the Presbyterian Church of England in 1876. Church of Scotland churches in England remained out of that union and 'England' is still one of the forty-nine Presbyteries of the National Church. Meanwhile the 'Scotch Baptist' movement of the early nineteenth century took root in both Lancashire and

Wales and still has congregations in Wales long after they were absorbed into the mainstream Baptist movement in Scotland.

The exile of Scots on religious grounds had its effects too; for the Roman Catholics there were communities in exile in France in particular and the French armies profited from the number of Scots who joined and sometimes led them after the failure of the Jacobite risings. Other exiles from Protestant camp found their way at an earlier period to Poland and Russia and their armies. As well as exiles, Scottish traders formed communities in northern Europe and some of these founded and preserved Scottish churches locally; references to support for them also occur regularly in Scottish Church records. Again some of these churches still exist, and the records of the Scots Kirk in Rotterdam for example are very substantial.

Scots did not just migrate to Europe though, and the diaspora of Scots in the New World shows churches of Scottish origin through Australia, New Zealand and North America still preserving their Scottish roots. The eighteenth century saw both Covenanters and Episcopalians make a new life in the American colonies. In due course the American Episcopalians received their ordination through a bishop consecrated by Scottish bishops after the American Revolution. The Covenanters and other Presbyterian groups took their own divisions with them, but in due course developed their own history of unions and splits which make the Scottish situation almost seem simple.

Mission activity took Scottish Church influence throughout the world and each of the churches tended to have its own sphere. Malawi is generally cited as the most 'Scottish' of ex-colonial countries as a result of the work of Church of Scotland and Free Church missions there, which despite the frictions at home, worked co-operatively and largely harmoniously. The Reformed Presbyterians took their mission to the New Hebrides, now Vanuatu, where one-third of the population is still Presbyterian, the Free Church took theirs to Peru, among other places; even South America had its Scottish religious heritage.

12

The Twentieth Century

In the years before the Great War, the last years of what some historians call the 'long 19th century', political debate began to impact on the churches. As well as the unresolved question of the churches' stance in labour disputes, the question of votes for women was beginning to take on importance and urgency in people's minds.

There was a considerable campaign to give the right to vote to women and many people within the Scottish churches were fully in favour of this. In fact, various branches of Presbyterianism had already sorted out the issue as much as a century and half previously. Despite their reputation as dyed-in-the-wool religious zealots, the Burgher branch of the Secession church allowed women to vote in the election of new ministers and despite some misgivings, this was enshrined in the agreement when they united with the majority of the Anti-burghers in 1820. Other churches were lagging behind, but the question was at least being considered by the Free Church in its early years, if not being acted upon. The Reformed Presbyterians were not concerned with parliamentary elections but within their own sphere they did enact in the eighteenth century that a congregation entirely made up of women had the right to vote for a minister. However, a congregational election for a minister in the 1860s was overturned on the grounds that women had voted, thus nullifying the result. As all Presbyterian Church courts were made up entirely of male elders and ministers, there was a complete absence of women in church government, just as there was in every major Christian denomination. In politics, however, many in the churches were fully in favour of women's suffrage. In 1895, the Principal of the Free Church College in Glasgow described the refusal give to women the right to vote as 'a survival of theoretical paganism, tending to perpetuate much of the practical paganism that lingers in legislation and social life'. Many ministers were to be seen on platforms associated with the campaign prior to the war. A Scottish Churches League for Woman Suffrage was formed in 1912, with its first meeting presided over by a Free Church minister. Its first president, Lady Frances Balfour, was a strong supporter of the Church of Scotland and it was said that she got as much enjoyment from attending the General Assembly as other women got from going to the theatre. Nor was it just the 'respectable' party in the suffrage movement that received church support; the platform party at a meeting addressed by Emmeline Pankhurst while out on bail and awaiting trial for incitement to violence contained at least ten clergy from a variety of Scottish denominations duly accompanied by their wives. It has to be said though that there was some backlash in the correspondence pages of the press. One minister responded by describing the movement as 'the greatest question of the day and the first practical attempt in this country to realise the Kingdom of God on earth'.

Nonetheless, such support did not prevent disruption of church meetings by militant suffragettes, including a demonstration during the United Free Church General Assembly in 1913. Each presbytery was asked to support the campaign in the winter of 1913–1914 and the refusal of some to entertain this on the grounds of the violent behaviour of some suffragettes led to further disruption. There was even the burning down of the mediaeval church at Whitekirk in East Lothian possibly as a response to the force feeding of suffragette prisoners in Scotland.

In general, although individual ministers in most of the major denominations were in favour of women's suffrage, the institutions, presbyteries in particular, hesitated to take sides and hid behind a disinclination to be involved in politics. The views of St Paul about the separate roles of men and women were still widely quoted by those opposing votes for women, as they were to be in later debates about ordaining women as ministers, priests or elders.

Ironically, for the supporters of women's suffrage it was the difference between men and women that made it important to instil the 'greater purity and spirituality' of women into the politics of the day to transform society, 'espousing the cause of the poor against the rich, the weak against the strong, the oppressed against the oppressor'. This view of the role of women then becomes remarkably similar to the social gospel of Christianity which was gaining ground at the same time.

In the event, the Great War settled the argument; hostilities against Germany immediately led to the suspension of radical action and the end of the War was followed by the extension of the franchise to women over the age of thirty.

Meanwhile, other politics of the time made their impact on the life of the churches. In the early years of the twentieth century, the biggest churches, the United Free Church and the Church of Scotland turned largely away from straightforward evangelism and instead turned to the social Gospel of reaching people through helping the most vulnerable in society, even giving cash-aid to unemployed people in the depression of 1908. This change of direction took the sting out of the militant secularism which was growing throughout Europe. Nonetheless, the opposition of the churches to the General Strike of 1926 showed the innate conservatism of many prominent churchmen and drove a wedge between the Church and the labour movement. There is no doubt that the post-Union Church of Scotland was met with suspicion as supporters of the political establishment even though nearly one-third of Scottish Labour Party leaders were members of the Church.

In 1914, the Great War broke out. It is perhaps impossible to overestimate the effect of the war on all aspects of Scottish life and the churches were not excluded. During the war, the churches recognized the immense effects of such widespread death, maiming and psychological damage on human emotions and spirit, beginning to make efforts to address them. All the churches though were taken up with the 'righteous cause' idea and according to some, patriotism became effectively the dominant religion of the country. Studies during the war suggested that Scottish soldiers were more than twice as likely to have a 'live' church connection as their English equivalents and indeed one battalion of a Glasgow regiment, the 16th Highland Light Infantry, was formed from members of the Boys' Brigade in the city.

The response of the churches included support for those going to war but also the active service of chaplains to the forces and the manning of recreation centres behind the lines. Chaplains seem to have been of variable experience and lacking in any training for the task ahead. There were also significant arguments between the Church of England, which naturally provided the huge majority of chaplains, and the other churches. About 5000 British chaplains served in the Great War, an unknown percentage was Scottish but at least 160 Scottish Presbyterian padres were serving on the Western front by 1917. Many ministers were also serving as combatants, as medical orderlies or as civilians behind the lines. Perhaps one unexpected result of this was the contact that they had with those of other varieties of faith or none. A Presbyterian minister might well have been providing rosaries or St Christopher medals for a Roman Catholic while wounded soldiers were being prayed over by Catholic or Anglican priests or by Presbyterian or Methodist ministers irrespective of their beliefs. Church of England chaplains at one stage were forbidden from going up the line with the men and this undoubtedly played a part in a widespread contempt for chaplains that was voiced in the aftermath of the war, with Robert Graves providing perhaps the best known example. Despite this, over 170 chaplains gave up their lives during the war. At home, some sermons equated the war with a holy crusade against the powers of evil; there is evidence that some German ministers preached in the same vein. The causes of war other than the breach of trust in invading Belgium seem rarely to have been considered. For most ministers, war was 'neither glorified nor welcomed' but instead denounced as barbarism, a throwback to a less enlightened period and an unavoidable waste of the nation's resources. Against this, there was sometimes a feeling that this was a punishment on the whole of Europe for its embrace of 'decadent and frivolous materialism' and therefore a cleansing resurgence of pure love for one's fellows and country.

That perhaps worked for those at home and those initially untouched by the horror; for those involved at closer quarters, such views gave little comfort. One early change in preaching was a further move away from the Calvinistic ideas of heaven and hell. Most Scottish churches realized that telling the families of the dead that their loved ones were not assured of a place in heaven was, to put it mildly, inappropriate. Instead, there came to be put round a view, almost an Islamic view, that death in battle in a righteous cause meant automatic entry to heaven. Not everyone agreed with this, though, with the Free Presbyterians in particular remaining true to their views and developing a form of comfort that did not conflict with their Calvinism.

In one sense, leaving aside the Free Presbyterians and organizational difficulties with the Church of England, individual denominations became less important. In the great national melting pot that was the British Army, there could be no guarantee that individual soldiers could have access to a chaplain of their own persuasion whilst it would seem that anti-Catholicism diminished as a result of the respect that RC Chaplains earned by their attitudes.

The experiences of the men in the trenches led to a great variety of attitudes, these might include political radicalization, espousing of atheism, a 'trench religion' that recognized an all-powerful God but had little to do with Christianity as well as more conventional strengthening or weakening of existing belief. Several soldiers came through the war decorated for bravery and became ministers, some of them ministers committed to future pacifism.

After the war, some recognized that it was justice that was required, not vengeance. There were enough links between the Scottish Protestant ministry and Germany to moderate the view that Germans were intrinsically evil, and some were conscious of Britain's own questionable moral stance in some previous wars.

Like everyone else, those who had influence in Scotland's churches were bewildered and out of their depth in how they should react to the War; they did their best to comfort the suffering and the bereaved, trying to make sense of their circumstances. What they did have though was a clear view that life and society had changed by the end of the war and an impetus to try to adapt to that.

In 1918, when it appeared that the war was grinding its murderous way to a conclusion, the General Assemblies of the two largest Scottish churches, Church of Scotland and United Free, committed to the idea of rebuilding their wounded country. There was a clear recognition that a new approach was needed; one prominent minister said that all old sermons needed to be scrapped so that ministers could look returning soldiers in the eye. There was equally a fear that the removal of the horror might lead to a reaction against discipline and morality.

It is perhaps in this context that the United Free Church condemned the rulers of the armed forces for being more interested in treating venereal diseases among the armed forces than preventing them. Prohibiting the sale of alcohol became a live political issue. Plebiscites in several areas of Scotland prevented or limited the sale of alcohol in those areas by considerable majorities. Although drunkenness was seen as a largely male vice at this point, the rise in female drunkenness during the war had added additional force to the argument.

Less focussed attention was paid to the need for 235,000 new houses within fourteen years, with the UF Church invited to 'keep the minds of the Christian community awake to the urgency of the matter'. At the same time, the church recognized the need for a new approach to employment in industry.

> It was now seen that the interests of employers and employees are identical and that for the future every man must think not only of his own trade and his own class but of the business and the industry and the service it could do the nation as a whole.

As a plea for the abolition of class strife, this statement made by the Moderator of the 1918 UF General Assembly did not carry much weight. Industrial strife was just around the corner.

Of course ministers felt the effects of the war too; the Moderator of the General Assembly of the Church of Scotland in 1919 had lost two of his three sons in battle; and his diary records how the constant round of dedicating war memorials around the country took its toll on him and his wife.

It was widely recognized that union with the UF Church and a return to one major Presbyterian national church was desirable, at least to those likely to be in that one national Presbyterian Church. Initial efforts in the aftermath of the union in 1900 had foundered partly on the question of breaking the links with the state that the UF Church was against and partly because the Great War had raised much more urgent issues. By the end of the War, though, the desirability had increased; the churches were much more used to working with each other and there was a realization that life was never going to be the same as it had been prior to the war.

From the perspective of eighty-five years on, it looks as though the UF Church got its way on most serious issues. The UF Church had two very solid planks of policy which underpinned the church: one was that the state had no right to meddle with ecclesiastical matters and the other was that no church had a right to state funding in any form. The first of these most obviously dealt with the Patronage question, but that had been dealt with finally half a century previously; so, by the 1920s, it was rather a reflection on whether Parliament could determine the Church's beliefs or whether that was a matter for the Church itself to decide. Both the (pre-1900) Free Church and the United Presbyterians had decided that they had the right to modify the role and text of the *Westminster Confession* and allow freedom of conscience for the parts that were not fundamental to faith. The demand was that the Church of Scotland should have that right too. That matter was settled by the 'Articles Declaratory', passed by the Church of Scotland in 1921, which remains as the Church's 'constitution'. The same year, Parliament passed the Church of Scotland Act of 1921, which recognized the spiritual independence of the Church for all time. The Church, of course, remains liable to the law of the land in any non-spiritual matters, and there have been occasional clashes as to what constitutes a non-spiritual matter.

The second matter that had to be cleared out of the way was the question of teinds and heritors. Although patrons no longer had the right to nominate a minister, the heritors still had the responsibility to pay for stipends and the upkeep of church property. In effect this was a land tax for the benefit of the Church of Scotland. Many of these responsibilities for payment had been split and re-split as land had been sold or leased so that, often, the cost of gathering the funds was uneconomic. It was also seen as unfair that landowners had to pay for a church that in many cases they did not support. After much ado, it was agreed that the teinds should be bought out and that every teind of less than a shilling a year (£0.05p) should be abolished, everyone responsible for paying between a shilling and a pound had to pay eighteen times the annual figure but have eighteen years to do so in order to be free of the responsibility. Those paying teinds of more than £1 had to make individual arrangements on much the same basis. The resulting funds were put under the control of a new body in the Church, the General Trustees, and still provide a tiny proportion of ministers' stipends. Amid great uncertainty and doubt, this too became enshrined in an Act passed by Parliament in 1925, owing to the then Moderator who successfully persuaded the House of Lords to sit on a Monday, a rarity indeed.

In the following four years, the administrative details were sorted out and so in October 1929, the two largest Presbyterian denominations in Scotland became one, with a minority remaining out of the Union and founding their own denomination, the United Free Church of Scotland (Continuing), with the proviso that the '(Continuing)' could be dropped from the title in after five years.

The arrangements for Union were made; the uniting churches had learned from the mistakes of 1900 and agreed on formulae for handing over church buildings to those who did not want to join the union on the basis of congregational voting. Both sides were fully agreed that a series of divisive and very expensive court cases would be to no one's advantage.

The national Church of Scotland kept its name, but in many other ways, it was the United Free ethos that prevailed. In presbytery, synod and General Assembly, elders for the first time equalled ministers in number. The Church was free from state control, but for the first time was responsible for its own financial affairs. Individual congregations, coming from a great variety of dissenting traditions, had the right to keep their own individual, and sometimes eccentric, constitutions.

In many ways, only one visible sign of the old relationship of Church and State remained in the appointment of the monarch's representative, the Lord High Commissioner which survived despite some opposition. It was nearly the cause of a last minute disruption though. The Duke of York, later King George VI, was to be the first Lord High Commissioner to the Union Assembly and his advisers were adamant that he process through the Assembly Hall to his 'Gallery'. The Church authorities insisted that the floor of the Assembly was entirely out of bounds to the monarch or his representative, just like the floor of the House of Commons. Stalemate ensued until the matter was reported to the Duke who told his advisors not to be silly and that he would not try to enter the floor of the Assembly in any circumstances.

One irony of the settlement, in view of the fact that one of the leading ministers of the UF Church was an MP and adamant in his opposition to the Union, was that the united Church of Scotland would have a regulation that forbade ministers from standing for Parliament. Curiously, there was never a regulation forbidding them from joining the House of Lords, but when the very Rev. George MacLeod was made a Life Peer in 1967, some felt it was inappropriate.

The newly united Church entered the 1930s full of hope; for the first time in nearly two hundred years, the great majority of presbyterians were members of the same denomination.

The statistics published in 1929 make for impressive reading, even allowing for the fact that they include around forty ministers who did not come into the union. There were 2897 ministers in active service in Scotland, over 200 divinity students, nearly 1.3 million communicant members, over 370,000 members of Sunday Schools, 112,000 older young people (14–18 years approximately) in Bible Classes, over 3000 buildings where worship was regularly conducted and over 800 missionaries abroad (including 214 missionary wives). The figures are impressive and the stated hope of the Church of Scotland's monthly *Record* was that with nearly 1.3 million members out of a population of three million, 'It is possible, and indeed probable, that with a few years' earnest work the present membership of the Church will be doubled.'

The page of figures which was published as the Union took place summed up the statistics of the two churches as they stood. However, the financial statistics/records were not as clear cut because of the vastly different methods in accounting of both the churches, rendering a comparison difficult, possibly deliberately. What was clear was that the UF Church had had an annual income almost twice as large as the Church of Scotland, and the unspoken reality was that because they were used to being self-supporting, old UF congregations contributed at a much higher level than those of the pre-Union Church of Scotland had contributed.

Despite all hopes, the newly united Church stagnated in the 1930s and, certainly, the brave hopes were not fulfilled. Partly, the economic climate debilitated efforts, partly the work of uniting churches locally took both time and emotional effort. The Church of Scotland was built on the parish principle and therefore when UF and Auld Kirk came together, the whole of Scotland had to have its parish maps and boundaries redrawn to accommodate all the constituent congregations of the united church. Each of these 3000 congregations had to have its own parish; and the members were not always pleased to find that they were not necessarily living in the parish of the church in which they worshipped.

There were other plans and issues that went by the board; during the 1920s, moves towards the ordination of women as elders and ministers had begun to gather pace. The UF Church (Continuing) allowed it; the post-1929 Church of Scotland briefly debated the matter in the 1930s and then ignored it for thirty years. The only sop to women's involvement in the leadership of the Church was that they were allowed to join the lowest courts of the church, 'Congregational Boards' or the other variants that were allowed to continue; 'Deacons' Courts' or 'Boards of Managers'. A small number began to appear on the national committees of the church; by 1929, in the new committee structure of the church, 160 out of 1752 members were women, with the highest proportion being found on the Foreign Mission Committee where 36 out of 120 were women.

One topic that remained, and remains, an embarrassment to Scottish Churches was anti-Catholicism, something which came to the fore periodically, often triggered by changes in the political climate. Demonstrations against the Roman Catholic activities were frequent; in some ways, this was little different from what the early Salvation Army suffered, or indeed the Methodists, but it was accompanied by political antagonism. It is perhaps surprising to see it become such an issue in the 1930s but it was an issue powerful enough to dominate Edinburgh elections and cause rioting in that byword of Edinburgh respectability, Morningside. The chief protagonist was one John Cormack, former soldier and son of a Baptist preacher. He had served in Dublin during the

Easter Rising and brought back from his experience a deep distrust and dislike of the Church that he saw there. With as many relatives in Ireland, the Scottish people were deeply concerned about Irish nationalism with supporters on both sides of the argument and the partition of Ireland was one of the major issues of the day. In Scotland, further signs that Catholicism was gaining ground were seen in the incorporation by the state of Catholic schools and the future state funding of them. 'Protestant ratepayers subsidising Catholic schools' was a battle-cry, despite the fact that Catholics had been paying rates for schools their children did not attend. The Protestant churches had given their schools into the care of the state some forty-six years previously, but these schools were officially 'non-denominational' though with a strong Protestant bias. A combination of these factors led to John Cormack founding the 'Protestant Action' group after being expelled from a Protestant pressure group because of his support for violent action. In 1934, he became a Town Councillor for North Leith, standing on the 'Protestant Action' platform. He moved to South Leith two years later and held that seat for many years. His party had several Edinburgh Councillors and polled a significant proportion of the votes.

In 1935, the Roman Catholic Church organized a 'Eucharistic Congress' in Edinburgh. This meeting of clergy and laity has at its centre the celebration of the 'Real Presence' of Christ in the Communion Bread. As such, it was a perfect target for the anti-Catholics, as the rejection of the Real Presence was one of the central planks of the Reformation.

Public halls were hired for various events and the climax was to be held in the grounds of a priory in Morningside; violent demonstrations ensued both outside the Waverley market in the centre of town and in Morningside, where thousands rallied outside the Priory at the call of Cormack. Buses carrying people to and from events were stoned and their windows smashed, although the main weapon of choice seems to have been spitting. Despite the thousands of people involved, there were no serious injuries; but many in Scotland, including many in the Protestant churches, felt a deep sense of shame. Amid all the turmoil, even a ceremony to honour the Prime Minister of Australia with the freedom of the City of Edinburgh was disrupted by Councillor Cormack shouting 'no popery'. The Catholic Herald's take on the incident was that;

> ...no one could suppose that the anti-Catholicism displayed in Edinburgh was a Protestant (let alone a Presbyterian) explosion. Ministers and others wrote thoroughly Christian disclaimers to the press. The inciters to public misdemeanour were well-known, and no one associated their names with piety or even belief.

The author of that article put the turmoil down to atheistic communists in the guise of militant Protestants.

Sectarianism remained an issue long after this time. Segregated schools made for a segregated population, and social mixing was rare in the decades after the Second World War. Masonic Lodges were a stronghold of what might be called a non-religious Protestantism and the Northern Irish Orange Order's parades kept the issues alive. Even Boys' Brigade parades in the 1960s were likely to burst into 'spontaneous' renditions of Orange songs as they matched past Catholic churches. The sectarianism still endemic in Scotland's football industry falls beyond the scope of this book, but for most church-going Christian Protestants, the Catholic Church is seen locally as an ally with the same concerns rather than the enemy at the door as it was regarded in the past.

The other issue with long roots in Scotland was that of Temperance. The Great War had seen a further strengthening of the Temperance position and it too became a political issue. It is a matter for some amusement that Dundee, not known as a stronghold of teetotalism, voted for a Scottish Prohibition Party candidate in 1922, thus depriving Winston Churchill of his seat in Parliament. The MP, Edwyn Scrymgeour, held his seat until 1931. In general, Temperance became a local and personal issue rather than one to pursue as a national campaign.

Despite the churches' stance during the General Strike, the social Gospel of the Church was not forgotten. It reached its most famous project in the foundation of the 'Iona Community'. Founded in 1938 by the Rev. George Macleod, the Community initially provided employment for workmen in rebuilding the ruined Iona Abbey, but it also provided rehabilitation employment for young offenders and soon spread its help in other directions, such as drug rehabilitation, support for homeless people. Allied to this strongly social programme, the Community developed a spiritual aspect and an inclusiveness which did not sit comfortably with conservative parts of the church. In later years, it has also nailed its colours firmly to the mast of social justice, notably in its anti-nuclear stance and its anti-apartheid stance. More recently, it has been involved in experiments in worship and in church music.

In one sense, 1960 was a high point for the churches in Scotland: membership was at a historic high; the 400th anniversary of the Reformation was duly celebrated, with the Queen herself attending the General Assembly of the Church of Scotland rather than sending a Lord High Commissioner. The churches were fragmented as they had always been, but at the centre was a national church which claimed nearly 38 per cent of the adult population as members. A further 7 per cent were members of other Protestant churches, some eighteen of them, and 15 per cent were Roman Catholics. Thus, two-thirds of the population was Christian in some form.

This was much the same total figure as it had been a hundred years previously, but the proportion of Roman Catholics was higher by 1960, an increase put down to continuing immigration from Ireland; a war-time influx of Poles who remained after the Second World War; and a higher birth rate in the Catholic community. But even then huge numbers of nominal members were just that, nominal members who rarely if ever crossed the threshold of a church.

Women outnumbered men both in membership and in activity. In fact, this had always been the case; communicants' rolls show a consistent pattern of men being in the minority even though they filled every position of power. By 1960, though, the first women had succeeded in inserting a toe into the hitherto closed door to ministry and eldership. Women ministers could now be found; it began with the tiny Church of the Nazarene in 1912, the Congregational Church and UF Church followed suit in the years that followed and by 1960, the Church of Scotland was seriously contemplating it. Women began to be ordained as elders in 1962 and as ministers in 1966. That battle has still not entirely been won; fifty years on, there are still a few congregations in the Church of Scotland which are yet to ordain a woman elder.

Post-war worries about the future led to what one participant called 'the greatest evangelistic campaign in the history of Scotland', the *Tell Scotland* campaign of 1955. In this campaign, seven Protestant churches worked together to evangelize and educate people with considerable success. There was a measurable increase in Church attendance after the campaign, and, more importantly, half of the new members were still attending a year later. In the midst of this came the first of the campaigns of the American evangelist, Billy Graham. This made a huge impression at the time and was linked to the *Tell Scotland* campaign. It has to be said that Graham had decided that he was coming anyway and *Tell Scotland's* decision to invite him was more damage limitation than actual enthusiasm. Many, including the influential George MacLeod of the Iona Community, saw his approach as completely at odds with the grassroots, congregation-based evangelism that the campaign was trying to nurture. Hindsight suggests that Billy Graham's intervention did long-term damage to the work that the Scottish churches were doing by concentrating on a short-term emotional response that did not actually lead into a long-term commitment and by imposing a foreign style that did not fit the local circumstances. Having said that, there are many Christians who, nearly sixty years later, still look back fondly to the heady days of Billy Graham's first Scottish tour. *Tell Scotland* and Billy Graham together did give the post-war church in Scotland a boost of publicity and energy. The rallies gave way to visitations around parishes; about 600 campaigns took place but there was a confusion as to the relative merits of 'congregation-based' evangelism versus 'big-name' evangelism, and the campaign finally fell between two stools. By

1960, it was clear that this huge effort had not translated into a revitalized church involvement, attendance or membership and a long decline was starting which still continues. The work of the churches in putting together the campaign was evidence that local churches were beginning to work better together. To some extent, they always had worked better at a local level away from the rigidity of church courts and hierarchies. By the 1950s, though, some form of organic unity was sought by some; to the many still-active ministers and members who had gone through the union of 1929, further union seemed possible and even desirable. Reports and discussions were the order of the day; the one that made the most waves just at the end of the 1950s was a report that considered the possibility of the eventual union between the Church of Scotland and the Church of England with the concept of 'bishops in presbytery', allowing the Scottish Episcopal Church to accept membership in the National Church once more. The whole affair was doomed to failure and finally sank without trace. It was largely ignored by the English press and was never important in England, but in Scotland, the press made hay, led largely by the *Scottish Daily Express* whose editor was an active elder in the Church of Scotland and saw it as his destiny to keep bishops as far from the Kirk as possible.

Relationships with the Roman Catholics too were improving. As a sweeping generalization, the continuing cancer of sectarianism between Protestant and Catholic factions is largely a tribalism that has nothing to do with religion beyond the names. Where there were doctrinaire anti-Catholic or anti-Protestant views within the churches, they were generally conducted in a reasonably courteous manner and cooperation at local levels was seen to be increasing, for example, in some areas, the local gatherings of ministers, 'fraternals' as they were called, began to include the local Catholic priests. In 1960, though, change was in the air; the formality of services was beginning, just beginning, to fade. It was beginning to be recognized that 'Sunday clothes' were not an absolute prerequisite for salvation. Sunday observance still ruled but more by society's unwritten rules than by law. But the Church which had been so central to much of Scotland's life for four hundred years, while still numerically strong, was no longer the unchallenged determining force in Scotland's spiritual and moral life.

Tables and Maps

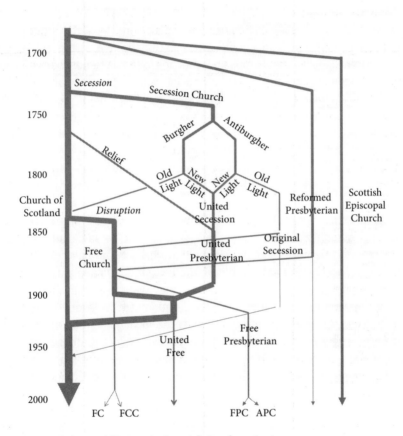

FIGURE 1 *Splits and Unions in Scottish Presbyterianism.*

TABLE A.   -   -   -   -   -

SUMMARY OF THE

Population

RELIGIOUS DENOMINATIONS.	Number of Places of Worship.*			Number of Sittings.†				Number of Attendants‡ at Public Worship on Sunday, March 30, 1851.		
	Separate Buildings.	Not separate Buildings.	TOTAL.	Free.	Appropriated.	Not distinguished.	TOTAL.	Morning.	Afternoon.	Evening.
TOTAL - -	2,694	220	2,914	490,213	696,841	235,984	1,422,438	740,794	499,349	153,785
PROTESTANT CHURCHES :										
Presbyterians—										
Established Church -	898	6	904	206,170	209,489	114,105	529,764	298,767	119,888	20,023
Reformed Presbyterian Church -	36	1	37	3,812	8,262	1,850	13,924	6,946	5,290	1,733
Original Secession Church -	29	1	30	3,195	6,124	3,455	12,774	5,286	4,611	1,312
Relief Church -	2	..	2	370	650	..	1,020	220	250	275
United Presbyterian Church -	423	4	427	45,724	159,971	48,329	254,024	143,443	131,227	27,763
Free Church -	786	38	824	139,658	241,296	40,853	421,787	235,482	173,565	65,946
Episcopal Church -	106	6	112	7,811	16,596	5,460	29,867	21,130	9,072	4,300
Independents, or Congregationalists	134	34	168	32,310	21,467	5,070	58,817	22,131	20,851	14,484
Baptists -	61	39	100	15,632	1,255	650	17,537	7,196	6,045	3,138
Society of Friends -	6	..	6	430	..	800	1,230	108	122	..
Unitarians -	4	1	5	800	1,150	..	1,950	690	104	684
United Brethren, or Moravians -	1	..	1	200	..	..	200	16	..	55
Wesleyan Methodists—										
Original Connexion -	50	11	61	7,687	8,174	200	15,961	6,347	2,173	7,011
Primitive Methodists -	6	4	10	1,730	160	..	1,890	527	494	715
Independent Methodists -	1	..	1	400	200	..	600	190	150	180
Wesleyan Reformers -	..	1	1	..	..	..	..	11	..	11
Glassites, or Sandemanians -	5	1	6	800	..	..	800	429	554	100
New Church -	4	1	5	310	250	150	710	211	67	120
Campbellites -	1	..	1	80	..	..	80	11	14	..
Evangelical Union -	18	9	27	2,146	3,325	1,900	7,371	3,756	4,343	2,093
Isolated Congregations—										
Various -	5	3	8	350	..	1,100	1,450	715	77	406
Common -	2	..	2	360	..	..	360	..	..	..
Unsectarian -	1	..	1	..	..	320	320	200	220	..
City Mission -	2	5	7	330	..	450	780	70	40	686
Christian -	3	4	7	716	..	415	1,131	417	216	280
Christian Disciples -	3	11	14	1,008	39	..	1,047	503	495	188
Christian Reformation -	..	1	1	50	..	..	50	..	11	..
Reformed Christians -	1	..	1	..	..	..	..	8	8	8
Free Christian Brethren -	1	..	1	340	..	..	340	180	261	..
Primitive Christians -	..	2	2	60	..	150	210	57	74	..
Protestants -	4	..	4	1,210	..	..	1,210	230	400	935
Reformation -	1	..	1	250	..	..	250	10	18	..
Reformed Protestants -	1	..	1	725	..	..	725	130	..	105
Separatists -	..	1	1	..	..	..	..	11	..	..
Christian Chartists -	1	..	1	220	..	..	220	100	80	..
Denomination not stated -	4	2	6	330	..	..	330	..	70	318
OTHER CHRISTIAN CHURCHES :										
Roman Catholics - - -	85	19	104	12,510	18,413	10,117	41,040	33,377	15,909	11,268
Catholic and Apostolic Church -	3	..	3	450	..	..	450	272	128	190
Latter Day Saints, or Mormons -	5	15	20	1,393	39	..	1,432	1,239	1,164	834
Jews - - - - -	1	..	1	36	31	..	67	28	..	7

* From the lists forwarded to the Census Office, it appears that there were 481 other places of worship existing at the time of the Census, but from which no returns were procured. For the denominations to which these belonged, see next page.

† The returns afford no information as to the number of *sittings* in 285 of the above-mentioned 2,914 places of worship. Of these, 87 belonged to the Established Church ; five to the Reformed Presbyterian Church ; two to the Original Secession Church ; 17 to the United Presbyterian Church ; 67 to the Free Church ; 12 to the Episcopal Church ; 20 to the Independents ; 20 to the Baptists ; two to the Society of Friends ; five to the Unitarians ; five to the Wesleyan Original Connexion ; one to the Wesleyan Reformers ; one to the Glassites ; seven to the Evangelical Union ; 13 to Isolated Congregations ; 13 to Roman Catholics ; one to the Catholic and Apostolic Church ; and 11 to the Latter Day Saints.

‡ The number of *attendants* was not stated in the case of 242 of the above-mentioned 2,914 places of worship. Of these, 134 belonged to the Established Church ; six to the Reformed Presbyterians ; one to the Original Secession ; eight to the United Presbyterians ; 47 to the Free Church ; seven to the Episcopal Church ; seven to the Independents ; seven to the Baptists ; one to the Unitarians ; four to the Wesleyan Original Connexion ; three to Isolated Congregations ; 15 to the Roman Catholics ; and one to the Latter Day Saints.

FIGURE 2 *The Churches of Scotland in 1851 showing the variety of churches available and the relative numbers of those worshipping in them. Taken from the Census of Great Britain, 1851, Religious Worship and Education. Scotland. Report and tables. BPP 1854 LIX (1764).*

Aberdeen	0.9
Angus	0.7
Argyll	0.4
Ayr	1.7
Banff	3.8
Berwick	0.0
Bute	0.9
Caithness	0.0
Clacks.	0.0
Dumfries	1.8
Dunbarton	3.4
East Lothian	0.0
Fife	0.3
Inverness	2.9
Kincardine	0.0
Kinross	0.0
Kirkcudbright.	1.2
Lanark	5.3
Midlothian	2.2
Moray	1.0
Nairn	0.0
Orkney	0.0
Peebles	1.3
Perth	0.9
Renfrew	4.2
Ross & Crom.	0.0
Roxburgh	0.3
Selkirk	0.0
Shetland	0.0
Stirling	1.6
Sutherland	0.0
West Lothian	0.0
Wigtown	1.8

0.1%–2%	
2%–5%	
5%–10%	
10% +	

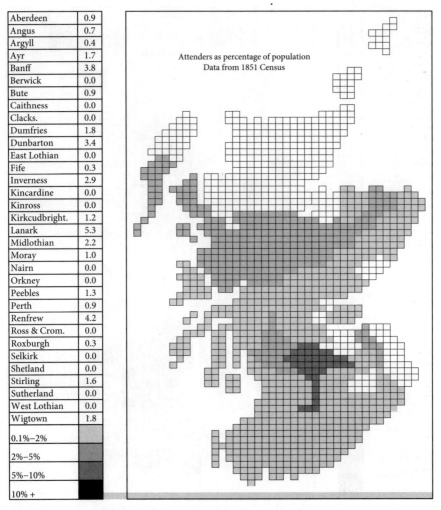

Attenders as percentage of population
Data from 1851 Census

FIGURE 3 *Roman Catholics in 1851.*

TABLES AND MAPS

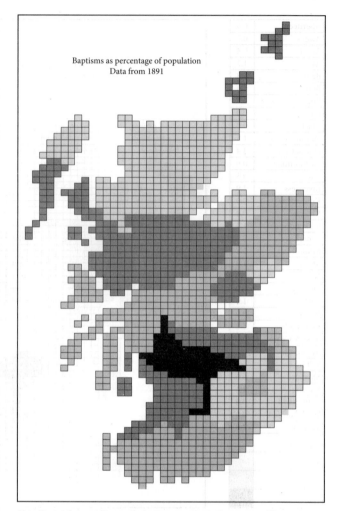

Aberdeen	2.5
Angus	8.9
Argyll	4.4
Ayr	7.0
Banff	2.9
Berwick	0.6
Bute	7.1
Caithness	0.8
Clacks.	4.2
Dumfries	4.0
Dunbarton	14.3
East Lothian	3.4
Fife	2.2
Inverness	9.7
Kincardine	0.4
Kinross	0.0
Kirkcudbright.	2.5
Lanark	15.7
Midlothian	6.6
Moray	1.0
Nairn	1.8
Orkney	8.3
Peebles	1.6
Perth	2.8
Renfrew	16.5
Ross & Crom.	0.6
Roxburgh	1.7
Selkirk	3.5
Shetland	8.3
Stirling	9.9
Sutherland	0.7
West Lothian	8.1
Wigtown	2.7

under 2%	
2%–5%	
5%–10%	
over 10%	

Baptisms as percentage of population
Data from 1891

Note: Due to infant mortality, counting baptisms overestimates the percentage of Roman Catholics in the population, but statistics of 'membership' were not kept.

FIGURE 4 *Roman Catholics in 1891.*

Aberdeen	5.2
Angus	1.7
Argyll	0.4
Ayr	0.2
Banff	0.9
Berwick	0.0
Bute	1.5
Caithness	0.0
Clacks.	0.5
Dumfries	0.4
Dunbarton	0.4
East Lothian	0.5
Fife	0.5
Inverness	0.8
Kincardine	3.0
Kinross	0.0
Kirkcudbright.	0.0
Lanark	1.1
Midlothian	2.2
Moray	0.6
Nairn	0.0
Orkney	0.0
Peebles	0.8
Perth	0.7
Renfrew	0.4
Ross & Crom.	0.3
Roxburgh	1.7
Selkirk	0.0
Shetland	0.0
Stirling	0.6
Sutherland	0.0
West Lothian	0.0
Wigtown	0.4

0%–0.25%

0.25%–0.5%

0.5%–1%

1% Up

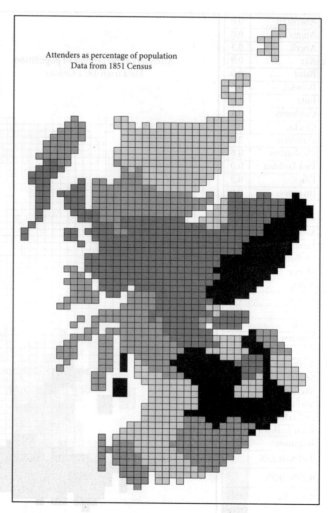

Attenders as percentage of population
Data from 1851 Census

FIGURE 5 *Scottish Episcopal Church.*

Aberdeen	0.0
Angus	0.0
Argyll	0.3
Ayr	0.9
Banff	0.0
Berwick	0.6
Bute	1.6
Caithness	0.1
Clacks.	0.0
Dumfries	2.2
Dunbarton	0.6
East Lothian	0.0
Fife	0.3
Inverness	0.0
Kincardine	0.0
Kinross	0.0
Kirkcudbright.	1.6
Lanark	0.8
Midlothian	0.5
Moray	0.0
Nairn	0.0
Orkney	0.0
Peebles	0.0
Perth	0.0
Renfrew	1.2
Ross & Crom.	0.0
Roxburgh	0.0
Selkirk	0.0
Shetland	0.0
Stirling	0.4
Sutherland	0.0
West Lothian	0.0
Wigtown	2.3
0.01%–0.25%	
0.25%–0.5%	
0.5%–1%	
1% Up	

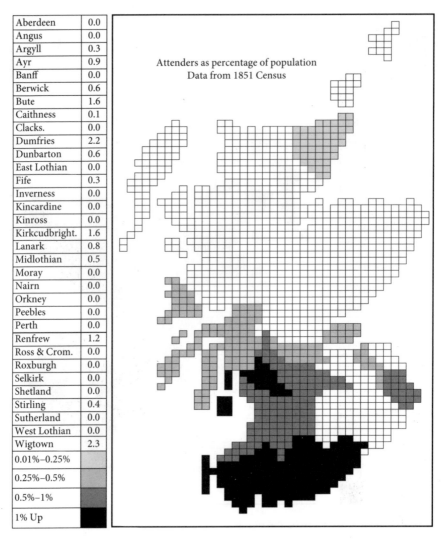

Attenders as percentage of population
Data from 1851 Census

FIGURE 6 *Reformed Presbyterians 1851.*

Aberdeen	3.3
Angus	9.5
Argyll	3.9
Ayr	11.2
Banff	2.4
Berwick	26.0
Bute	3.1
Caithness	1.9
Clacks.	14.4
Dumfries	11.3
Dunbarton	18.9
East Lothian	10.2
Fife	18.5
Inverness	1.7
Kincardine	3.5
Kinross	33.5
Kirkcudbright.	3.0
Lanark	11.4
Midlothian	14.0
Moray	15.1
Nairn	21.2
Orkney	17.4
Peebles	15.4
Perth	13.1
Renfrew	10.8
Ross & Crom.	1.3
Roxburgh	8.9
Selkirk	14.0
Shetland	17.4
Stirling	12.7
Sutherland	0.0
West Lothian	9.8
Wigtown	7.9
0%–5%	
5%–10%	
10%–20%	
20% +	

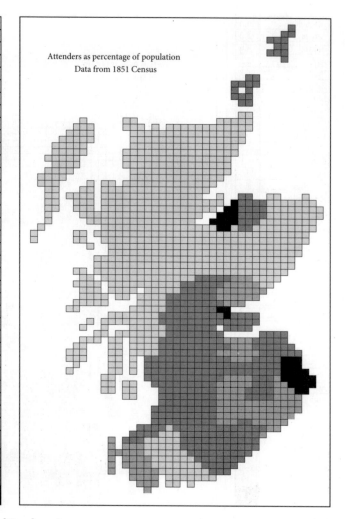

Attenders as percentage of population
Data from 1851 Census

FIGURE 7 *United Presbyterians.*

Aberdeen	14.4
Angus	18.2
Argyll	7.6
Ayr	15.8
Banff	16.5
Berwick	23.8
Bute	19.6
Caithness	2.5
Clacks.	12.2
Dumfries	9.6
Dunbarton	13.8
East Lothian	14.6
Fife	25.6
Inverness	7.4
Kincardine	22.7
Kinross	24.2
Kirkcudbright.	12.9
Lanark	8.0
Midlothian	10.1
Moray	17.4
Nairn	6.3
Orkney	16.4
Peebles	18.9
Perth	17.3
Renfrew	11.5
Ross & Crom.	4.2
Roxburgh	6.9
Selkirk	4.0
Shetland	16.4
Stirling	16.4
Sutherland	1.8
West Lothian	6.6
Wigtown	8.1
0%–5%	
5%–10%	
10%–20%	
20% +	

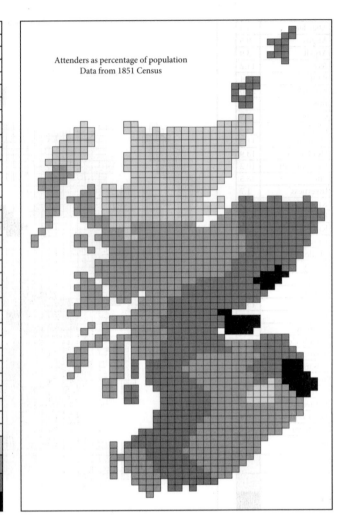

Attenders as percentage of population
Data from 1851 Census

FIGURE 8 *Established Church.*

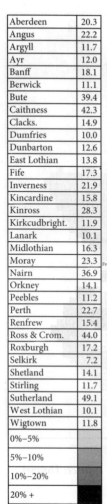

Aberdeen	20.3
Angus	22.2
Argyll	11.7
Ayr	12.0
Banff	18.1
Berwick	11.1
Bute	39.4
Caithness	42.3
Clacks.	14.9
Dumfries	10.0
Dunbarton	12.6
East Lothian	13.8
Fife	17.3
Inverness	21.9
Kincardine	15.8
Kinross	28.3
Kirkcudbright.	11.9
Lanark	10.1
Midlothian	16.3
Moray	23.3
Nairn	36.9
Orkney	14.1
Peebles	11.2
Perth	22.7
Renfrew	15.4
Ross & Crom.	44.0
Roxburgh	17.2
Selkirk	7.2
Shetland	14.1
Stirling	11.7
Sutherland	49.1
West Lothian	10.1
Wigtown	11.8
0%–5%	
5%–10%	
10%–20%	
20% +	

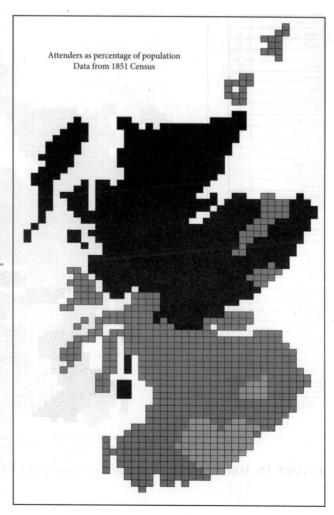

Attenders as percentage of population
Data from 1851 Census

FIGURE 9 *Free Church.*

Aberdeen	f
Angus	f
Argyll	f
Ayr	e
Banff	f
Berwick	e
Bute	f
Caithness	f
Clacks.	f
Dumfries	u
Dunbarton	u
East Lothian	e
Fife	e
Inverness	f
Kincardine	e
Kinross	u
Kirkcudbright.	e
Lanark	u
Midlothian	f
Moray	f
Nairn	f
Orkney	u
Peebles	e
Perth	f
Renfrew	f
Ross & Crom.	f
Roxburgh	f
Selkirk	u
Shetland	u
Stirling	e
Sutherland	f
West Lothian	f
Wigtown	f
Established	
Free Church	
United Pres.	

The best attended denomination in each county as recorded in 1891.

FIGURE 10 *Majority Denominations in Each County in 1891 (Source: Howie).*

Aberdeen	3.9
Angus	4.0
Argyll	2.5
Ayr	1.9
Banff	1.8
Berwick	0.7
Bute	2.0
Caithness	1.7
Clacks.	1.6
Dumfries	2.2
Dunbarton	1.9
East Lothian	1.4
Fife	1.5
Inverness	1.3
Kincardine	2.9
Kinross	0.7
Kirkcudbright.	1.0
Lanark	1.9
Midlothian	3.6
Moray	2.5
Nairn	1.6
Orkney	2.0
Peebles	1.4
Perth	3.5
Renfrew	2.0
Ross & Crom.	0.4
Roxburgh	2.3
Selkirk	4.4
Shetland	3.7
Stirling	1.8
Sutherland	0.0
West Lothian	0.5
Wigtown	1.9

0.01%–1%	
1%–2%	
2%–3%	
3% Up	

Combined membership as percentage of
population
Data from Howie

Note: 'Smaller Protestant Churches' includes Episcopalian, Presbyterian outwith the three main
churches, Congregational, Baptist and Methodist Churches. It excludes Brethren and similar churches.

FIGURE 11 *Smaller Protestant Churches in 1891.*

Further Reading

Note: *RSCHS* – Records of the Scottish Church History Society

General

Brown, C. G. (1993), *The People in the Pews; Religion and Society in Scotland since 1780*. Glasgow: Economic and Social History of Scotland.

Burleigh, J. H. S. (1960), *A Church History of Scotland*. London: OUP.

Burns, T. (1892), *Old Scottish Communion Plate*. Edinburgh: Clark.

Cheyne, A. C. (1999), *Studies in Scottish Church History*. Edinburgh: Clark.

Donaldson, G. (1960), *Scotland; Church and Nation Through 16 Centuries*. London: SCM Press.

Dunlop, I. A. (1988), *The Kirks of Edinburgh; 1560–1984*. Edinburgh: Scottish Records Society.

Henderson, G. D. (1935), *The Scottish Ruling Elder*. London: Clarke.

Herron, A. (1985), *Kirk by Divine Right*. Edinburgh: St Andrews Press.

———. (1999), *Kirk Lore*. Edinburgh: St Andrews Press.

———. (2007), *Historical Directory to Glasgow Presbytery: Brief Historical Notes Regarding Congregations and Their Buildings within the Presbytery of Glasgow*. (Revised and updated by Andrew Wale) [online] Available at http://www.presbyteryofglasgow.org.uk/resources2/historical-document.html [Accessed 24 February 2014].

Kirk, J. (2001), *The Scottish Churches and the Union Parliament 1707–1999*. Edinburgh: Scottish Church History Society.

MacLean, C. (1997), *Going to Church*. Edinburgh: NMS.

——— and Veitch, K. (2006), *Scottish Life and Society; A Compendium of Scottish Ethnology*. Volume 12; Religion, Edinburgh: John Donald.

Marshall, J. S. (1976), 'Scottish Trade Incorporations and the Church', *RSCHS*, 19.2, 93–109.

Sanderson, E. C. (2004), 'Hidden from History? Piecing Together the Working Lives of Ministers' Wives and Daughters', *RSCHS*, 34, 28–47.

Scott, Hew. (1915 onwards), *Fasti Ecclesiae Scoticanae: The Succession of Ministers in the Church of Scotland from the Reformation*. 11 volumes, Edinburgh: Oliver and Boyd.

Smout, T. C. (1969), *A History of the Scottish People 1560–1830*. Glasgow: Collins.

———. (1986), *A Century of the Scottish People 1830–1950*. Glasgow: Collins.

Wright, D. F. (1988), *The Bible in Scottish Life and Literature*. Edinburgh: St Andrews Press.

Chapter 1; Overview: Reformation to revolution

Bardgett, F. D. (1986), 'Four parische kirkis to ane preicher', *RSCHS*, 22.3, 195–209.

Cowan, I. B. (1982), *The Scottish Reformation; Church and Society in Sixteenth Century Scotland*. London: Weidenfeld and Nicolson.

Dawson, J. E. A. (2007), *Scotland Re-formed 1488–1587*. Edinburgh: Edinburgh UP.

Dilworth, M. (1974), 'Monks and Ministers after 1560', *RSCHS*, 18.3, 201–221.

Dunbar, L. J. (1998), 'An Early Record from the Synod of Fife', *RSCHS*, 28, 217–238.

Foster, W. R. (1966), 'The Operation of Presbyteries in Scotland, 1600–1638', *RSCHS*, 15.1, 21–34.

Gardiner, G. (2004), *The Scottish Exile Community in the Netherlands*. East Linton: Tuckwell.

Haws, C. H. (1973), 'The Diocese of St Andrews at the Reformation', *RSCHS*, 18.2, 115–132.

Heron, A. I. C. (1982), *The Westminster Confession in the Church Today*. Edinburgh: St Andrew Press.

Kirk, J. (1974), 'The Influence of Calvinism on the Scottish Reformation', *RSCHS*, 18.3, 157–179.

———. (1989), *Patterns of Reform; Continuity and Change in the Reformation Kirk*. Edinburgh: Clark.

———. (1992), 'Iconoclasm and Reform', *RSCHS*, 24.3, 366–383.

Knight, A. F. (1935), 'The Bible in Scotland after the Reformation', *RSCHS*, 5.3, 214–226.

MacPherson, H. (1926), 'The Political Ideals of the Covenanters 1660–1688', *RSCHS*, 1.3, 223–232.

Makey, W. H. (1970), 'The Elders of Stow, Liberton, Canongate and St Cuthbert's in the Mid-seventeenth Century', *RSCHS*, 17.2, 155–167.

Marshall, R. K. (2008), *John Knox*. Edinburgh: Birlinn.

McGrath, A. (2001), *In the Beginning; The Story of the King James Bible*. London: Hodder and Stoughton.

McInnes, J. (1966), 'The Historical Background of the Westminster Confession', *RSCHS*, 15.1, 57–76.

Rhodes, E. (2011), 'Paper, Parchment and Protestants: Reformers and the Preservation of Catholic Ecclesiastical Documents in the Parish of St Andrews C1550–80', *Scottish Archives*, 17, 44–55.

Sanderson, M. H. B. (1987), *Mary Stewart's People*. Edinburgh: Mercat Press.

———. (1999), 'The Printing and Distribution of the Bible and Psalm Books in Sixteenth-century Scotland: Some Additional Documentation', *RSCHS*, 29, 139–149.

———. (2002), *A Kindly Place? Living in Sixteenth Century Scotland*. East Linton: Tuckwell Press.

Spurlock, R. S. (2007), 'Anie Gospell Way; Religious Diversity in Interregnum Scotland', *RSCHS*, 37, 89–119.

Stevenson, D. (1973), 'Conventicles in the Kirk', *RSCHS*, 18.2, 99–114.

———. (1988), 'The National Covenant: A List of Known Copies', *RSCHS*, 23.2, 255–299.

———. (1993), 'The Solemn League and Covenant: A List of Signed Copies', *RSCHS*, 25.1, 154–187.

Wormald, J. (1981), *Court, Kirk and Community; Scotland 1470–1625*. Edinburgh: Edinburgh UP.

Chapter 2; Dissenting voices backing Bishops: Roman Catholics and Episcopalians

Any study of the history of the Catholicism before and after the Reformation should take as its starting point the copious amount of material contained within the *Innes Review* from its foundation in 1950.

Aspinwall, B. (1986), 'Popery in Scotland, Image and Reality. 1820–1920', *RSCHS*, 22.3, 235–257.

Bradley, J. M. (1995), 'Religious Cleavage and Aspects of Catholic Identity in Modern Scotland', *RSCHS*, 25.3, 442–468.

Cosh, M. (2003), *Edinburgh; The Golden Age*. Edinburgh: John Donald.

Edwards, R. (2010), 'Terror and Intrigue: The Secret Life of Glasgow's Episcopalians', *RSCHS*, 40, 31–68.

———. (2012), 'Pomp or Circumstance; Glasgow's Episcopalians and the Uprising of 1745', *RSCHS*, 41, 1–30.

Foskett, R. (1967), 'The Drummond Controversy', *RSCHS*, 16.2, 99–109.

Goldie, F. (1951), *A Short History of the Episcopal Church in Scotland*. London: SPCK.

Handley, J. E. (1949), *The Irish in Scotland*. Glasgow: Burns.

Hay, M. V. (1929), *The Blairs Papers, 1603–1669*. London: Sands.

Kehoe, S. K. (2010), *Creating a Scottish Church; Catholicism, Gender and Ethnicity in Nineteenth Century Scotland*. Manchester: Manchester UP.

Knight, C. (1989), 'The Anglicising of Scottish Episcopalianism', *RSCHS*, 23.3, 361–377.

McCaffrey, J. F. (1983), 'Roman Catholics in Scotland in the 19th and 20th Centuries', *RSCHS*, 21.3, 275–300.

———. (1995), 'The Roman Catholic Church in the 1890s: Retrospect and Prospect', *RSCHS*, 25.3, 426–441.

Roberts, A. (1997), 'Popery in Buchan and Strathbogie in the Early 17th Century', *RSCHS*, 27, 127–155.

Strong, R. (2003), 'The Reconstruction of Episcopalian Identity in Scotland: The Renunciation of the Stuart Allegiance in 1788', *RSCHS*, 33, 143–164.

White, G. D. (1998), 'The Nine Lives of the Episcopal Cat; Changing Self-images of the Scottish Episcopal Church', *RSCHS*, 28, 78–92.

———. (1998), *The Scottish Episcopal Church: A New History*. Edinburgh: General Synod of the Scottish Episcopal Church.

Chapter 3; Overview: After the revolution

Brown, C. G. (1997), *Religion and Society in Scotland Since 1707*. Edinburgh: Edinburgh UP.

Clarke, T. (1990), 'The Williamite Episcopalians and the Glorious Revolution in Scotland', *RSCHS*, 24.1, 33–51.

Drummond, A. L. and Bulloch, J. (1975), *The Scottish Church 1688–1843*. Edinburgh: St Andrews Press.

Dunlop, A. I. (1967), *William Carstares and the Kirk by Law Established*. Edinburgh: St Andrews Press.

Inglis, W. (2003), 'The Impact of Episcopacy and Presbyterianism, Before and After 1690, on One Parish: A Case Study of Dunblane Kirk Session Minutes', *RSCHS*, 33, 35–61.

Knox, R. B. (1989), 'Establishment and Toleration During the Reigns of William', *RSCHS*, 23.3, 330–360.

MacIntyre, J. (1963), 'John McLeod Campbell; Heretic and Saint', *RSCHS*, 14.1, 49–66.

Paton, D. (2006), *The Clergy and the Clearances*. Edinburgh: John Donald.

Smith, D. (2008), *God, the Poet, and the Devil: Robert Burns and Religion*. Edinburgh: St Andrews Press.

The New Statistical Account of Scotland, 1834–1845 [online] Available at http://stat-acc-scot.edina.ac.uk/sas/sas.asp?action=public& [Accessed 24 February 2014].

The Statistical Account of Scotland, 1791–1799 [online] Available at http://stat-acc-scot.edina.ac.uk/sas/sas.asp?action=public& [Accessed 24 February 2014].

Chapter 4; Dissenting voices: The covenanting and secession traditions

Brown, C. G. (1996), 'To Be Aglow with Civic Ardours; The Godly Commonwealth in Glasgow', *RSCHS*, 26, 169–195.

Couper, W. J. (1925), 'The Reformed Presbyterian Church in Scotland', *RSCHS*, 2, 1–174.

Drummond, R. J. (1942), 'Traditions of the Relief Church', *RSCHS*, 8.1, 42–54.

———. (1943), 'Later Story of the Relief Congregations', *RSCHS*, 8.2, 171–183.

———. (1948), 'The Significance of the United Presbyterian Church', *RSCHS*, 10.1, 1–7.

Jardine, M. (2009), *United Societies: Militancy, Martyrdom and the Presbyterian Movement in Late-restoration Scotland, 1679 to 1688*. PhD. University of Edinburgh. Available at https://www.era.lib.ed.ac.uk/handle/1842/3842 [Accessed 21 February 2014].

Mackerrow, J. (1839), *History of the Secession Church*. Edinburgh: Fullarton.

McKelvie, W. (1873), *Annals and Statistics of the United Presbyterian Church*. Edinburgh: Oliphant.

McMillan, W. (1934), 'The Hebronites', *RSCHS*, 5.2, 157–174.

———. (1950), 'The Covenanters after the Revolution of 1688', *RSCHS*, 10.3, 141–153.

McWhirter, A. (1944), 'The Last Anti-burghers; A Footnote to Secession History', *RSCHS*, 8.3, 254–291.

Muirhead, A. T. N. (1986), 'A Secession Congregation in Its Community; The Stirling Congregation of the Rev. Ebenezer Erskine, 1731–1754', *RSCHS*, 22.3, 211–233.

Paton, H. (1908), *Register of the Rev. John MacMillan*. Edinburgh: Lorimer and Chalmers.

Scott, D. (1886), *Annals and Statistics of the Original Secession Church Till Its Disruption and Union with the Free Church of Scotland in 1852*. Edinburgh: Elliot.

Small, R. (1904), *History of the Congregations of the United Presbyterian Church from 1733 to 1900 2 vols*. Edinburgh: Small.

Smith, R. M. (2004), 'The United Secession Church in Glasgow 1820–1847', *RSCHS*, 34, 48–90.

———. (2009), 'The Lord Helps Those Who Help Themselves: The U.P. Laity in Glasgow', *RSCHS*, 39, 35–68.

Whatley, C. A. (2000), *Scottish Society, 1707–1830*. Manchester: Manchester UP.

Chapter 5; Governing lives: The churches' impact on personal life

Boyd, K. M. (1980), *Scottish Church Attitudes to Sex, Marriage and the Family, 1850–1914*. Edinburgh: John Donald.

Brackenridge, R. D. (1969), 'The Enforcement of Sunday Observance in Post-revolution Scotland', *RSCHS*, 17.1, 33–45.

Buchanan, J. L. (1793), *Travels in the Western Hebrides from 1782–1790 (reprinted 1997)*. Skye: Maclean Press.

Cameron, A. (2008), 'The Fate of the Old Parish Registers under the Registration Act of 1854', *Scottish Archives*, 14, 62–72.

di Folco, J. (1977), 'Discipline and Welfare in the Mid 17th Century Scots Parish', *RSCHS*, 19.3, 169–183.

Hanham, A. (2005), *The Sinners of Cramond; The Struggle to Impose Godly Behaviour on a Scottish Community*. Edinburgh: John Donald.

Leneman, L. (1986), *Living in Athol*. Edinburgh: Edinburgh UP.

———. (1998), *Alienated Affections; The Scottish Experience of Divorce and Separation*. Edinburgh: Edinburgh UP.

———. (2000), 'Marriage as Interpreted by Church and State in Eighteenth Century Scotland', *RSCHS*, 30, 103–123.

——— and Mitchison, R. (1993), 'Acquiescence in and Defiance of Church Discipline in Early-modern Scotland', *RSCHS*, 25.1, 19–40.

——— and Mitchison, R. (1998), *Sin in the City; Sexuality and Social Control in Urban Scotland*. Edinburgh: Scottish Cultural Press.

Lumsden, C. (2008), 'Church Discipline in Nineteenth Century Edinburgh; Contrasts and Comparisons', *RSCHS*, 38, 83–104.

Marshall, J. S. (1972), 'Irregular Marriages in Scotland as Reflected in Kirk Session Records', *RSCHS*, 18.1, 10–25.

Mitchison, R. (2000), *The Old Poor Law in Scotland; The Experience of Poverty. 1574–1845*. Edinburgh: Edinburgh UP.

Survey of Scottish Witchcraft [online] Available at http://www.shc.ed.ac.uk/Research/witches/ [Accessed 24 February 2014].

Withrington, D. J. (1970), 'Non-church-going, c1750–c1850; A Preliminary Study', *RSCHS*, 17.2, 99–113.

———. (1991), 'Non-church-going, Church Organisation and "Crisis in the Church", c1880–c1920', *RSCHS*, 24.2, 199–236.

Chapter 6; Non-Presbyterian dissent: The major lines

Balfour, I. L. S. (2009), 'Charlotte Chapel, Edinburgh: Evangelical Social Involvement', *RSCHS*, 39, 69–88.

Batty, M. (2010), *Scotland's Methodists, 1750–2000*. Edinburgh: John Donald.

Beaton, D. (1928), 'The Old Scots Independents', *RSCHS*, 3.2, 135–145.

Bebbington, D. W. (1988), *The Baptists in Scotland; A History*. Glasgow: Baptist Union of Scotland.

Campbell, J. (1937), 'The Berean Church', *RSCHS*, 6.2, 138–146.

Escott, H. (1960), *A History of Scottish Congregationalism*. Glasgow: Congregational Union of Scotland.

Fisher, J. S. (1996), *Impelled by Faith; A Short History of the Baptists in Scotland*. Stirling: Scottish Baptist History Project.

Hillis, P. (2000), 'The 1891 Membership Roll of Hillhead Baptist Church', *RSCHS*, 30, 170–192.

Lovegrove, D. W. (1999), 'Pope Haldane, Bishop Ewing and the Troubled Birth of Scottish Independency', *RSCHS*, 29, 23–38.

MacWhirter, A. (1966), 'The Early Days of Independentism and Congregationalism in the Northern Islands of Scotland', *RSCHS*, 16.1, 63–87.

McKelvie, W. (1873), *Annals and Statistics of the United Presbyterian Church*. Edinburgh: Oliphant.

McNaughton, W. (1993), *The Scottish Congregational Ministry, 1794–1993*. Glasgow: Congregational Union of Scotland.

———. (2003), 'Revival and Reality; Congregationalists and Religious Revival in Nineteenth-century Scotland', *RSCHS*, 33, 165–216.

Murray, D. B. (1977), *The Social and Religious Origins of Scottish Non-presbyterian Protestant Dissent from 1730–1800*. PhD. St Andrews University. Available at http://research-repository.st-andrews.ac.uk/handle/10023/2660 [Accessed 25 February 2014].

———. (1984), 'The Influence of John Glas', *RSCHS*, 22.1, 45–56.

Talbot, T. (2005), *Standing on the Rock; A History of Stirling Baptist Church, 1805–2005*. Stirling: Privately printed.

———. (2008), 'The Use of the Scottish Baptist Church Archive in Writing a History of Stirling Baptist Church', *Scottish Archives*, 14, 47–61.

Chapter 7; Overview: Disruption to diversity

Black, A. (2006), *Gilfillan of Dundee; 1813–1878; Interpreting Religion and Culture in Mid-Victorian Scotland*. Dundee: Dundee UP.

Cheyne, A. C. (1983), *The Transforming of the Kirk; Victorian Scotland's Religious Revolution*. Edinburgh: St Andrews Press.

Denny, N. D. (1988), 'Temperance and the Scottish Churches', *RSCHS*, 23.2, 217–239.

Dineley, M. (2005), 'Continuities and Discontinuities: Reaction to the Disruption in Three Highland Parishes', *RSCHS*, 35, 142–162.

Drummond, A. L. and Bulloch, J. (1975), *The Church in Victorian Scotland;
    1843–1874*. Edinburgh: St Andrews Press.
———. (1978), *The Church in Late Victorian Scotland; 1874–1900*. Edinburgh: St
    Andrews Press.
Enright, W. G. (1978), Urbanization and the Evangelical Pulpit in Nineteenth-
    Century Scotland. *Church History* [e-journal] 47.4, 400–407. Available at http://
    journals.cambridge.org/action/displayAbstract;jsessionid=1D424C6EB722DAE
    B21F678D0582E9964.journals?fromPage=onlineandaid=2226352 [Accessed
    24 February 2014].
Great Britain, (1854), Census of Great Britain Religious Worship and Education
    (Scotland) Report and Tables 1854. in *Parliamentary Papers Session
    31 January 1854 –12 August 1854*, 301–346, Vol. LIX [online] Available at
    http://www.histpop.org/ohpr/servlet/PageBrowser2?ResourceType=Census&
    ResourceType=Essays&SearchTerms=religious scotland 1851&simple=
    yes&path=Results&active=yes&titlepos=0&mno=34&pageseq=1
    [Accessed 24 February 2014].
Hillis, P. (2007), *The Barony of Glasgow; A Window Onto Church and People in
    19th Century Scotland*. Edinburgh: Dunedin Academic Press.
Howie, R. (1893), *The Churches and the Churchless in Scotland; Facts and
    Figures*. Glasgow: Bryce.
Johnston, J. (1874), *The Ecclesiastical and Religious Statistics of Scotland* [online]
    Available at https://archive.org/details/ecclesiasticalre00john [Accessed
    24 February 2014].
Lumsden, C. (2012), *Class, Gender and Christianity in Edinburgh 1850–1905:
    A Study in Denominationalism*. PhD. Edinburgh University. Available at https://
    www.era.lib.ed.ac.uk/handle/1842/6440 [Accessed 24 February 2014].
Marwick, W. H. (1952), 'Social Heretics in the Scottish Churches', *RSCHS*, 11.3,
    227–240.
McCraw, I. (2002), *Victorian Dundee at Worship*. Dundee: Abertay Historical Society.
Mechie, S. (1960), *The Church and Scottish Social Development*. London: OUP.
Muirhead, I. A. (1974), 'Churchmen and the Problems of Prostitution in
    Nineteenth-century Scotland', *RSCHS*, 18.3, 223–243.
Thomson, E. P. (2006), 'The Impetus Given to the Use of Instrumental Music in
    Scottish Churches by the Visit of Moody and Sankey to Scotland in 1873–74',
    RSCHS, 36, 175–194.
Withrington, D. J. (1973), 'The 1851 Census of Religious Worship and Education',
    RSCHS, 18.2, 133–148.
———. (1977), 'The Churches in Scotland c1870–1900; Towards a New Social
    Conscience?', *RSCHS*, 19.3, 155–168.

Chapter 8; Dissenting voices:
The disruption tradition

Ansdell, D. (1991), 'The 1843 Disruption of the Church of Scotland in the Isle of
    Lewis', *RSCHS*, 24.2, 181–197.
———. (1996), 'The Disruptive Union, 1890–1900, in a Hebridean Presbytery',
    RSCHS, 26, 55–103.

————. (2003), 'A Chapter of Free Church History That Is Yet to Be Written: Dr John White and the Free Church Behind Closed Doors', *RSCHS*, 33, 217–232.
Collins, G. N. M. (1974), *The Heritage of Our Fathers*. Edinburgh: Knox Press.
Fowler, J. (2006), *Mr Hill's Big Picture; The Day That Changed Scotland Forever; Captured on Canvas*. Edinburgh: St Andrews Press.
MacLaren, A. A. (1974), *Religion and Social Class; The Disruption Years in Aberdeen*. London: Routledge and Kegan Paul.
Macleod, D. (1978), *Hold Fast Your Confession; Studies in Church Principles*. Edinburgh: Knox Press.
MacLeod, J. L. (1995), 'The Influence of the Highland-lowland Divide on the Free Presbyterian Disruption of 1893', *RSCHS*, 25.3, 400–425.
Ritchie, L. A. (1985), 'The Floating Church of Loch Sunart', *RSCHS*, 22.2, 159–173.
Ross, K. R. (1988), 'The Union of 1900 and the Relation of Church and Creed in Scotland', *RSCHS*, 23.2, 241–253.
Tallach, S. F. (1996), *The Open Door*. Thurso: Weydale Press.
Whyte, I. (2012), *Send Back the Money; The Free Church of Scotland and American Slavery*. Cambridge: James Clark.
Withrington, D. J. (1993), 'The Disruption: A Century and a Half of Historical Interpretation', *RSCHS*, 25.1, 118–153.
————. (1966), 'The Free Church Educational Scheme', *RSCHS*, 15.2, 103–116.

Chapter 9; Non-Presbyterian dissent: other small churches

Couper, W. J. (1933), 'The Moravian Brethren in Scotland', *RSCHS*, 5.1, 50–72.
Dickson, N. (1993), 'Modern Prophetesses; Women Preachers in the Nineteenth Century Scottish Brethren', *RSCHS*, 25.1, 89–117.
————. (2002), *Brethren in Scotland 1838–2000; A Social Study of an Evangelical Movement*. Milton Keynes: Paternoster Press.
————. (2009), 'Researching the Brethren Movement in Scotland; Problems and Possibilities', *Scottish Archives*, 15, 42–56.
The Faith Mission Archives [online] Available at www.faithmission.org [Accessed 24 February 2014].
Long, J. *Diary* in *Telling the Truth* [online] Available at http://www.tellingthetruth.info/home/he diary of John Long [Accessed 24 February 2014].
Watters, A. C. (1997), *History of the British Churches of Christ* [online] Available at http://www.simplychristians.eu/eusebos/zpayne3/watters1.htm#contents [Accessed 24 February 2014].
Wilson, A. (1970), *The Chartist Movement in Scotland*. Manchester: Manchester UP.

Chapter 10; Non-Trinitarian Churches

Buchanan, F. (1987), The Ebb and Flow of Mormonism in Scotland, *BYU Studies*, 27.2 [e-journal] Available at https://ojs.lib.byu.edu/spc/index.php/BYUStudies/article/view/5663 [Accessed 24 February 2014].

Burton, P. F. (2007), *A Social History of Quakers in Scotland, 1800–2000*. Lampeter: Mellen.

———. (2008), 'Using Quaker Records for Social History', *Scottish Archives*, 14, 39–46.

MacWhirter, A. (1956), 'The Church of the New Jerusalem in Scotland', *RSCHS*, 12.3, 202–219.

———. (1959), 'Unitarianism in Scotland', *RSCHS*, 13.2, 101–144.

Marwick, W. H. (1967), 'Studies in Scottish Quakerism', *RSCHS*, 16.2, 89–98.

McHaffie, A. (2003), *150 Years: A Very Brief History of Edinburgh Christadelphian Ecclesia; 1853–2003*. Edinburgh: Edinburgh Christadelphian Ecclesia.

Chapter 11; The geography of faith in Scotland

Ansdell, D. (1998), *The People of the Great Faith; The Highland Church; 1690–1900*. Stornoway: Acair.

Brooks, C., Saint, A. (1995), *Victorian Church Architecture and Society*. Manchester: Manchester UP.

Ferguson, F. (1969), 'The Problems of the Established Church in the West Highlands and Islands in the Eighteenth Century', *RSCHS*, 17.1, 15–31.

Kirk, J. (1998), *The Church in the Highlands*. edited by James Kirk, Edinburgh: Scottish Church History Society.

MacInnes, J. (1942), 'The Origin and Early Development of the "Men"', *RSCHS*, 8.1, 16–41.

———. (1951), *The Evangelical Movement in the Highlands of Scotland*. Aberdeen: Aberdeen UP.

MacLeod, J. (2008), *Banner in the West; A Spiritual History of Lewis and Harris*. Edinburgh: Birlinn.

Mearns, A. B. (1990), 'The Minister and the Bailiff: A Study of Presbyterian Clergy in the Northern Highlands During the Clearances', *RSCHS*, 24.1, 53–75.

Meek, D. E. (1996), *The Scottish Highlands; The Churches and Gaelic Culture*. Geneva: WCC.

Paton, D. M. M. (2001), 'The Myth and the Reality of the "Men"; Leadership and Spirituality in the Northern Highlands', *RSCHS*, 31, 97–144.

Porter, J. D. (1980), Thomas Telford's Parliamentary Churches, *Caithness Field Club* [online] Available at http://www.caithness.org/caithnessfieldclub/bulletins/1980/october/thomas_telfords_parliamentary_churches.htm [Accessed 24 February 2014].

Ritchie, L. A. (2009), 'The "naval policy" of the Free Church of Scotland', *Scottish Archives*, 15, 57–66.

Chapter 12; The Twentieth Century

Bardgett, F. D. (2008), 'The Tell Scotland Movement; Failure and Success', *RSCHS*, 38, 105–150.

Brown, S. J. (1990), 'The Social Vision of Scottish Presbyterianism and the Union of 1929', *RSCHS*, 24.1, 77–96.

Dunlop, A. I. (1980), 'The Paths to Reunion in 1929', *RSCHS*, 20.3, 163–178.

Leneman, L. (1991), 'The Scottish Churches and "Votes for Women"', *RSCHS*, 24.2, 237–252.

Madonald, C. M. M. and McFarland, E.W. (1999), *Scotland and the Great War*. East Linton: Tuckwell Press.

Macdonald, L. O. (1999), 'The Most Potent Force of the Future: The Ministry and Citizenship of Presbyterian Women in the Aftermath of the Great War', *RSCHS*, 29, 119–138.

———. (2000), *A Unique and Glorious Mission; Women and Presbyterianism in Scotland*. Edinburgh: John Donald.

Matheson, P. (1971), 'Scottish War Sermons 1914–1919', *RSCHS*, 17.3, 203–213.

Ritchie, D. (Summer 2012), *A Very Edinburgh Riot; the John Cormack Phenomenon* [online] Available at http://www.academia.edu/1079621/A_Very_Edinburgh_Riot [Accessed 24 February 2014].

Stephen, J. (2001), 'The Kirk and the Union', *RSCHS*, 31, 68–96.

Walker, G., Gallagher, T. (1990), *Sermons and Battle Hymns; Protestant Popular Culture in Modern Scotland*. Edinburgh: Edinburgh UP.

Index